PRIVATE MONEY LENDING:

Learn How To Consistently Generate
A Passive Income Stream

Also by Gustavo J. Gomez:

HAIR LOSS: Options for Restoration & Reversal
(Multi-Award-Winning Book)

Terapéutica Respiratoria: Normas y Aplicaciones

Balding: Hair Loss and Restoration

Medical Necessity Guidelines for Ordering
Respiratory Care Services:
A Physician's Pocket Reference

Acknowledgements

I want to extend my most sincere thanks and gratitude to my wife for her endless support and valuable assistance during the undertaking of this project. Margot is a special woman who completes my life in countless ways, too numerous to enumerate. I would also like to thank Professors Dr. Benny Rodriguez, academic coordinator, and Dr. Anthony B. Portigliatti, former Chancellor and President of Florida Christian University (FCU). Their guidance, support, recommendations, and encouragement were invaluable and greatly appreciated.

Additionally, there are individuals in everyone's life whose mere presence makes one's life substantially better. Thus, I would like to thank a few of these individuals whose special friendships have made my worldly existence much more enjoyable. They are Manuel A. Soler-Perez, M.D., Daniel Hernandez, Jack A. Arce, Dr. Jose Valle, Dr. Frank Batista, and the late Justo J. Ruiz and Albert G. Blanco. I especially would like to thank Ralph Rovirosa, a highly decorated IRS Agent for writing the foreword to this updated and revised edition.

I would be remised if I didn't thank the United States of America for all the opportunities she has afforded me to make all my dreams come true—and in many instances—exceed them. What an exceptional country to live in and what a wonderful life she has allowed me to have. Finally, I would like to thank my late parents, grateful immigrants who never had the opportunity to achieve their dreams. Instead, they sacrificed all so that I could have all.

Chapter 9
Minimizing Private Mortgage Investment Risk 218

Foreword

It was an honor when Dr. Gomez approached me and asked if I would be willing to review his book. He also requested that once reviewed, if I felt the information it contained described a safe, useful, valuable, and sound investment strategy to write the foreword to the second edition of his multi-award-winning book. As he explained it to me, he wanted the perspective of a former Criminal Investigation Division (CID) IRS agent with forensic accounting expertise, which has been my experience for the past 35 years.

As a CID IRS agent, my experience has been concentrated on the examination of complex personal and business tax returns, including corporations, partnerships, and trusts, to determine possible tax liability. I also have extensive experience assisting and supporting attorneys at the Department of Justice, the United States Attorney's Office, and IRS Special Agents, during criminal investigations and prosecutions of violations of Federal laws by providing auditing and forensic accounting services and reviewing and analyzing financial transactions. Thus, I'm qualified to interpret the soundness of the financial structure employ in the investment strategy Gomez describes in his well-researched book.

Needless to say, after reading Dr. Gomez's book, I accepted the task of writing the foreword as I felt the information contained was rigorously researched, valuable, safe, and structurally financially sound. Therefore, let me begin by saying that every learned investor knows that learning how to generate a consistent, substantial, and predictable passive income stream is the ultimate goal for anyone who wants to retire early and in comfort. In fact, creating a consistent passive cash flow sufficient to cover all monthly expenses, is considered the *"Holy Grail"* of personal financial independence.

It is essential to understand that many investments can generate passive income. However, not all passive incomes are created equal. Readers of this book should be mindful of the fact that Dr. Gomez has produced the first how-to guide emanating from a university research study addressing the investment topic to be described. This book succinctly explains the importance of learning how to create a safe and consistent passive income stream to ensure not only a comfortable and tranquil retirement but also a financially abundant life.

Gomez's book is an important and timely research study that explores a little-known but crucial area of passive income investing, which is that of *private mortgage lending*. The critical aspect of investing in private mortgages is the fact that this is a non-stock market correlated investment that works under all market conditions if properly structured and executed. A non-stock market correlated investment, also known as an alternative investment, is an investment that does not move lock-step with the direction of the overall stock market.

This alternative investment is significant and timely because of the monetary policy adopted by the Federal Reserve back in 2008 when the financial crisis began as the result of the ***"bursting of the housing bubble."*** During this time, the United States and the world were subjected to the most intense period of global financial strains since the Great Depression of the 1930s. This economic crisis led to a deep and prolonged worldwide recession that lasted more than a decade. When economic downturns like these occur, the Federal Reserve is tasked with conducting monetary policy that will achieve maximum employment, price stabilization, and moderate long-term interest rates.

Consequently, under the Obama administration, the Federal Reserve—in response to the financial crisis and to help stabilize the

Preface

This book is an important and timely research study that explores a little-known area of investing, which is that of private mortgage lending. The reason for undertaking the study is twofold: 1) for the past 19 years, retirement portfolios have been devastated by stock market fluctuations resulting from a greater prevalence of boom and bust economic cycles; and 2) The policy adopted by the Federal Reserve of creating an artificially low-interest-rate environment in an attempt to sustain the continued growth of the stock market and support the current real estate recovery efforts.

These two economic conditions primarily affect the already and soon-to-be-retired individuals because of their inability to generate a safe income stream from the typically available fixed-income investments, such as bonds, CDs, savings, and money-market accounts. The combination of a low-interest-rate environment and increased stock market volatility has dramatically impacted the livelihood of the fixed-income investor. Moreover, it has forced these investors to seek greater levels of investment risk by incentivizing them to search for higher yields by investing in the stock market—in essence, forcing them to return to the place that has created most of their financial problems.

It is a fact that the current economic environment has imposed tremendous limitations on the income investor to find investments that could potentially generate sufficient passive income to adequately sustain a retirement lifestyle, or produce an adequate cash flow. Thus, the reason for undertaking this qualitative research study was to explore the viability of private mortgage investing as a safe, consistent, and suitable investment vehicle that could be used to meet the needs of the income investor.

The study participants in this research project were purposefully selected to include individuals who possessed the unique richness of information, relevant to extract the detailed research information as recommended by Patton (1980). The focus of purposive sampling in qualitative research, also called judgmental sampling, involves the specific selection of study participants who possess the appropriate knowledge according to the purpose or needs of the study (Glaser & Strauss, 1967; Morse, 1991). For the data collection process, the instruments used were interviews and questionnaires that adhered to the guiding principle of saturation. Saturation has attained widespread acceptance as a methodological principle in qualitative research. It means that based on the data that have been collected or analyzed hitherto, further data collection and analysis are unnecessary (Saunders et al., 2018).

The topic explored by this study is vital because the contention of the economic assessment of the Federal Open Market Committee (FOMC) is that maintaining the current target range for the federal funds rate will continue to be necessary. In other words, this means that a low-interest-rate environment will continue to be maintained. Therefore, this study is both relevant and timely. Exploring the safety and viability of private mortgage investing as an alternative source of income generation will be crucial information for the income investor to survive and sustain their projected investment goals, in spite of the improved economic environment created by the Trump administration.

In contrast to other books that are available on the market on this particular subject, this book is not intended to promote any other business the author is engaged in. The objective is strictly educational, which essentially is to create awareness about this type of investment vehicle. Learning about this investment class, if properly applied and executed, could provide investors and the and manifest themselves in different degrees of severity (see Appendix A).

A detailed explanation of business cycles is beyond the scope and objective of this book. However, the author contends that it is important for the reader to understand this economic concept in order to become a better and safer investor. The most comprehensive research undertaken regarding business cycles, as known today, was done by Arthur F. Burns and Wesley C. Mitchell in their book entitled, *"Measuring Business Cycles."*

Dr. Burns is best known for having been the tenth chairman of the Board of Governors of the Federal Reserve from February 1, 1970, to March 8, 1978. Furthermore, Burns also served as the ambassador to West Germany from 1981 to 1985. Burns's book, published in 1946 by the National Bureau of Economic Research (NBER), is an extensive study of previous business cycles. In this massive research undertaking, Burns and Mitchell distilled and clarified a large number of statistical indicators of expansions (booms) and recessions (busts) into one signal of turning points in the U.S. business cycle (Burns & Mitchell, 1946).

The NBER is a private, nonprofit research institute that is now the organization that announces when recessions begin and end (see Appendix A). Much of the Institute's approach is based on the work done by Burns and Mitchell. The book by Arthur Burns, more than any other single accomplishment, gave him a reputation as the preeminent expert in business cycle forecasting in the United States.

As was previously mentioned, stock market downturns are devastating events for all investors. However, they are more damaging to individuals who are already retired or are near retirement age. The reason these market downturns are so destructive to this class of investors is because these individuals do not have the necessary years to wait for a market recovery. This fact, essentially, is the reason why it is crucial to rebalancing investment portfolios to a more conservative capital preservative approach, the closer an investor gets to retirement age.

Another dilemma affecting the retired and soon-to-be retiring individuals is finding a suitable alternative investment that could be used to generate an adequate passive income stream with increased safety to sustain their retirement goals. Furthermore, because markets will continue to be volatile and uncertain, fluctuating between boom and bust cycles. The objective of this book—and the reason for undertaking the qualitative research study—was to explore and uncover the availability of a safe and consistent passive income-generating investment that could mitigate both market and investment risks.

Nothing has hurt the retired individual more than the current, intentionally created, low- interest-rate environment. This strategy that began under Obama and continues under Trump is designed to sustain the continued growth of the stock and real estate markets. The objective of this monetary policy by the Federal Reserve has forced many investors to invest in riskier investment vehicles in search of a higher rate of return to generate an income stream, placing their retirement portfolio in even greater danger.

As mentioned above, one of the objectives of the research undertaken to write this book is precisely because of this artificially low-interest-rate environment purposefully created by the Federal Reserve that specifically hurts the retired investor who lives on the returns of fixed- income investments. The information contained throughout this book will demonstrate to the reading audience that private mortgage investing is a good, income-generating strategy that is quite suitable to include in a retirement portfolio or used as a passive cash flow generating business.

While it is well-established that no single investment vehicle is without risk, the author's research has focused explicitly on an alternative investment vehicle that possesses some unique characteristics. These favorable features make it a suitable hopefully. Thus, I decided to use some repetition to emphasized specific points I considered necessary.

I subscribe to an old philosophical Latin phrase that states, *"Repetitio est mater studiorum."* What this means is that repetition is the mother of all learning. Therefore, as you embarked on the journey to read this book, understand that a degree of redundancy is essential for learning. It is especially crucial when learning about investment strategies that carry a significant financial risk if inadequately learned. Thus, repetition helps to improve speed, increases confidence, and strengthens the connections in the brain that support the learning process. In essence, it ensures reception by the audience.

2

Types of Liquid Investments

T he research objective of this book is to explore and create awareness regarding the investment vehicle of private mortgage investing as a suitable, safe investment practice to generate an income stream, either as a business, for retirement, or both. However, before addressing the topic of private mortgage investing, it is appropriate first to review the most common types of investment vehicles customarily available to the investor.

An investment vehicle can be anything that a person can invest their money in and generate a return on investment (ROI). There are no shortages of investment vehicles for those wishing to invest their money. The premise behind selecting any investment vehicle is to identify those that will allow money to grow while minimizing the risk of losing the invested funds. It is also important to distinguish between investing and saving. Investing is the proactive use of money to make additional money. In essence, investing is making the money grow, or appreciate, for the long-term financial objectives of the investors. It is a way of saving money to be used for something in the future, such as retirement. Therefore, the goal of investing is focused on the return, which can follow the investment spectrum from conservative to aggressive in terms of assuming the investment risk. Thus, investing is different from saving because penalty for transactions that require more funds than are available in the account.

In some cases, the bank will cover the check presented for payment and debit the amount on the account, resulting in a negative balance. The bank can also reject the check. No matter which situation occurs, the overdraft fee will still be incurred, unless the account holder has some form of overdraft protection arranged with the bank. It sometimes takes longer to transfer money from a savings account than from a checking account. A transfer from a savings account can take up to five days while transferring money from a checking account customarily will be executed by the next business day.

There are several types of checking accounts. Two common types of checking accounts are joint checking, which is owned by two or more people, and express checking, which was created for customers who seldom need to enter the bank building. An express checking account would be appropriate if the account holder is comfortable using an ATM, telephone, or computer to make bank transactions. These accounts typically have low minimum balance requirements and no monthly fees.

A checking account is insured by the FDIC for up to $250,000. However, if an individual has money in excess of that amount, it would be a prudent practice to deposit the majority of the funds into a savings account or another type of investment vehicle that pays interest, where the funds could be used more efficiently. Although some banks do offer interest-bearing checking accounts, the rates they pay are typically lower than a savings account. That is why a checking account should generally hold the amount of money that an individual would normally need for their day-to-day transactions.

When a person opens a checking account, the bank will run a quick background credit check on the potential depositor. If the person has been reported to ChexSystems, which is a consumer credit reporting agency similar to Experian, Equifax, TransUnion, or Innovis, the consumer will not be allowed to open an account until the credit issue has cleared. While most credit agencies' broker data about how a consumer handles their credit relationships, the difference with ChexSystems is that it provides data related to how a consumer has handled deposit accounts at banking institutions.

The bank customarily uses the ChexSystems service to mitigate their risk of losing money on account holders with a poor record of handling their deposit accounts.

Advantages of Checking Accounts

- ❖ Safe and convenient
- ❖ Use of a debit card
- ❖ Use of ATM's
- ❖ Access to online and mobile banking services
- ❖ Can be used for direct deposits
- ❖ FDIC insured, thus providing safety and security

Disadvantages of Checking Accounts

- ❖ Most checking accounts do not pay interest on the money deposited.
- ❖ Many of these accounts impose a minimum balance requirement and may charge a fee if—the balance goes below that minimum.
- ❖ Might charge an array of fees, such as monthly maintenance fees, overdraft fees, ATM withdrawals fees from third party machines, etc.

Savings Accounts

The primary feature of a savings account is that the account holder earns interest on the funds deposited into the account. The bank pays interest on this type of account because it uses those funds to make loans and conduct other business, which earns the bank a higher interest rate than the one they pay their account holders. Savings accounts usually limit the number of withdrawals that can be made per statement cycle and require a minimum balance to ensure that the bank has enough funds at its disposal.

There are several types of savings accounts. Two common types of savings accounts are passbook accounts and high-yield savings accounts. A passbook savings account is a bank account that uses a specific kind of record-keeping method. With a passbook savings account, it is the responsibility of the account holder to keep track of all transactions made in a small passbook type ledger that the bank provides to the client. The bank will check the balance against the balance recorded by the account holder for accuracy during the account holder's visits to the bank, or as requested by the account holder. This type of account is good for someone who performs a limited number of transactions.

A high-yield savings account is an account the bank offers only to certain clients because it earns a higher interest rate than other accounts. To qualify for this type of account, the account holder must make a sufficiently large initial deposit and maintain a high minimum balance.

Advantages of Savings Accounts

❖ Pays interest

❖ FDIC insured, thus providing safety and security

❖ Accessibility to the funds especially through online banking

❖ Savings accounts retain their importance because it is always critical to have money set aside for emergencies.

Disadvantages of Savings Accounts

❖ Generally, these accounts pay a low interest rate. In fact, savings accounts pay the lowest interest rates of any interest-bearing accounts other than a checking account.

❖ Some banks charge monthly maintenance fees.

Money-Market Accounts

Money-market accounts (MMAs) or money-market deposit accounts (MMDAs) are a type of financial account offered by banks and credit unions similar to regular checking accounts. MMAs typically pay a higher rate of interest and require a larger minimum balance, usually ranging from $1,000 to $2,500; $10,000; $25,000; or greater, to earn interest or avoid paying monthly service fees. Customarily, the bigger the account's balance, the more the interest it pays. These types of accounts also impose a limit on the amount of withdrawals or checks that can be written per month.

MMAs offer many of the same benefits as CDs with the added feature of a checking account. This investment strategy is similar to, and it is meant to compete with, the money-market funds offered by the brokerage house. Bank MMAs should not be confused with money-market funds. MMAs are bank alternatives to money-market mutual funds. A money-market fund or money-market mutual fund is an open-ended mutual fund that invests in short-term debt securities such as U.S. Treasury bills and commercial paper. It is presumed that money-market mutual funds are just as safe as regular bank money-market or savings accounts that pay a higher yield. However, this is not an entirely accurate presumption, because money-market mutual funds do have some market risk exposure and are not FDIC insured, making them a riskier investment.

A money-market fund is a mutual fund that attempts to keep its share price at a constant net asset value (NAV) of one dollar. Professional money managers will take the funds that have been deposited into these money-market accounts and invest them in government T-bills, savings bonds, CDs, and other safe and conservative financial instruments. Subsequently, a portion of the interest earned is paid to the account holder in the form of dividends, less a management fee for the mutual fund company. These money-market funds are an important source of liquidity for financial intermediaries. They are regulated in the United States under the Investment Company Act of 1940, just like any other mutual fund.

The Investment Company Act (ICA) of 1940 is an act of Congress that, together with the Securities Exchange Act of 1934 and the Investment Advisers Act of 1940, forms the backbone of the United States financial regulatory system. These acts were updated by the Dodd-Frank Act of 2010 (see Chapter 6). ICA, often known as the Company Act or the 1940 Act, is the primary source of regulation for mutual funds and closed-end funds, an investment industry that has currently grown to a multi-trillion-dollar industry (Lemke, Lins & Smith, 2002).

Advantages of Money-Market Accounts

An MMA, or money-market deposit account, is a government-insured bank account that pays relatively high interest-rates and provides cash withdrawal privileges. This type of account offers both the benefits of savings and checking accounts at higher interest rates than regular savings and checking accounts. The following are some advantages of MMAs:

- ❖ FDIC insured, thus providing safety and security
- ❖ Liquidity (funds are readily available)
- ❖ Low risk
- ❖ Pays higher interest rates
- ❖ Check writing and debit card access privileges
- ❖ Possess a degree of growth potential

Depositing money into an MMA is as easy as depositing cash into a savings or checking account, and the investor's funds are immediately available, making these types of accounts very convenient and liquid.

Disadvantages of Money-Market Accounts

Some financial institutions place a limit on the number and amount of checks that can be drawn against the account in any given month. The rate of interest earned is directly proportional to the size of the investor's level of deposited funds and not the maturity, as is the case with CDs. Hence, MMAs are disproportionately beneficial to the wealthier investors.

Some of the disadvantages associated with MMAs are:

- ❖ High balance requirements.
- ❖ Limited number of withdrawals and transfers.
- ❖ Interest rate fluctuations and other fees.

Although both CDs and MMAs can be useful for those who need access to their capital, MMAs are considered a far superior investment vehicle. Brokerage houses sometimes have an account that automatically sweeps their customers' uninvested cash into MMAs so investors can earn interest between investments. This is a convenient solution if the investor regularly invests because the funds can be used immediately to purchase stocks, bonds, mutual funds, or any other preferred types of investments.

Certificates of Deposit

A certificate of deposit (CD) is a time deposit, which is a financial product commonly sold in the United States by banks, thrift institutions, and credit unions. CDs are similar to savings accounts in that they are insured and are therefore virtually risk-free. They are insured by the FDIC for banks and by the National Credit Union Administration (NCUA) for credit unions.

CDs are different from savings accounts in that CDs have a specified, fixed holding term, such as one month, three months, six months, one year, five years, or longer, with each term typically paying an established interest rate. The lengthier the holding period or term, the higher the interest rate the account will pay. It is intended that CDs be held until maturity, at which time the money may be withdrawn, together with the accrued interest.

However, withdrawals before the specific maturity are typically subjected to a substantial penalty. The imposition of these penalties is intended to ensure that it is not in the account holder's best interest to withdraw the money before the maturity date. Insured CDs are required by the Truth in Savings Act (TISA) Regulation DD, to state at the time of account opening the penalty for early withdrawal.

TISA was enacted as Title II of the Federal Deposit Insurance Corporation Act FDIC of 1991, Public Law. No. 102-242,105, Stat. 2236 (1991), (12 USC § 4301, et sequentes), and is implemented by the Federal Reserve's Regulation DD, and by the NCUA regulations for credit unions. The intended purpose of the law is to enhance economic stability, improve competition between depository institutions, and allow consumers to make informed decisions.

TISA is primarily a disclosure law, intended to encourage comparative shopping for deposit products. The purpose of Regulation DD is to enable consumers to make informed decisions about their accounts at depository institutions through the use of uniform disclosures. These disclosures aid comparison shopping by informing consumers about the fees, annual percentage yield, interest rate, and other terms for deposit accounts. TISA only applies to deposit accounts held at a depository institution by individuals for personal, household, or family use. Thus, business accounts are not covered, nor are financial relationships other than deposit accounts. Moreover, TISA does not apply to money-market mutual funds offered by securities brokers and dealers (Gallagher, 2011, June 9).

Under TISA, a consumer is entitled to receive disclosures for the following:

- ❖ When an account is opened
- ❖ Upon request
- ❖ When the terms of the account are changed
- ❖ When a periodic statement is sent
- ❖ For most time accounts, before the account matures

The TISA regulation also includes requirements on the payment of interest, the methods of calculating the balance on which interest is paid, the calculation of the annual percentage yield, and advertising (Regulation DD Truth in Savings, n. d.).

In exchange for keeping the money on deposit for the agreed-upon terms, institutions usually will grant higher interest rates than they do on accounts from which money may be withdrawn on demand. Fixed rates are common, but some institutions may also offer CDs with variable rates. For example, if interest rates are expected to increase, banks and credit unions may offer CDs with a bump-up feature. This strategy allows for a single readjustment of the interest rate at a time of the customer's choosing, during the term of the CD.

Advantages of CDs

Certificates of deposit (CDs) have always been a safe haven type of investment for investors and retired individuals who simply want to park their money and earn an adequate rate of return.

Some of the advantages of Certificate of Deposit accounts are:

- ❖ Limited Safety Guarantee and FDIC insured, thus providing safety and security
- ❖ Opening account with ease
- ❖ Account flexibility
- ❖ Higher rates of return
- ❖ Maturity date selection options

There are different types of stock shares, which include the following:

- ❖ Common stock
- ❖ Preferred stock
- ❖ Convertible preferred stock
- ❖ Unlisted stock

Common Stock

Common stock is one form of security issued by a public corporation. Essentially, purchasing shares of stock provides the shareholder with a specified amount of equity ownership in the issuing company. Common stock is also referred to as voting or ordinary shares, which grant the shareholder a proportion of the company's dividends, earnings growth, and voting rights. In the event of company liquidation or bankruptcy, the common shareholders are customarily the last creditors to be paid. Therefore, common stock investors will only receive funds after the bondholders, creditors, employees, and preferred stockholders have been paid. What this means is that common stock investors will not receive any money after a company bankruptcy.

Preferred Stock

Preferred stock differs from common stock in that it typically does not carry voting rights, but it is legally entitled to receive a certain level of dividend payments before any dividends can be issued to other shareholders. It is a special type of stock that grants the holder priority over common stockholders in terms of dividends and bankruptcy rights.

Moreover, the price of preferred stock does not fluctuate as often as a company's common stock. It is classified as a fixed-income security. Therefore, a preferred stock is a security with characteristics that are similar to a bond and a common stock. These characteristics mean that dividends are usually guaranteed, and the owner can also participate in share price appreciation, if the preferred share is convertible stock. If the preferred stock misses a dividend payment, the company is required to pay that dividend before any future dividends are issued on common stock.

Convertible Preferred Stock

As mentioned above, convertible preferred stocks are a form of corporate fixed-income securities that investors can choose to convert into a certain number of shares of the company's common stock after a predetermined amount of time or on a specified date. The fixed-income component of the security offers investors a consistent passive income stream, similar to a bond, with some downside protection to the investors' capital. However, the option to convert these securities into common stock provides the investor with the opportunity to participate in gains from a rise in the company's share price.

Therefore, convertible stocks are particularly attractive to those investors who want to participate in the rise of growth in the companies, while being protected from a drop in the share price in the event that the company stocks do not live up to their expectations. Convertible preferred shareholders, unlike common stock shareholders, rarely have voting rights.

Unlisted Stock

Unlisted securities are shares in companies that are not listed on a stock exchange licensed by the Financial Services Board. Unlisted securities are issued by companies that either cannot or do not wish to meet the requirements of a licensed exchange, such as the New York Stock Exchange or the NASDAQ.

Unlisted stock can be either common or preferred shares. They may also pay higher dividends because of the greater risk associated with it. Moreover, they are less liquid than publicly traded stocks. For these reasons, investors are not as protected as they would normally be when trading stocks through a licensed stock exchange.

Advantages of Stock Investing

Some of the advantages of stock investing include the following:

- ❖ Potential for higher returns
- ❖ Greater earnings benefits
- ❖ Liquidity
- ❖ Limited liability protection

Potential for Higher Returns

Stock investing has the potential of delivering higher returns compared with other types of investments over the long term.

Greater Earnings Benefits

Stocks offer two ways for the owner to profit: by way of capital gains and by dividend payments, which can help to cushion a drop in the share price.

Liquidity

Most stocks are very liquid, which makes them easy to buy and sell should access to the funds be required.

Limited Liability Protection

Stocks possess limited legal liability because stockholders are considered passive investors who are not directly involved in the day-to-day operation of the company. Thus, they are protected against any liability stemming from the company's action beyond their financial investment in the corporation.

Disadvantages of Stock Investing

Some of the disadvantages of stock investing include the following:

- ❖ Volatility exposure
- ❖ Last to be paid

- ❖ Limited safety of the investment
- ❖ Traumatic psychological experience

Volatility Exposure

Stock prices can rise and fall dramatically, which can arise from multiple economic variables, including detrimental and favorable company news.

Last to be Paid

Because common stock represents ownership in the business, the stockholder is the last one to get paid in the event of insolvency, just like all other owners.

Limited Safety of the Investment

Stocks are volatile, which means they fluctuate in value daily. When an investor purchases a stock, they are not guaranteed a return on investment (ROI). In spite of the level of skill an investor might attain, there is always an asymmetry of information that instills risk in any investment. The most that can be achieved from investment skill is the mitigation of risk.

Traumatic Psychological Experience

Stock volatility could be a psychologically damaging experience for the investor. Since greed and fear are determining psychological factors of the market, they can produce mental trauma for most investors who are inappropriately trained or prepared to experience such sudden market changes.

Stock values can sometimes change for no apparent reason, which can be psychologically very painful for the investor. Investors in a publicly-traded company may not be privy to all that there is to know about the company. Therefore, stockholders could be subjected to the internal corruptive practices of the companies they invest in.

Bonds

A bond is a type of debt issued by a company to raise capital to expand its business. In essence, a bond is a debt security, similar to an "I owe you" (IOU), which essentially is a promissory note used to cover the payment of a debt. When an investor purchases a bond, they are lending money to a government, municipality, corporation, federal agency, or other entity, which is known as the issuer. In return for lending the money, the issuer provides the investor with a bond in which it promises to pay a specified rate of interest during the life of the bond and to repay the principal, which is the bond's face value, when it matures at a specific maturity date.

The terms "treasury bills," "notes," "debt securities," and "debt obligations" are all used synonymously to represent bonds. This book, for the sake of simplification, will be referring to bonds when any of these terms are used. Bonds will typically have a face value, a coupon rate, and a maturity date. Bonds are issued by corporations to the public, and are subsequently purchased by investors who collect the original principal amount in addition to a predetermined interest rate when the bond matures at a specified date.

Furthermore, federal, state, and municipal governments also issue bonds to raise money for public works programs and projects. For example, municipal bonds are issued by a state, city, or local government to fund municipal projects and offer tax advantages. The federal government does not count earnings from municipal bonds as part of taxable income, and bonds bought by a resident of the issuing state are typically exempt from taxes on the interest. This favorable tax treatment helps incentivize individual investors to purchase municipal bonds. However, yields on municipal bonds are often lower than other types of bonds because of the tax-free advantages.

Bonds are considered a less risky form of investment than stocks because they have less volatility. Even though bonds are considered more predictable than stocks, they are not without risk. They possess credit risk, prepayment risk, liquidity risk, and interest-rate risk. If the bond is sold before its maturity date, the investor risks losing capital, but if the bond is held to maturity, the investor will receive the entire principal amount that was originally invested.

The Effect of Market Interest Rates on Bond Prices and Yield

The interest-rate risk of bonds is a very important concept for the bond investor to understand. This concept relates to the fundamental principle of bond investing, which states that market interest rates and bond prices generally move in opposite directions. In other words, there is an inverse relationship between interest rates and bond prices. For example, when market interest rates increase, the price of fixed-rate bonds decreases. This inverse relationship between interest rates and bond prices moving in opposite directions can be illustrated by a drawing of a seesaw, as shown in Appendix G. In fact, this is the illustration that is disseminated by the U.S. Securities and Exchange Commission (SEC) to educate investors on this important topic. According to the SEC Office of Investor Education and Advocacy, this interest rate and bond price movement is a phenomenon known as interest-rate risk (Investor Bulletin Interest Rate Risk, n. d.).

Appendix I illustrate, by way of tables 1 and 2, how a 1% increase or decrease in the market interest rates will affect bond prices and their yield to maturity. Because of this inverse relationship between interest rates and bond prices and subsequent yields to maturity, the SEC recommends that it is imperative for investors always to consider interest-rate risk when they purchase bonds in a low-interest-rate environment.

Advantages of Bond Investing

Some of the advantages of bond investing include the following:

- ❖ Less volatile investment
- ❖ Can provide income stability
- ❖ Can provide both income stability and liquidity

Less Volatile Investment

Bond prices tend to rise and fall to a lesser degree than stocks, which means their prices fluctuate less than that of stocks. Therefore, bonds are not as volatile an investment as stocks.

Can Provide Income Stability

Certain bonds can provide a level of income stability. However, with a bond, the guarantee or income stability is only as good as the financial strength of the issuer. If the issuer runs into financial difficulty, they may default, and the investor could lose all or part of their money.

Can Provide Both Income Stability and Liquidity

When an investor begins to build a portfolio of investments, they need to consider their short and long-term goals. This decision should involve the inclusion of bonds, such as U.S. Treasuries and short maturity bonds that can provide both stability and liquidity to the portfolio. The liquidity from bonds, is provided because they are considered cash equivalents, which can be easily converted to cash relatively quickly.

Disadvantages of Bond Investing

Some of the disadvantages of bond investing include the following:

- ❖ Lower long-term returns
- ❖ Interest rate inverse relationship of bonds
- ❖ Loss of principal if the sale of bonds occurs before maturity

Lower Long-Term returns

Historically, bonds have provided lower long-term returns on investment than stocks. The reason for the reduced returns generated by bonds is attributed to the lesser volatility of the investment; thus, bonds carry less risk than stocks. Consequently, for any investment, the less risk the investor assumes, the lower the returns that will be attained.

Interest Rate Inverse Relationship of Bonds

Bonds have an inverse relationship with interest rates, which means that bond prices fall when interest rates increase and vice versa. Long-term bonds, especially the 30-year bond, suffer more from price fluctuations as interest rates rise and fall, than bonds with shorter maturities. This is an important concept for investors to remember.

Loss of Principal if Sale of Bonds Occurs before Maturity

If the investor holds the bond to maturity, the investor will receive the entire amount invested. However, if interest rates increase and the investor needs to sell their bond before its maturity date, then the sale of the bonds will be made at a loss of principal.

Consequently, each type of investment has its own potential rewards and risks. Stocks offer an opportunity for higher long-term returns compared with bonds but come with a greater degree of risk. In contrast, bonds are usually more stable than stocks but generate lower long-term returns.

One of the goals of this book is to demonstrate to investors that private mortgage investing is similar to bond investing, but with the potential to generate a higher rate of return or ROI. As the reading audience will see, the research study demonstrated that private mortgage investing as an alternative investment vehicle is worthy of consideration for investors who are seeking to generate a consistent income stream with a high degree of safety and reduced volatility.

The objective of the study undertaken is not to promote this form of investing, but rather to create awareness of the availability of such an investment as a suitable investment vehicle for passive cash flow generation. It is a well-known investment strategy that by owning a mixture of different investment vehicles, diversification of the investment portfolio can be achieved. Following this type of *"diversify"* investment strategy will help mitigate the risks associated with putting all the investor's money into a single type of investment.

Mutual Funds

A mutual fund is a type of professionally managed, collective investment strategy that pools money from many investors to purchase a variety of investment securities. Mutual funds are the most common type of investment for individual investors. These mutual funds are popular investment vehicles because they offer portfolio diversification for investors, allowing professional money managers to handle the buying and selling of individual stocks, bonds, and other investment vehicles.

A mutual fund is controlled by a fund manager who invests money based on a strategy that guides the objective of each particular fund. The mutual fund investment objective is described and explained in the fund's prospectus. For example, the objective of a mutual fund can be to invest only in stocks, bonds, or in a balanced portfolio of stocks, bonds, commercial paper, and other securities. In a balanced type of fund, the small investors will benefit from the diversification of this type of mutual fund objective because of the holding of several types of assets, which may reduce portfolio and market risk. In other words, many different types of investments in one portfolio decrease the investor's risk of loss from any one of those investments. There are three different types of U.S. mutual funds:

❖ Open-ended fund

❖ Unit investment trust (UIT)

❖ Closed-end fund

Open-Ended Fund

Open-end funds are the most common type of mutual fund. The fund is classified as open-ended because there is no limit to the number of shares the fund can have. Thus, the fund can sell as many shares as it wants. When the fund sells more shares, the new money is used to expand the fund's portfolio. Open-ended mutual funds must be willing to buy back their shares from their investors at the end of every business day at the *net asset value (NAV)* computed for that particular day.

This type of fund is managed by professional money managers that oversee the buying and selling of the portfolio's securities. The total investment in the fund will vary based on share purchases, share redemptions, and fluctuation in market prices, or valuation.

Unit Investment Trust (UIT)

Unit investment trusts (UITs) are open-ended investments similar to an open-ended mutual fund. Therefore, the underlying value of the assets is always directly represented by the total number of units issued, multiplied by the unit price, less the transaction or management fee having been charged (and any other associated costs). Each UIT fund has a specified investment objective to determine the management aims and limitations (Unit Investment Trusts (UITs), n. d.; Unit Trust, n. d.).

Unlike open-ended mutual funds, UITs issue their shares to the public only once, which is when the trusts are created. In other words, a UIT will make a one-time *"public offering"* of only a specific, fixed number of units, similar to closed-end funds. UITs generally have a limited life span, which is established at creation.

Investors can redeem their shares directly with the fund at any time, similar to an open-ended fund, or they can wait to redeem upon the termination of the trust. The reason this function can be executed is because UIT sponsors will maintain a secondary market that allows owners of UIT units to sell their shares back to the sponsors, as well as allowing other investors to buy UIT units from the sponsors. Even though selling shares back to the sponsor is not the customary practice, it is important to be aware that there is an open market available to facilitate this process.

As mentioned above, the portfolio of securities in a UIT is established when the UIT is created, and it will not change during the life span of the trust. Thus, a UIT does not require the services of a professional investment manager to oversee the investment portfolio because UITs behave similarly to an index fund. Therefore, UITs do not have a board of directors, corporate officers, or an investment adviser to render advice during the life span of the trust (Unit Investment Trusts (UITs), n. d.; Unit Trust, n. d.).

The first UIT was created and launched in 1931 in the United Kingdom by Municipal and General Securities Company (MGSC). The creation of this first UIT was attributed to the inspiration of Ian Fairbairn, a British financier and Olympic rower who competed in the Summer Olympics of 1924. The rationale behind the launch of this UIT was to emulate the comparative robustness of United States mutual funds through the 1929 Wall Street crash. This initial trust, which was called the *"First British Fixed Trust,"* held the shares of 24 leading companies in a fixed portfolio that was not changed for the established life span of 20 years. The trust was re-launched again in 1951 as the M&G General Trust, which was subsequently renamed the *"Blue-Chip Fund"* (M&G, n. d.; Sin, 1998).

Closed-End Fund

A closed-end, or *closed-ended* fund is a collective investment arrangement or strategies composed of a fixed number of shares, which are not directly redeemable from the fund. Unlike open-ended funds, new shares or units in a closed-end fund are not created by managers to meet the investors' demand. Instead, the shares can be purchased and sold only in the open market; thus, the selling and redeeming of the fund shares are subject to the laws of supply and demand. This is the original design of the mutual fund, which predates open-end mutual funds but offers the same actively managed pooled investment securities.

Publicly sold, closed-end funds must be registered under both the Securities Act of 1933 and the Investment Company Act of 1940. The Securities Act of 1933, also known as the Truth in Securities Act, was enacted as a result of the market crash of 1929. It was the first major piece of federal legislation to apply to the sale of securities. The objectives of the fund were to require that investors receive significant or material information about the securities being offered for public sale, and to prohibit deceit, misrepresentations, and other fraud in the sale of securities to the public (Lemke, et al., 2002).

Similar to open-ended funds, are usually sponsored by a fund management company that controls how the fund is invested. The fund begins by soliciting money from investors in an initial offering, which may be public or limited. The investors are given shares corresponding to their initial investment. The fund managers pool the collected money and purchase securities or other assets. The investments that the fund manager can invest in will depend on the fund's charter, prospectus, and the applicable governmental regulations. The funds will typically invest in stocks, bonds, a combination of both, or in some other very specific investments, such as tax-exempt bonds issued by the various states like Florida, New York, and California, to name just a few.

Therefore, in summary, closed-end or closed-ended funds generally issue shares to the public only once when they are created, similar to UITs, through the initial public offering (IPO). The fund's shares are then listed for trading on a stock exchange. Investors who no longer wish to invest in the fund cannot sell their shares back to the fund, as can be done with an open-end fund.

The investor must sell their shares to another investor in the open market. The price the investor receives may be significantly different from NAV. It may be at a premium to NAV, which is higher than NAV, or at a discount to NAV, lower than NAV. The fund is managed by a professional investment manager that oversees the fund's portfolio by executing the buying and selling of securities as appropriate.

Advantages of Mutual Fund Investing

Mutual funds are popular investment vehicles that provide several advantages, which include the following:

- ❖ Convenience
- ❖ Diversification
- ❖ Professional money management
- ❖ Investment size
- ❖ Liquidity
- ❖ Economies of scale

Convenience

Mutual funds are an easy way for the average investor to buy and participate in stock market investments that would be too complex for most individual investors to manage on their own.

Diversification

Mutual funds can own thousands of individual securities that span across various asset classes and industry sectors, which gives investors broad diversification, thus providing mitigation of portfolio risks.

Professional Money Management

Mutual funds differ from index funds and UITs in that they are managed by experienced industry professionals who follow the funds' stated investment objectives with oversight from the federal government.

Investment Size

Investors can invest small or large amounts of money in mutual funds, even if they do not have much financial or investing experience.

Liquidity

Liquidity is determined by the degree to which an asset or security can be bought or sold in the market without affecting the asset's price. Investors can sell their mutual funds' shares at any time since they are as liquid as regular common stocks. Liquidity is also known as marketability, which is simply the ability to convert an asset to cash quickly.

Economies of Scale

Mutual funds can take advantage of their buying and selling capability, and thereby can reduce transaction costs for investors. When an investor buys a mutual fund, they are able to diversify without incurring numerous commission charges.

Disadvantages of Mutual Fund Investing

Again, as with any kind of investment vehicle, there are also disadvantages, and mutual funds are no exception. Some of the disadvantages include the following:

- ❖ Management and expense fees
- ❖ Share price calculation
- ❖ Capital gains
- ❖ Phantom gains
- ❖ Past performance is not a reliable indicator of future performance.
- ❖ Mutual funds are not guaranteed, or FDIC insured

Management and Expense Fees

Mutual funds can be expensive to manage. Therefore, they charge investors sales commissions, or what they call *"loads,"* in addition to annual fees, regardless of the fund's performance. Even if the funds are considered "no loads," they compensate for the lack of an up-front commission by charging higher management fees, which can actually be more than the load or commission. In other words, the mutual fund will make money even if the investor loses money. Mutual funds' fees can be reduced by buying the funds directly from the funds' family instead of buying them from a broker that will charge a commission.

Share Price Calculation

Mutual fund share prices are calculated and made public once per day. Stock prices are updated throughout the day, allowing the investor to take advantage of market movements if investors trade frequently. Because the mutual fund shares are composed of multiple investments, their price will depend on the NAV of all the underlying securities. Therefore, if investors place a buy or sell order for a mutual fund, the price is not set until the official end of the market day.

Capital Gains

Mutual funds must distribute capital gains to their shareholders, regardless of how long the investor has owned their shares. It is not unusual for mutual fund investors to lose money while at the same time paying taxes on capital gains. However, if the investor owns individual securities instead of mutual funds, they can control when to sell the investment, which makes it simpler to control the capital gains taxes that will have to be paid.

Phantom Gains

Mutual funds that need to raise cash can sell profitable investments, which will create capital gains. These capital gains get passed to investors, which means that even if the fund performed poorly, the investor would end up paying capital gain taxes.

Past Performance is Not a Reliable Indicator of Future Performance

Therefore, investors should not be impressed by, or purchase a fund based on, its historical performance. In essence, do not be impressed by the previous year returns on investment. However, according to the Securities and Exchange Commission, past performance is not a guarantee of future performance. Still, this historical track record can help the investor assess a fund's volatility over time.

Mutual Funds are not Guaranteed, or FDIC insured

Most mutual fund investors have access to three different types of protection for their fund investments. They have insurance against investment firm failure, security guarantees in the case of fraudulent activity, and litigation in the case of management negligence or malpractice. However, there is no protection against the risks of poor market performance.

Insurance for mutual fund accounts is provided by the Securities Investors Protection Corporation (SIPC), in which most investment firms are members. If the investment company fails, the SIPC insurance will make sure that all customers are made whole, either by the investment company itself, or through the reserve funds of the SIPC, up to a limit of $500,000 per account. After the failure of a company, the SIPC will either move the investor's account to another SIPC member firm, or the investor has the choice to select a firm of their choice. Therefore, mutual funds are not riskless investments (US Securities and Exchange Commission, n. d.).

When choosing mutual funds, be sure to compare expense ratios. The total expense ratio (TER) equals all the fees and fund expenses divided by the average net assets. High expense ratios will reduce the return the investor can earn from a mutual fund. Researchers have found that the best way to maximize profits from a mutual fund is to reduce the fees paid by choosing no-load funds, which offer low expense ratios. In other words, look at every expense in the prospectus because expenses can determine, to a large extent, the return that can be generated from an investment.

Exchange Traded Funds (ETFs)

Exchanged traded funds (ETFs) are a relatively recent innovation in the mutual fund industry. ETFs have been available in the U.S. since 1993 and in Europe since 1999. ETFs are open-ended funds or UITs that trade on an exchange. Open-ended funds are the most common, but ETFs have been rapidly gaining in popularity. ETFs essentially combine the characteristics featured in both the UIT and open-ended mutual funds. They can be bought and sold at the end of each trading day for their net asset value (NAV), with the tradability feature of a closed-end fund, which trades throughout the trading day at prices that may be more or less than its NAV.

Therefore, like closed-end funds, ETFs are traded throughout the day on a stock exchange at a price determined by the market. However, as with open-ended funds, investors normally receive a price that is close to NAV. To keep the market price close to net asset value, ETFs issue, and redeem large blocks of their shares with institutional investors. ETFs are similar in many ways to traditional mutual funds, except that shares in an ETF can be bought and sold throughout the day like stocks on a stock exchange through a broker-dealer (ETFs, n. d.).

ETFs are baskets of securities that are often structured to mimic a market index. These funds are traded on national stock exchanges and are available for purchase through any broker. They encompass the benefits of open-end index mutual funds and provide diversification. Moreover, they have low operating costs with the potential for tax efficiency and the trading flexibility of individual stocks.

ETFs are funds that track indexes like the NASDAQ-100 Index, S&P 500, and Dow Jones, just to name a few. When an investor purchases shares of an ETF, they are buying shares of a portfolio that tracks the yield and return of its native index. The main difference between ETFs and other types of index funds is that ETFs do not try to outperform their corresponding index, but instead simply replicate its performance. Thus, most ETFs are index funds that do not attempt to beat the market, but rather, they try to be the market.

In the United States, the majority of ETFs are designed as open-ended management investment companies, which is the same arrangement or structure used by the mutual funds' industry. However, some ETFs, including a few of the largest ones, are constructed as UITs. ETFs that are arranged or structured as open-ended funds have greater flexibility in constructing a portfolio and are not prohibited from participating in securities lending programs or from using futures and options in achieving their investment objectives (Sec Concept Release # IC-25258, 2001, November 8).

Under the existing regulations, to create a new ETF, the ETF must receive an order from the Securities and Exchange Commission, giving it relief from provisions of the Investment Company Act (ICA) of 1940 that would not otherwise allow the ETF structure. This act, often known as the Company Act or the 1940 Act, is the primary source of regulation for mutual funds, closed-end funds, and investment industry, which currently is an impressive multi-trillion dollar industry (Lemke, et al., 2002). The primary emphasis of the ICA of 1940 is to regulate mutual funds and other companies that engage primarily in investing, reinvesting, and trading in securities, and whose own securities are offered to the investing public (*15 U.S.C. §§ 80a-1-64*). The purpose of the ICA is to require disclosure to the investing public about the fund, its investment objectives, and its structure and operations.

The ICA of 1940 is an act of Congress that passed as U.S. Public Law 76–768 on August 22, 1940. This act, in combination with the passage of the Securities Exchange Act of 1934—which was the act that established the Security Exchange Commission (SEC) to regulate the secondary market for the trading of securities (such as stocks, bonds, and debentures) and the Investment Advisers Act (IAA) of 1940 that was created to regulate the actions of investment advisers—together provide the legal foundation or backbone of the United States financial regulations. All of these acts have been updated to incorporate provisions of the newly instituted Dodd-Frank Act of 2010 as the result of the 2008 financial housing crisis (Title I-Investment Companies, n. d.).

As previously mentioned, to create a new ETF, it is required to request an exemptive relief order from the SEC. However, the SEC has proposed rules that would allow the creation of an ETF without the need for an exemptive order. Under this SEC proposal, an ETF would be defined as a registered, open-ended management investment company that performs the following functions:

- ❖ Issues or redeems creation units in exchange for the deposit (or delivery) of basket assets, the current value of which is disseminated per share by a national securities exchange at regular intervals during the trading day.
- ❖ Identifies itself as an ETF in any sales literature.
- ❖ Issues shares that are approved for listing and trading on a securities exchange.
- ❖ Discloses each business day, on its publicly available website, the previous business day's net asset value and the closing market price of the fund's shares, and the premium or discount of the closing market price against the net asset value of the fund's shares as a percentage of net asset value.
- ❖ An ETF can be classified either as an index fund, or an actively managed fund that discloses each business day on its publicly available website the identities and weighting of the component securities and other assets held by the fund.

The SEC rule proposal would allow ETFs to be either an index fund or a fully transparent, actively managed fund. In 2008, the SEC issued their first exemptive order to the Power Actively Managed Exchange-Traded Fund Trust (Investment Company Act of Shares 940 Release No. 28171, 2008, February 27). Most ETFs are passively managed, meaning the fund manager makes only minor and periodic adjustments instead of continually and actively trading assets.

Investors seeking to be involved with ETF-type investments have a variety of asset classes as options, which include the following underlying investment vehicles:

- ❖ Foreign stocks
- ❖ Equities
- ❖ Fixed income
- ❖ Commodities
- ❖ Real estate

ETFs have been around since January 1993, when the S&P 500 SPDR (SPY) was first launched with relatively little fanfare. However, this ETF in the 21 years since its debut, has accumulated more than $100 billion in assets (Johnston, 2014, May 22). ETFs often have lower costs than mutual funds and are tax-efficient because they generally have less turnover than other securities. Only authorized participants, which are usually big institutional investors, buy or sell ETFs directly from or to the fund manager, typically done in huge blocks of shares. Other investors trade shares on the secondary market just like stock investors.

Advantages of ETF Investing

- ❖ ETFs have low annual expenses, especially in relation to mutual fund charges. Customarily, ETF administrative costs are less than two-tenths of one percent (or 20 basis points) per annum, compared to the more than 1% yearly costs of some mutual funds, according to the NASDAQ.

❖ ETFs can also be more tax-efficient. They only generate taxable capital gains when sold, unlike actively-traded mutual funds that annually pass through taxable capital gains.

❖ ETFs can be bought and sold through a broker without restriction during the trading day. Thus ETFs give investors more flexibility, especially when compared to mutual funds, which only trade at the end of the day.

❖ Because ETFs trade like stocks, it is easier for ETF investors to use risk-management strategies like *stop-loss orders*. This type of order calls for the buying or selling of securities when they reach a particular price and *limit orders*, which set the maximum and minimum purchasing and selling prices.

Disadvantages of ETF Investing

❖ The bid-ask spread, which is the difference between the bidding and asking price, on ETFs can be large, with fewer assets under management. The smaller the ETF spread, the lower the cost. ETFs are not as liquid as small-cap stocks, so the investor may not get the ETF at net asset value. What this means is that the investor could overpay for the portfolio or sell it for less than it is worth.

❖ Emotional reactions to events in one major company within the sector can amplify the short-term trading of ETFs. For example, a price drop in companies like Google or Apple can trigger the sale of ETFs that include its stock, potentially resulting in increased volatility.

Derivatives

A derivative is a financial contract whose value is based upon some other asset. In other words, it derives its value from something else. It is a contract between two or more parties whose value is based on an agreed-upon, underlying financial asset, index, or security. Derivatives are one of the three main categories of financial instruments, the other two being equities, such as stocks or shares, and debt securities, such as bonds and mortgage-back securities (MBSs) (Derivatives, n. d.).

Some of the common underlying instruments for the derivatives include the following investment vehicles:

- ❖ Bonds
- ❖ Commodities
- ❖ Currencies
- ❖ Interest rates
- ❖ Market indexes
- ❖ Stocks

Futures contracts, forward contracts, options, swaps, and warrants are common types of derivatives. For example, a futures contract is a derivative because its value is affected by the performance of the underlying contract. Similarly, a stock option is a derivative because its value is derived from the performance of the underlying stock.

Derivatives are used for speculating and hedging purposes. Speculators seek to profit from changing prices in the underlying asset, index, or security. For example, a trader may attempt to profit from an anticipated drop in an index's price by selling the related futures contract, which is a process that is called *"going short"* or *"selling short."* Derivatives used as a hedge allows the risks associated with the underlying asset's price to be transferred between the parties involved in the contract.

Derivatives are traded on national securities exchanges and are regulated by the SEC. Other derivatives are traded over-the-counter (OTC), which are individually negotiated agreements between two parties without any supervision of an exchange. OTC, or off-exchange trading, does not possess the benefits of trading in a regulated stock exchange that facilitates liquidity, mitigates all credit risk concerning the default of one party in the transaction, provides transparency, and maintains the current market price.

Although the use of derivatives appears to be an investment instrument used in this modern era, its origins trace back several centuries. One of the oldest derivatives is rice futures, which have been traded on the Dojima Rice Exchange since the eighteenth century (Dojima Rice Exchange, n. d.). Derivative securities are a useful and necessary investment tool, and the advantages of derivative trading typically far outweigh the disadvantages.

Advantages of Derivatives Investing

- ❖ Speculation
- ❖ Hedging for risk mitigation
- ❖ Contract flexibility
- ❖ Leveraged

Disadvantages of Derivatives Investing

- ❖ Misuse of these investment vehicles can result in large losses.
- ❖ Inadequate training and skill level to use these products

This chapter has addressed the topic of liquid investments, which refers to investments that can easily be converted to cash without any loss of value. The level of liquidity an investor should keep readily available depends largely upon the estimated monthly expenses of the individual. While most financial planners recommend that at least six months of cash reserve be kept on hand to cover unexpected emergencies, this goal is not always achievable for most people. However, this is an important objective that should be followed by everyone. Investors should be cognizant of the fact that national emergencies are less likely to occur than personal emergencies; thus, having a certain level of liquidity on hand will allow the individual to maintain their monthly financial stability with far fewer worries.

3

Types of Illiquid Investments

A s previously mentioned, illiquid investments are assets or investments that cannot be readily converted into cash, in contrast with liquid assets, which are investments either in the form of cash or easily convertible into cash. Therefore, the main disadvantage of illiquid investments is that when cash is required in a hurry, these are unsuitable investments unless the investor is willing to sell at a discount because of the pressing need to sell the investment quickly. The investments that will be described below are considered illiquid-type investments.

Annuities

Annuities are an investment vehicle typically used for retirement purposes that can also be tax-deferred. An annuity is any continuing payment with a fixed total annual amount. It is an investment product designed to provide an accumulation of funds or an income stream for retirement. Annuities provide similar tax benefits to IRAs, and like other types of investments, have unique advantages and disadvantages. Fundamentally, an annuity is an insurance product that pays out income and can be used as part of a retirement strategy.

However, annuities can also be an effective funding source for educational purposes where the annuity is held in the child's name under the provisions of the Uniform Gifts to Minors Act.

The negative aspect of this strategy is that the child would then pay a 10% tax penalty on the earnings when the time came for withdrawals. Moreover, another drawback is that the child is free to use the money for any purpose, not just education costs.

Annuities are a popular choice for investors who want to receive a consistent income stream during retirement. Thus, an annuity essentially is a contract between the investor and an insurance company. When the investor purchases an annuity, they can either pay a large lump sum upfront—this type of annuity is called an immediate annuity—or the investor can make a regular series of deposits over a set, scheduled amount of time.

If the selection is an immediate annuity, the insurance company then agrees to start paying the annuitant (the investor) money on a specified date, and will continue to make those payments or distributions to the investor for a fixed amount of time (e.g., 15 or 20 years), or until the death of the investor. The investor can choose for the payments to be a fixed dollar amount or a variable amount that will fluctuate based on market performance. The investor can also choose a deferred annuity, which will provide for scheduled distributions. In this case, the investments will grow, similar to an IRA account, until the investor is ready to receive the money.

Various Types of Annuities

The type of annuity selected by the investor will be determined by the amount of income the annuitant would like to receive, and by the degree of risk, the investor is willing to accept. There are three basic annuity options to choose from, which are as follows:

❖ Fixed annuity

❖ Variable annuity

❖ Indexed or equity-indexed annuities

Fixed Annuity

Fixed annuities behave very similarly to certificates of deposit (CDs). Investors are guaranteed their principal and interest by the insurance company.

Variable Annuity

This type of annuity is similar to a mutual fund. Therefore, the investor can lose both principal and interest, but has the potential to earn double-digit returns when the stock market is rising.

Indexed or Equity-Indexed Annuities

These annuities combine features of both fixed and variable annuities. The principal is guaranteed by the insurance company. However, the return is determined by the performance of the stock market index, such as the Standard and Poor's 500 (S&P 500). While the payout can vary, the principal remains protected, even when the equity market experiences losses.

Insurance Companies

Insurance companies—the issuers of annuities—like any other enterprises are in business to make a profit on the annuities they issue or sell. These companies project how much they can potentially expect to earn from investing the investors' funds, and although the insurance company distributes the majority of the earnings to the investors, they retain a portion of the earnings as expenses and management fees. Like banks, insurance companies generate their profits by investing other people's money (OPM) and making a spread between the earned interest and the payout interest to the investors.

There are over 2000 insurance providers in the United States, of which approximately 200 offer annuities (Freeannuityrates.com, n. d.). Since purchasing an annuity is a serious decision that will have a positive or negative impact on the investor's life, the decision should be embraced with the importance it deserves. Because the selection of an annuity product is a consequential decision, only a superior, A-rated insurance company should be selected. Once the selection has been made, the various options available should be discussed with an objective financial planner who is not involved in the selling aspect of the annuity to avoid any conflict of interest.

Advantages of Annuities Investing

- ❖ Tax deferral
- ❖ Lifetime payments
- ❖ Asset accumulation and protection
- ❖ Guaranteed payout
- ❖ Estate planning (probate avoidance)
- ❖ Protection from creditors
- ❖ Exemption from Free Application of Student Aid (FAFSA) Asset Status

Disadvantages of Annuities Investing

- ❖ Threat of inflation
- ❖ Hidden fees
- ❖ Annuity withdrawal penalties
- ❖ Complexity
- ❖ Taxation
- ❖ Illiquidity
- ❖ Outliving your payments
- ❖ Stability of the insurance company underwriting the annuity

When the purchase of an annuity has been considered, the investor should seek the advice of a competent, independent, certified financial planner (rather than an insurance agent) to help review the contract because of the potential conflict of interest inherent in all these types of financial transactions.

Insurance agents typically are more interested in selling the annuity than ensuring that investors acquire the best possible annuity option because of the hefty commission they receive. Although this might not be the case with all insurance agents, it is important for the investor to realize that there is an inherent conflict of interest situation any time someone is trying to sell a product or a service to a prospective client or customer. Moreover, the investor should be pre-educated (i.e., be familiar) regarding this investment vehicle before signing the contract.

Understanding Conflict of Interest

Understanding the existence of a conflict of interest situations should be very important to all investors because it can help mitigate unnecessary risk-taking. There are many definitions used to describe what a conflict of interest is. In this book, the author will use a universally accepted definition that states: *"A conflict of interest is a set of circumstances, which creates a risk that professional judgment or actions regarding a primary interest will be unduly influenced by a secondary interest"* (Lo & Field, 2009).

"Primary interest" refers to the principal goals of the profession or activity, such as the protection of clients, the health of patients, the integrity of research, and the duties of public office. *"Secondary interest"* includes not only financial gains, but also such motives as the desire for professional advancement and the wish to do favors for family and friends. However, conflict of interest rules usually focus mostly on financial relationships because they are relatively more objective, reciprocated, and quantifiable. The secondary conflicts of interest are not treated as wrong in and of themselves, but become objectionable when they are believed to have greater weight or importance than the primary interests.

The *"conflict"* in a conflict of interest scenario exists whether or not a particular individual is actually influenced by the secondary interest. It is assumed to exist if the circumstances are reasonably believed—based on past experience and objective evidence— to create a risk that the decisions might be unduly influenced by the secondary interests. In other words, a conflict of interest is a situation where an individual or firm has an incentive to serve one interest at the expense of another interest or obligation. The conflict could simply be serving the interest of the firm over that of a client, or serving the interest of one client over the interest of other clients, or an employee or group of employees serving their own interests over those of the firm or the firm's clients (di Florio, 2012).

Another way of expressing it in more general terms is that conflicts of interest can be defined as any situations in which an individual or corporation—either private or governmental—is in a position to be able to exploit in a professional or official capacity in some way for their personal or corporate benefit. According to Carlo di Florio (2012), former director of the Securities and Exchange Commission (SEC) Office of Compliance Inspections and Examinations, conflict of interest should be a topic of perpetual importance to all aspects of compliance and ethics programs. Therefore, understanding the concept of conflict of interest should be of paramount importance to all investors. In fact, it is the key to risk mitigation in the opinion of the author. The potential for the existence of a conflict of interest permeates all business transactions. Conflicts of interest exist throughout the commercial world.

Failure to manage conflicts of interest has been a continuing theme of most financial crises and scandals since before the inception of the federal securities laws. During the early 1930s, the Pecora hearings held by the Senate Committee on Banking and Currency revealed a vast array of self-dealing and other conflicts of interest throughout the financial markets. For example, such as the use of bank loans to support bank affiliates, and incentives on the part of banks to give investment advice that supported affiliate-underwritten securities.

The Pecora hearings were a financial investigation of Wall Street that commenced on April 11, 1932, under the leadership of three different head counsels who were all dismissed because of their ineffectiveness in resolving the investigation. Ferdinand Pecora, an Italian-American assistant district attorney from New York County, was hired on January 24, 1933, by Senator Peter Norbeck, who was chairman of the Senate Committee on Banking and Currency during the Depression-era. Therefore, in 1933, Pecora became the head counsel for the Senate Committee on Banking and Currency, and within six weeks of his hiring, he had unraveled all the secrets that had created the financial scandal.

Pecora was so successful during these hearings that the investigation became synonymous with his name, becoming known as the *"Pecora hearings"* and not with Senator Peter Norbeck, the chairman of the Senate committee who initiated the investigation. The Pecora hearings ended on May 4, 1934, and soon after that, Pecora was rewarded for his stellar performance during the investigation with an appointment to the commissionership of the Securities and Exchange Commission (SEC) (Ruggeri, 2009, September 29; Pecora Commission, n. d.). Pecora, like Dodd-Frank, most recently, in essence, investigated the main causes that led to the market crash of 1929, which resulted in the Great Depression.

According to Ruggeri (2009, September 29), these types of investigations rarely result in any criminal charges being imposed on the perpetrators. However, they usually lead to the creation of new legislation intended to prevent a similar crisis from occurring again in the future. What resulted from the Pecora hearings by the close of the investigation in June of 1934, was the creation of the following legislation: the Glass-Steagall Act of 1933, the Securities Act of 1933, and the Securities Exchange Act of 1934. The creation and implementation of this legislation dramatically improved and reshaped the American financial system.

The Glass-Steagall Act alone created the Federal Deposit Insurance Corporation (FDIC), which guaranteed consumers' bank deposits. It also gave the Federal Reserve greater oversight over banks, as well as separating banks from insurance companies and investment firms. Some economists currently speculate that the repeal of the Glass-Steagall Act in 1999 helped bring about the current financial crisis (Ruggeri, 2009, September 29).

A well-known quote from philosopher Jorge Agustín Nicolás Ruiz de Santayana y Borrás, better known as George Santayana, is entirely appropriate at this juncture because of its applicability to the situation just described. Santayana, a well-known philosopher, is known for the famous saying that states, *"Those who cannot remember the past are condemned to repeat it."* However, it seems that not remembering the past is a chronic affliction of humanity, for it appears that humankind continues to repeat the same mistakes from the lessons it has not learned from the past.

Conversely and somewhat cynically, it is entirely possible—but difficult—to prove that humankind has, in fact, learned from the mistakes of its previous experiences. If this observation is correct, then it is possible to conclude that the problem of repeating past mistakes lie not with the incapability of humans to learn from their past mistakes, but rather with the corruptive nature of humans to take conscious risks, believing that they will get away with it, in spite of those lessons, which, in fact, were learned.

Real Estate Investing

Real estate investing involves the purchase, ownership, management, rental, or sale of real estate for profit. Improvement of realty property as part of a real estate investment strategy is generally considered to be a sub-specialty of real estate investing classified as "real estate development."

Real estate is an asset form with limited liquidity relative to other investments, like stocks, bonds, and mutual funds. It is also considered a capital intensive form of investment, although capital can be acquired through mortgage leverage, either through conventional or private mortgage lenders, and it's highly cash-flow dependent. If these elements of real estate investing are not well understood and appropriately managed by the investor, real estate becomes a risky investment. The primary cause of real estate investment failure is for the investor to generate negative cash flow from the investment for an unsustainable period of time, which will force the investor to either resell the property at a loss or become insolvent.

Real estate assets are expensive in comparison to other widely available investment vehicles such as stocks, bonds, and CDs. Rarely will real estate investors pay the entire amount of the purchase price of a property in cash. Customarily, a large portion of the purchase price will be financed using some sort of financial instrument, such as a mortgage loan collateralized by the property itself.

The amount of the purchase price financed by debt is referred to as *"leverage."* The amount financed by the investor's own capital, through cash or other asset transfers, is referred to as *"equity."* The ratio of leverage to total appraised value, referred to as the *"loan-to-value (LTV) ratio,"* for a conventional mortgage is a mathematical measure of the risk an investor is taking by using leverage to finance the purchase of a property.

The objective of real estate investors is typically to seek to decrease their equity requirements and increase the leverage component of the investment so that their return on investment (ROI) can be maximized. Conversely, for the lenders and other financial institutions, their objective is to maximize the equity requirements for the real estate investments they will finance, which customarily is approximately 20% of the appraised value for traditional lending institutions, or an LTV ratio of 80/20.

If the property to be financed is a rehab-type project, which requires extensive repairs, traditional lenders like banks will usually not lend on these properties. In this type of situation, the investor may be required to borrow from a private or hard money lender utilizing a short-term bridge loan. The unavailability of conventional loans from traditional banks creates a financial vacuum that results in one of the reasons why private money lenders are needed.

Private money loans are usually short-term loans where the private lender charges a higher interest rate, customarily in the range of 9% to14%. Additionally, private money loans are underwritten at lower LTV ratios to help mitigate investment risk. The typical LTVs for these types of loans are between 65/35% and 70/30%, which depend on the underwriting guidelines the investor wants to adhere to. The LTV ratio is a financial term used by lenders to express the ratio of a loan to the value of an asset purchased. Loan-to-value is one of the key risk factors that both private and traditional lenders assess when qualifying borrowers for a mortgage.

The risk of default is always at the forefront of the lending decisions, and the likelihood of a lender absorbing a loss increases as the amount of equity decreases. This is the reason private money lenders will not lend more than 65% to 70% of the appraised value of the property. The loan-to-value ratio is a crucial tool used by private money lenders to mitigate investment risk; thus, the lower the LTV ratio, the safer the investment.

Therefore, for conventional lenders, as the LTV ratio of a loan increases, the qualification guidelines for certain mortgage programs become stricter. For borrowers of high LTV loans, the lenders can require borrowers to purchase mortgage insurance to protect the lender from the possibility of the buyer's default. Usually, borrowers who do not provide at least a 20% down payment on their loan, or borrowers who choose an FHA loan product, will be required by the lender to buy private mortgage insurance (PMI).

Private mortgage insurance will no longer be required once the borrower has paid the balance of the mortgage down to where the value of the home exceeds the mortgage balance by 20%, and the borrower has demonstrated a willingness to pay the loan on time.

Real Estate Risk Management

Inadequate risk management can result in severe consequences for companies as well as individuals. For example, the recession that began in 2008 was mainly the result of loose credit risk management of financial institutions. Therefore, risk management is the identification, assessment, and prioritization of risks, followed by coordinated and economical application of resources to minimize, monitor, and control the probability and impact of unfortunate events, or to maximize the realization of opportunities (ISO/DIS 31000, 2009; Hubbard, 2009).

Risks can come from uncertainty in financial markets or threats from project failures, which can be at any phase in design, development, production, or sustainment life cycles. They can also come from legal liabilities, credit risk, accidents, natural causes, and disasters, as well as a deliberate attack from an adversary, or events of uncertain or unpredictable root cause. Several risk management standards have been developed, including the Project Management Institute, the National Institute of Standards and Technology, actuarial societies, and the International Organization for Standardization (ISO).

Risk management is simply a practice of systematically selecting cost-effective approaches for minimizing the effect of threat realization to the organization. Risks can never be fully avoided or mitigated merely because of financial and practical limitations. Therefore, all organizations have to accept some level of residual risks (Kumar & McDonough, June 29, 2013).

Whereas risk management tends to be preemptive, business continuity planning (BCP) was invented to deal with the consequences of realized residual risks. The need to have BCP in place arises because even improbable events will occur if given enough time. Risk management and BCP are often mistakenly seen as rivals or overlapping practices. In fact, these processes are so tightly tied together that such separation seems artificial. The risk-management process creates important inputs for business continuity planning, such as assets, impact assessments, and cost estimates. Risk management also proposes applicable controls for the observed risks. Therefore, risk management covers several areas that are vital for the BCP process. However, the BCP process goes beyond risk management's preemptive approach and assumes that the disaster will happen at some point (Stratis & Snow, n. d.).

Methods, definitions, and goals vary widely according to whether the risk-management method is in the context of project management, security, engineering, industrial processes, financial portfolios, actuarial assessments, or public health and safety. The strategies to manage threats, which are uncertainties with negative consequences, typically include transferring the threat to another party, avoiding the threat, reducing the negative effect or probability of the threat, or even accepting some or all of the potential or actual consequences of a particular threat (Risk Management, n. d.).

Risk is ever-present in every facet of human endeavor, and while it is an uncomfortable state of mind, without risk, there would not be any opportunities. Management and evaluation of risk are a major part of any successful real estate investment strategy. Real estate risks can occur in many different ways at every stage of the investment process. Therefore, risk cannot be avoided; however, it can be mitigated and managed to levels of great certainty. Being a successful real estate investor, or any type of investor for that matter, essentially means that calculated risks are being taken at all times. To mitigate and minimize the level of real estate risk, investors must be knowledgeable in every aspect of the investing field they are engaged in.

Being involved in real estate investment means performing the proper due diligence process, not overpaying for properties by being aware of market prices in any economic business cycle, and adhering to flexible strategies to be able to adjust to changing market conditions.

In conclusion, the most prosperous investors or firms in any field of endeavor become successful not because they are avoiding risk, but rather because they are actively seeking it and then exploiting it to their own advantage.

Table 1 below shows some common real estate risks that can occur, along with the subsequent mitigation strategy to resolve them.

Table 1

Type of Risks and Their Appropriate Mitigation Strategies

Type of Risks	Risk Mitigation Strategy
Fraudulent sale	Verify ownership, purchase title insurance.
Adverse possession	Obtain a boundary survey from a licensed surveyor.
Environmental contamination	Obtain environmental survey, test for contaminants (lead paint, asbestos, soil contaminants, etc.)
Building component or system failure	Complete full inspection prior to purchase, perform regular maintenance.
Overpayment at purchase	Obtain third-party appraisals and perform discounted cash flow analysis as part of the investment pro forma, do not rely on capital appreciation as the primary source of gain for the investment.
Cash shortfall	Maintain sufficient liquid or cash reserves to cover costs and debt service for a period of time.
Economic downturn	Purchase properties with distinctive features in desirable locations to stand out from competition, control cost structure, have tenants sign long-term leases.
Tenant destruction of property	Screen potential tenants carefully, hire experienced property managers.

Type of Risks	Risk Mitigation Strategy
Underestimation of risk	Carefully analyze financial performance using conservative assumptions, ensure that the property can generate enough cash flow to support itself.
Market decline	Purchase properties based on a conservative approach that the market might decline, and rental income may also decrease.
Fire, flood, personal injury	Insurance policy on the property.
Tax planning	Plan purchases and sales around an exit strategy to save taxes.

Source: http://en.wikipedia.org/wiki/Real_estate_investing

Advantages of Real Estate Investing

Like any other investments, real estate has advantages and disadvantages. What follows are considered the advantages of owning real estate:

- ❖ Real estate is a tangible asset
- ❖ Diversification strategy
- ❖ Yield enhancement
- ❖ Holds value despite economic health
- ❖ Inflation hedge
- ❖ Opportunities in open-market Systems disequilibrium

Real Estate is a Tangible Asset

Real estate is a tangible asset; consequently, an investor can influence the asset performance. For example, the investor can do things to a property to increase its value or improve its performance, such as replacing a leaky roof, improving the exterior, and re-tenanting the building with higher-quality tenants. An investor has a greater degree of control over the performance of a real estate investment than other types of investments. Real estate is a tangible form of investing. The investor is investing in properties that can physically be seen and felt.

Diversification Strategy

The positive aspect of diversifying an investment portfolio in terms of asset allocation is a well-documented strategy. One of the important attributes of real estate investing is that it is a non-correlated market asset, unlike stocks and bonds, which are influenced by the performance of the market. Therefore, including real estate in an investment portfolio will enhance portfolio diversification and mitigate investment portfolio risk.

Yield Enhancement

The inclusion of real estate as part of a diversified portfolio will allow the investor to achieve higher returns for a given level of portfolio risk.

Holds Value Despite of Economic Health

Another positive aspect of real estate investing is that no matter if an investor overpaid for a property or obtained a good price, the investor still owns a piece of property in spite of market conditions. Real estate will always have value, even in the worst of times, because real estate is a tangible asset and is one of our basic needs.

Inflation Hedge

Real estate returns are directly linked to the rents that are received from tenants. Some leases contain provisions for rent increases to be indexed to inflation. In other cases, rental rates are increased whenever the lease term expires, and the tenant is renewed. Either way, real estate income tends to increase faster in inflationary environments, allowing an investor to maintain its real returns.

Opportunities in Open-Market Systems Disequilibrium

Management consultant and economist Sahil Alvi (2010, August 7), proposed the hypothesis of the *"Perpetual Market Disequilibrium."* Alvi's contention is that in an open-market system where the market is perpetually dynamic, a state of balance cannot be achieved even for the briefest of moments. The reason for this disequilibrium is because of the continuous, competing influences of the market, which are attributed to the individual elements and collective interactions of an endless array of internal and external factors.

Alvi further contends that what causes this perpetual motion is attributed to influences such as investor sentiments, the psychology of human emotions, social perceptions, economic cycles, and data inaccuracies. Moreover, other causes of this perpetual-motion can be attributed to the influences of systemic inefficiencies, structural problems, asymmetric information, competing interests, global capital flows and trade, policy and regulatory changes, and central bank interventions.

Furthermore, among market participants in an open system, the market is also influenced by an unlimited number of variables, whose interactive impact is constantly changing and morphing the state of the markets in profound ways. Therefore, according to Alvi (2010, August 7), markets are in a perpetual state of disequilibrium and inefficiency.

The real estate market is considered an open-market system. Therefore, it is subjected to the same state of disequilibrium and inefficiencies as the stock market or any type of open-market system. The author believes that what Alvi is attempting to demonstrate is the fact that disequilibrium or imbalance creates volatility, which in turn results in market opportunities— albeit with substantially higher risk. These volatility-created opportunities could potentially be as much of an advantage in real estate investing as it is for stock market investing.

Disadvantages of Real Estate Investing

Virtually all types of investment vehicles possess a variety of advantages and disadvantages, and real estate investing is no exception. In the previous section, the advantages of real estate were described.

What follows are considered to be some of the disadvantages of real estate investing:

- ❖ Illiquid investment
- ❖ Steep learning curve
- ❖ Significant liabilities

Illiquid Investment

In contrast to the stock market, real estate investing is an illiquid investment, which is not subject to a quick buy-and-sell atmosphere unless the real estate is purchased through a real estate investment trust fund. Even if the investor bought a property and had a buyer ready and willing to buy on the next business day, the closing transaction would still take approximately a month on average.

Steep Learning Curve

Real estate investing requires knowledge and experience in many different ways to overcome the oversights or difficulties that will often arise. Knowledge is required in every sub-category of real estates, such as mortgages, title research, insurance requirements, construction, negotiations, market familiarity, appreciation potential, and income potential.

Significant Liabilities

In real estate investing, the investor will need insurance to protect themselves from the frivolous lawsuits of tenants who might try to reach into the landlord's pocket, or when someone accidentally hurts themselves on the property that was entirely their own fault. Investing in real estate is not for the faint of heart;

however, there are many variables that make real estate investing significantly profitable. Conversely, the same variables may cost investors far more than what they bargained for. Therefore, before investing in real estate, a complete understanding of the workings of the real estate market is essential in making the right investment decisions.

Real Estate Investment Trusts (REITs)

For investors who would like to invest in real estate but do not feel compelled to explore all the potential problems associated with owning the real estate itself, real estate investment trusts (REITs) can facilitate that process. A REIT is a type of real estate company modeled after mutual funds. A REIT is a company that owns, and in most cases, operates income-producing real estate.

A REIT is considered a liquid type investment because the investor can sell their shares at the end of the business day just the same as with any mutual fund. However, the degree of liquidity for these funds is starting to become a focus of controversy. The reason for this controversy is that the REIT market is relatively small, encompassing approximately 200 publicly-traded REITs, with about 80% of them possessing a market value of less than $500 million.

Therefore, in essence, this market value is considered a small-capitalization market, which could lead to a liquidity problem for the REIT fund industry should there be a significant real estate market downturn—like the one that occurred in 2008—and investors decide to sell their shares en masse. This potential illiquidity of REITs and the fact that these funds invest in real estate is the reason this investment vehicle has been included in this section.

REITs own many types of commercial real estate, ranging from office and apartment buildings to warehouses, hospitals, shopping centers, and hotels, and some even include timberlands. This type of REIT is classified as an equity REIT or eREIT. Conversely, some REITs are also engaged in the business of mortgage financing, which is categorized as mortgage REITs or mREITs. The REIT structure was designed to provide a real estate investment similar in fashion to the structure mutual funds provide for investment in stocks.

How REITs Were Created

REITs were created in the United States when President Dwight D. Eisenhower signed into law the REIT Act title, which was contained within the Cigar Excise Tax Extension of 1960. REITs were created by Congress in order to facilitate to all investors the opportunity to invest in large-scale, diversified portfolios of income-producing real estate in a way they typically invested in other asset classes— through the purchase and sale of liquid securities. While available to the real estate investment community, they languished unused as an investment vehicle for over three decades. Then, in the early 1990s, the REIT marketplace grew dramatically.

The growth of REITs has been so extensive that currently, more than 30 countries around the world have established their own REIT investments, with more countries preparing to embrace the concept. The spread of the REIT approach to real estate investment around the world has also increased awareness and acceptance of investing in global real estate securities.

A comprehensive index for the REIT and the global listed property market is the FTSE EPRA/NAREIT Global Real Estate Index Series. This index was created jointly in October 2001 by the index provider FTSE Group, the National Association of Real Estate Investment Trusts (NAREIT), and the European Public Real Estate Association (EPRA). The FTSE EPRA/Nareit Global Real Estate Index is a free-float adjusted, market capitalization-weighted index designed to track the performance of listed real estate companies in both developed and emerging countries worldwide. As of January 23, 2020, this global index included approximately 500 public real estate companies from 40 countries. This global real estate index currently represents an equity market capitalization of approximately two trillion dollars of prime real estate property worldwide. (EPRA/NAREIT Global Real Estate Index Series, 2020, January 23; Real Estate Investment Trust, n. d.).

REIT Tax Implications

REITs allow investors to invest in a professionally managed portfolio of real estate properties. REITs, under Internal Revenue Service (IRS) rules, qualify for what its call a pass-through entity. A pass-through entity is a company that is able to distribute the majority of its income cash flows to investors without taxation at the corporate level.

REITs are allowed to deduct the dividends paid to the shareholders from its corporate tax bill under the following conditions:

- ❖ The company's assets must be primarily composed of real estate held for the long term.
- ❖ The company's income must be derived mainly from real estate.
- ❖ The company must payout at least 90% of its taxable income to the shareholders.

A corporation or trust that qualifies as a REIT customarily does not pay corporate income taxes to the IRS. This is a unique feature and one of the most attractive aspects of a REIT-type investment. Most states also honor this federal tax treatment and do not require REITs to pay state income tax. Not paying federal or state taxes means that nearly all of a REIT's taxable income—at least 90%—can be distributed to shareholders, and there is no double taxation of the income to the shareholder. In contrast to a partnership, a REIT cannot pass its tax losses onto its investors (EPRA/NAREIT Global Real Estate Index Series, 2012, December 18; Real Estate Investment Trust, n. d.).

Advantages of REIT Investing

Like with any other investment vehicle, there are always advantages and disadvantages, and REIT investing is no exception. A REIT offers several advantages to both stock and real estate investors. The following are some of the advantages of REIT investing:

- ❖ REITs must payout at least 90% of their income as dividends.
- ❖ Large payouts result in higher-than-average yields.
- ❖ REITs help diversify an investment portfolio.
- ❖ The investor can own real estate without the costs and hassles associated with real estate investing.
- ❖ REITs own physical assets with an intrinsic value that can appreciate over time.
- ❖ REITs are more liquid than typical real estate investments.

REITs must payout at least 90% of their income as dividends.

This requirement is the number one reason why investors buy REITs. Management can raise the payout to more than 90%, but by law, they cannot lower it below 90%. In other words, management is prohibited from reducing the dividend payment.

Large payouts result in higher-than-average yields.

For dividend investors, high yield is a primary consideration in REIT investing. However, it is important to be cognizant of the fact that high dividend yields equate to high risk, and REITs have some of the highest yields on stock exchanges, which also means they are among the riskiest of investments.

REITs help diversify an investment portfolio.

Real estate values do not generally correlate with stock prices. Unless a real estate downturn triggers a financial crisis or vice versa, a portfolio that contains both stock and real estate holdings may provide a certain degree of protection in situations that affect one or the other asset class.

REITs help diversify a real estate portfolio.

Money pooled from many investors allows the trust to purchase more buildings than an individual would be able to buy alone. If an investor purchases real estate on his own, a large amount of—or all of—the investor's funds could be tied up in a single property. However, a REIT investment provides the investor diversification by facilitating a piece of ownership in many different properties instead of just one, which means that one underperforming building won't affect the portfolio significantly.

The investor can own real estate without the costs and hassles associated with real estate investing.

The investor does not have to find and research properties; the REIT's managers do that for the investors.

REITs own physical assets with an intrinsic value that can appreciate over time.

Since the REIT investor will own tangible assets that have the tendency to increase in value over the long-term, this will provide a certain degree of investment value protection for the investors. Therefore, the market value of the properties owned by the REIT will offer some protection as long as the values of the properties do not go down as it happened during the real estate crash of 2008.

REITs are more liquid than typical real estate investments.

Instead of selling the property to cash out, as an investor would do with property ownership, the REIT investor can just simply sell their shares. Therefore, even though REITs have been included with real estate investment—an illiquid asset—when owned through a REIT, the real estate investment behaves like mutual fund shares, which means that shares can be sold quickly, making this investment liquid.

Disadvantages of REIT Investing

Because REITs allows investors to invest in real estate through a fund-type vehicle, they carry some of the same risks associated with real estate investing, as well as stock investing, which include the following:

❖ Falling occupancy rates and increasing vacancies hurt revenues.

❖ Share prices can drop when property values fall.

❖ Share prices can fall with the broader stock market based on supply and demand of shares.

❖ High dividend payouts for REITs force management to take on debt to expand real estate holdings.

❖ Rising interest rates hurt profitability.

It is important to know that not all REIT dividends' qualify for the current 20% capital gains tax rate that was increased from 15% in 2014. It is crucial for investors to understand that tax rates are always on the table. Therefore, they will probably change, which typically depends on the political party that is in power. Even though there was a 5% increase in the capital gains tax for 2014, some believe it is likely that these rates will continue to rise. Additionally, some dividends are taxed as ordinary income.

Moreover, beginning in 2013, high-income investors have also been subjected to a 3.8% Medicare surtax on investment income as the result of the enacted Health Care and Education Reconciliation Act of 2010. The purpose of this surtax was simply to create revenue to offset the cost of health care legislation. However, nowhere in the act does there seem to be a reason that the funds from this surtax must be used for Medicare.

There is a challenge pending before the United States Supreme Court to the Patient Protection and Affordable Care Act, as amended by the Health Care and Education Reconciliation Act of 2010.

The 3.8% surtax was a part of that second law, but the provision enacting the 3.8% surtax did not amend the first law; it appears to be a stand-alone provision. Therefore, it is unclear whether the 3.8% surtax is implicated in the Supreme Court case, and it is vague how the Supreme Court's decision might affect the 3.8% surtax (Wealth Strategy Report.ustrust.com, n. d.).

These last two chapters have covered many different investment classes, all possessing advantages and disadvantages, and various levels of risk. Suffice it to say; no investment vehicle can offer returns with zero risks, not even the investment vehicle that is the focus of this book. It is a well-known fact that the lower the returns, the less risk, and conversely that the higher the returns, the greater the risk.

The author believes it is appropriate to end this chapter with some investment advice from the United States Securities and Exchange Commission and some other well-known successful investors. The Securities and Exchange Commission encourages investors to always thoroughly evaluate the background of any financial professional with whom the investor intends to do business before handing over the investor's hard-earned money.

It does not matter if the investor is a beginner or has been a seasoned investor for many years. It is never too early or late to start asking questions. In fact, the SEC contends that it is impossible to ask a dumb question about how investors are investing their money. A well-known Chinese proverb said it best: *"He who asks a question is a fool for five minutes; he who does not ask a question remains a fool forever."* Do not feel intimidated. Investing is not a game; it is a serious business with potentially grave consequences to the investor's psyche and future well-being. The investor should be mindful of the fact that it is their money at stake. It is a safer strategy to do nothing if the investor does not fully understand the risks involved in the investment that is being contemplated. The investors are paying for the assistance and expertise of the financial professional; they should make sure that the vetting process (due diligence) is comprehensive.

A competent financial professional will be receptive to questions, no matter how basic they might appear to be. Financial professionals understand that an educated client is an asset, not a liability. They would rather answer the investor's questions before they invest than confront their anger and confusion at a later date. According to famed value investor *Seth Klarman* (1957, 1991), it is very difficult to recover from one large loss, which could literally destroy, instantly, the beneficial effects of many years of investment success.

In other words, an investor will do much better by achieving a consistent return on investment with limited downside risk than by making spectacular returns in a volatile and considerably riskier market where the loss of principal can be substantial. For example, an investor who consistently earns 10% annual returns over a decade will generate more money than an investor who makes 15% a year for nine years and then incurs a sizeable 20 % loss in the tenth year. It is recommended that the reader perform the calculation so that they can visualize the results. See appendix E for an explanation of the importance of why it is necessary to embrace—as the core of any trading or investing strategy—the investment philosophy proposed by investor *Daniel Drew in the late 1800s,* who recommended that investor should, *"cut their losses short and let their winners run"*(Slagle, 2008).

Therefore, the next time a mutual fund or an investment advisor trumpets or proclaims their average returns, be very skeptical about such claims. Insist that they provide you with not only their geometric compounded returns, but also the range of their returns so the investor can see exactly how often, and to what degree, they incur damaging losses (Fink, 2011 December 7).

Furthermore, an essential point for investors to keep in mind when seeking financial advice or money managing services is the fact that the money manager or advisor will always earn money in spite of the investor losing their money. Because of this fact, the question that arises is this: *why would anyone pay a financial advisor a portfolio management fee so that the investor loses money while the advisor will make money, whether or not the investor earns money?* This fact alone should emphasize the importance of becoming an educated investor.

That is why the SEC encourages investors to ask questions and to thoroughly evaluate the background of the financial professional with whom they intend to do business before turning over their money to any advisor. The Securities and Exchange Commission contends that vetting the financial professional the investor plans to select is of paramount importance for several reasons.

The investor should thoroughly investigate before doing business with any financial professional or firm to determine if there has been a history of complaints or problems with regulators. Additionally, the investor should understand that if the financial professional or the firm becomes insolvent and declares bankruptcy, the investor might not be able to recover their money, even if an arbitrator or a court rules in the investor's favor.

As previously mentioned, investing is not a game; it is an extremely serious business that can have devastating consequences for the uninformed. Therefore, there is no better risk-mitigating strategy than to become a knowledgeable and well-informed consumer.

4

What is Private Money Lending?

P rivate money is a commonly used term in banking and finance. It refers to lending money to a company or person by a private individual or organization that is engaged in this practice. While banks are traditional sources of financing for real estate and other purposes, private money is provided by individuals or organizations specializing in this type of lending, which may apply nontraditional, qualifying guidelines to their underwriting process. There is traditionally less red tape, impediments, and regulation because it is the private investor who determines to a great extent, the regulation and guidelines they will impose upon themselves.

Private money lenders must comply and be familiar with the usury laws of the state they want to invest in, as well as federal usury laws. In the United States, usury laws are state laws that specify the maximum legal interest rate at which loans can be made. Each U.S. state has its own statute, which dictates how much interest can be charged before it is considered usurious or unlawful.

On a federal level, Congress has opted not to regulate interest rates on purely private transactions federally but instead based on past decisions. Arguably, the U.S. Supreme Court could grant it the power to do so under the interstate commerce clause of Article I of the Constitution. However, Congress opted to put a federal criminal limit on interest rates by the Racketeer Influenced and

Corrupt Organization Act (RICO Statute) definitions of unlawful debt. The RICO statute makes it a federal felony to lend money at an interest rate more than twice the local state's usury rate and then try to collect that unlawful debt (Commerce Clause, n. d.).

As stated above, each U.S. state has its own statute, which dictates how much interest can be charged before it is considered usurious or unlawful. *"Usury"* is defined as the act of lending money at an unreasonably high-interest rate. This rate is defined at the state level. For example, Florida has enacted a very liberal system when it comes to usurious lending practices. It ranks as one of the most tolerant laws in the country when it comes to what lenders can charge in the way of interest on personal loans. In some states, like New York, loans that carry an interest rate above what is legal are voided **ab initio**, which is a Latin term that means "from the beginning" (Usury, n. d.).

The State of Florida has established a two-tier system when it comes to usury limitations on personal loans. On personal loans under $500,000, the general usury limit that has been established in Florida is at 18% per annum. When loans greater than $500,000 are being considered, the usury limitation has been set at 25% per year. This rate is regarded as one of the highest usury maximum rates to be found anywhere in the United States at the present time. The rationale behind this high-interest rate is based on the premise that the lender has a greater degree of risk with a personal loan of this magnitude. Therefore, a more substantial interest rate is suitable and appropriate to the circumstances, according to the state of Florida.

Private money lenders (PMLs) are not entirely exempt from banking laws, which depend on how the PML has structured its lending operation. They may be exempt from routine banking regulations, and depending on their particular lending practice, might not even be required to have a license to become a private mortgage investor. However, in spite of these possible exemptions, the private lender will need to understand how the business works, the risks involved in this industry, and the potential rewards involved. Moreover, currently of paramount importance is the full understanding of the Dodd-Frank Act (DFA), the SAFE Act, and all pertinent laws, rules, and regulations that might apply to the investor's area of interest. The PML will also have to adhere to any local or state regulatory requirements for operating as a private mortgage business or sole mortgage lender/investor, which in Florida is Chapter 494.

There is an important distinction between a private mortgage lending business, which does require state licensure, and a sole independent private lending investor, who might or might not need a license. This distinction is a significant difference that needs to be understood because it will determine the number of loans an investor can make without a license. For example, in the states of Florida and New York, a sole independent private money lender may make no more than five loans per annum before being required to be a state-licensed lender. The regulatory guidelines that limit the number of loans a private money lender or mortgage lender originator (MLO) can make without being required to have a lender's license is regulated by the SAFE Act of 2008, through its *de minimis* exception provision (See Chapter 6).

Private money can be similar to the prevailing rate of interest, or it can be very expensive. When there is a higher risk associated with a particular transaction, it is a common practice for the private money lender to charge an interest rate above the going rate. Private money is customarily offered to clients in cases where the banks determine the risk to be too high, or the project presented was unacceptable for the bank underwriting guidelines.

Private money lenders (PMLs) are investors who seek alternative investments other than the customary stock, bonds, CDs, and mutual funds that most investors are familiar with. Private lenders are also known as *"hard money lenders"* (HMLs). HML is a relatively new term that is used to refer to loan professionals (broker/lenders) specializing in private money loans. Historically, these professionals have had a multitude of labels, including PMLs. Still, no matter which term is used, both hard money lenders and private money lenders essentially provide the same service. However, there is a slight difference between them, which will be explained below.

Difference between Hard Money and Private Money

It is important to understand that there is a subtle difference between the terms *"hard money and private money."* Both hard money and private money are typically asset-based type loans, which are loans backed more by the strength of the real estate to be purchased than the financial credentials or creditworthiness of the borrower. These loans are funded from non-traditional lending sources, such as individual investors engaged in the practice of lending their personal funds for real estate collateralized loans. Therefore, neither the hard money nor the private money lenders are banks or national lenders.

Hard Money Lenders (HMLs), despite their non-traditional status, are organized money lending businesses that are licensed to lend money. In contrast, private money lenders (PMLs) are exactly what their name implies: individual private lenders. For example, a private lender could be a family member, a business colleague, or just an individual who engages in private money lending activities as an investor. They could also be the lending source for the hard money broker.

The underwriting guidelines and due diligence process that these investors apply to evaluate their loan-funding opportunity is largely determined by them. However, with the imposition of the Dodd-Frank Act of 2010, the industry is in a state of flux; therefore, it is extremely important to keep abreast of all changing laws and regulations to avoid violating any new laws. In spite of the liberal evaluating guidelines used by private lenders, there are numerous lending criteria that most private money lenders apply to mitigate investment risk. However, as was previously mentioned, if an individual private lender makes more than a certain quantity of loans per annum, they might need to be licensed by the states in which they invest. This is one of the areas of the lending industry that is in flux, mostly attributed to the Dodd-Frank Act of 2010 and Secure and Fair Enforcement for Mortgage Licensing Act of 2008 (S.A.F.E. Act).

Hard money lenders follow certain underwriting lending criteria. Their loans customarily have defined durations, interest rates, and upfront points, all of which are known to the borrower prior to a loan ever being issued. In fact, these criteria are often used by the borrower to differentiate and select hard money lenders when they are shopping for available options.

Private money is much more flexible and usually cheaper than hard money because most HMLs received some of their funds from private sources, such as PMLs; therefore, they must mark up their interest rates and fees to make a profit. Thus, when a borrower deals directly with private lending sources of capital, they essentially eliminate the middleman from the transaction, which could result in better terms.

Another difference between private money lenders and hard money lenders is that private money lenders typically do not advertise because it could jeopardize their legal exemption of not requiring a license to operate. In contrast, hard money lenders will and often do, advertise because they are specifically engaged in the lending business.

The term *"hard money"* is often a misunderstood label and frequently carries with it a negative connotation. There are two explanations for the use of the word *"hard,"* as revealed by the literature review. One explanation is that because of the word "hard," most borrowers erroneously assume the loans are hard to get; however, it is actually used to describe that the loan is based on a hard or tangible asset.

In contrast, the second explanation for the use of the word *"hard"* is that when money is discussed between investors, it is considered to be either *"soft"* or *"hard"* money. Typically, soft money is easier to qualify for, and the terms are more flexible. Conversely, hard money is just the opposite, which means it is much more restrictive—not in the sense that it is more difficult to obtain—but in the sense that the terms are stricter and more specific. Most of the hard money comes from private individuals with a great deal of money on hand. This is why hard money is also referred to as "private money."

Thus, a hard money loan is a real estate or asset-based type loan that is collateralized against the appraised value of the property for which the loan is made. Most private lenders fund in the *"first lien"* position, meaning that in the event of a default, they are the first creditors to receive remuneration. Therefore, the purpose of lending on a first lien position is to mitigate the investment risk. In the opinion of the author, this should be the only type of loan that should be made if the objective is safety of principal.

Typically, hard money loans are arranged at much higher interest rates than the interest rate that can be attained with a conventional, commercial, or residential property loan. These types of loans are almost never issued by a commercial bank or any other type of traditional deposit institution. They are loans issued by PML investors. These loans are customarily arranged by local-area mortgage brokers or hard money lenders who specialize in private money loans.

A hard money loan, by definition, is a loan of last resort, or a short-term bridge loan. These types of loans, as mentioned before, are backed by the value or equity of the property, not by the creditworthiness of the borrower. Because the real estate property itself is used as the protection against a potential default by the borrower, hard money loans have lower loan-to-value ratios than traditional loans.

The loan-to-value (LTV) ratio is a financial term used by lenders to express the ratio of a loan to the value of the asset purchased. Loan-to-value is one of the key risk factors that lenders assess when qualifying borrowers for a mortgage. It is an essential tool to mitigate investment risk when issuing private money loans.

The risk of default is always at the forefront of the lending decision. The likelihood of a lender absorbing a loss increases as the amount of protective equity in the property decreases. That is why financing properties with lower LTVs is so crucial in the private mortgage lending business. Therefore, as the LTV ratio of the loan increases, the qualification guidelines for certain mortgage programs become much stricter. Traditional lenders customarily will require borrowers of high LTV loans to purchase private mortgage insurance to protect the lender from the possibility of a buyer's default. Consequently, buying private mortgage insurance will increase the costs of the mortgage for the borrower. In contrast, private lenders will only make loans with lower LTV ratios, customarily from 65% to 70%, which helps them to mitigate the possibility of default risk.

Safety of Private Money Lending

Every investor knows that there are no risk-free investments. There are risks associated with any investment, and investing in mortgages is no different. The most that can be achieved is to mitigate the risk of the investment vehicle. This risk mitigation can be accomplished through the acquisition of knowledge and experience, which is one of the objectives of this book.

Investors should not engage in private mortgage investing without learning how to perform a thorough due diligence research process before committing to a loan opportunity. This process requires real estate experience and knowledge, as it does in any viable business. Therefore, it is highly recommended that finding a knowledgeable and honest private broker/lender as a mentor is essential to the success of this business. In fact, associating oneself with individuals who possess experience in the field the investor wants to participate in is in itself a risk-mitigating strategy.

However, private money loans, if structured correctly, are safe investments because they are collateralized or protected by the tangible real estate asset that was purchased. Additionally, the investor's loan principal is further protected by following the underwriting guideline of only lending no more than 65% to 70% of the appraised value of the property. These LTV ratios are usually the amount that will be lent for residential-type properties. In contrast, for underdeveloped, raw land, the LTV ratios are approximately 30% to 50%, and for construction loans, and for purchasing buildable lots, the LTV ratios are about 55%.

It is important to understand that these are just guidelines that most private money lenders use to evaluate the various loan opportunities. Another strategy used to mitigate mortgage investment risk is to lend money on first-lien mortgages only. The risk-mitigating guidelines used to execute private mortgage investments are flexible and are essentially determined by each individual lender. However, this flexibility is rapidly changing because of the passage of the Dodd-Frank Act of 2010 and other regulatory laws.

Until a few short years ago, anyone who had money to lend on real estate could do so without too many restrictions. However, following the financial housing crisis of 2008, many new regulations were passed by Congress. The most influential of these was the SAFE Act of 2008 and the Dodd-Frank Act of 2010. These sweeping fiscal, regulatory reform bills were aimed at increasing consumer legislation were specific provisions placing limitations on the terms of mortgages, as well as restrictions on residential mortgage loans. Many broker/lenders, as well as individual money lenders, have serious concerns with this legislation that they claim will ultimately harm consumers through increased fees and fewer services and benefits. Chapter 6 provides an overview of the provisions of the Dodd-Frank Act and the SAFE Act, as well as a brief description of numerous other laws and regulations that determine the processes of the mortgage lending industry.

Every investor knows that there are no 100% risk-free investments, and private mortgage investing is no exception. However, the qualitative research study undertaken to evaluate the suitability and safety of private mortgage investing as a sound alternative investment vehicle has demonstrated that private mortgage investing can, in fact, accomplish both of these objectives. Thus, it is an excellent investment strategy to both generate a consistent passive income stream for retirement and business.

Furthermore, the research study also demonstrated that the reason private mortgage investing is considered a safe investment is because of the numerous hedging and risk-mitigating strategies available to the investor to reduce the level of investment risk. The feature that is most attractive about private mortgage investing is the use of hedging with the equity of a tangible real estate asset as collateral that ensures the mortgage is secured. This equity, in essence, is what makes it safer than other investments. Unlike stocks and bonds investing where investors can lose their entire investment, with private mortgage financing, the investor will consistently retain some value in the investment because it is a tangible asset. Real estate under the worst possible conditions will always maintain some degree of value.

Moreover, a curious finding from the study that was serendipitously discovered was the reason why private mortgage investing was not a well-known investment vehicle. The reason was that investors who have been fortunate enough to have been exposed to this investment concept were not inclined to broadcast or share this information with other potential investors. They seem to guard this information as a sort of secret that, if disseminated to others, will reduce the available investment opportunities for themselves.

Perhaps the lack of information sharing could be attributed to some form of selfishness or greed on the part of investors, which makes them reluctant to divulge valuable information that might have taken these investors a long time to learn. This assumption might be the source of the resistance to share and make it easy for other investors, who they feel are seeking to circumvent the learning process and piggyback on someone else's effort.

In subsequent chapters, the author will be introducing and addressing additional risk-mitigating strategies that will help to structure the loan opportunities in ways that will substantially minimize the risk associated with this type of investment.

Similarities of Private Mortgage and Bond Investing

Bond investing, or fixed income investing, is an investment strategy that is basically used when investors are seeking a predictable income stream or cash flow. This is primarily the same reason investors invest in private mortgage lending opportunities and hence, the similarities of the two investment vehicles.

Some of the features and benefits of bond investing include the following:

- ❖ Consistent income stream
- ❖ Diversification
- ❖ Capital preservation

Consistent Income Stream

If the investor is attempting to supplement their income or help fund their retirement, fixed-income investments may provide a steady stream of income on a monthly or quarterly basis with less volatility.

Diversification

Investment with low volatility and low correlation to stocks, such as bonds or private mortgage investments, can help balance a portfolio, helping to reduce portfolio volatility in uncertain markets.

Capital Preservation

Fixed income prices may fluctuate, but the investor can rely on receiving the invested amount when the fixed income investment matures if there is no investment default.

Investing in hard money loans is considered similar to investing in bonds. Bonds and mortgage loans are both considered debt securities. A bond is a type of loan, which is also called a *"debt securities"* or *"fixed income"* investment. It is used by corporations or governments to raise capital by selling IOUs (I owe you) to the general public.

In the case of bonds, the general public is the lender or creditor, and the corporations or the governments are the borrowers, which are called "issuers." The issuer is obligated to repay the holder of the bond the principal amount at a predetermined maturity date. Maturity is the time limit that has been fixed or set for the repayment of the loan. However, along with the contracted maturity date repayment, the borrowers will also have to make monthly or quarterly interest payments until the time of the maturity of the bond. In contrast, private mortgage loans are typically paid on a monthly basis. This feature makes private mortgage investing a very appealing investment to generate a consistent income stream during retirement.

One significant feature that private mortgage investing possess as compared to bond investing is that it is a non-market-correlated type of investment, which means that the return on investment (ROI) does not follow the market. Therefore, the interest rate that a private mortgage investor receives will always be higher than the interest rate that a bond will pay under normal economic circumstances.

Bonds differ from mortgage loans in that they are considered a liquid investment, which means they are tradable in the open market. If a bondholder does not want to continue holding their bond until its maturity date, they can sell their bond in the secondary market. The secondary market, or aftermarket, is the financial market in which previously issued financial instruments such as stock, bonds, and derivatives are bought and sold. In contrast, private mortgage loans are considered illiquid investments because they are not tradable in an open market. However, although considered an illiquid investment, there is a note-selling and buying market where mortgage notes can be sold or purchased by mortgage note investors. Therefore, there is some degree of liquidity available to the private mortgage investor, although the mortgage notes are typically sold at a discount, which, in essence, means at a loss.

In summary, both bonds and mortgage loans are similar in that they both have a fixed interest yield and a specific maturity date. For example, if a mortgage loan is made to a borrower for $100,000 at 8% interest and requires interest-only payments, the investor will earn $8,000 income per annum for the duration of the loan. If the borrower does not default, then the loan will be paid off at or before the maturity date, and the original principal will be returned to the lender/investor.

As a private money lender, the investor will discover that private loan investments require a skill set, which is considerably more involved than in bond investing. The expertise the investor will need is essential to mitigate any potential risks that could result from this type of investing. However, once the investor has acquired the appropriate skill set, the inherent risks associated with this type of investment vehicle are easily mitigated.

The acquirement of this skill set, in essence, could be considered another risk-mitigating feature of private mortgage investing because the mere fact that the investor has to be engaged in managing their investment will further mitigate investment risk. Disseminating the applicable information necessary to develop this skillset to invest in private mortgage lending safely is a goal of this book.

Most investors would love nothing more than to delegate their investment responsibility to a financial advisor, thus eliminating the arduous task of learning or acquiring the skill set necessary to become a knowledgeable and safe investor. The author contends that disregarding the responsibility of the investors to educate themselves in whichever type of investment endeavor they would like to engage in, is an extremely dangerous practice that will always result in investment losses.

While there is nothing wrong with seeking the assistance of a financial advisor and even delegating the investment function to them, the investor should do so only after they have become an educated consumer, which is a perpetual process. This practice, in essence, is risk mitigation at its best. Furthermore, it is of paramount importance for investors to understand that—the author emphatically contends—no one will protect the investor's money better than the investor. Unfortunately, this is a lesson that is only learned after investors have experienced investment losses so substantial that it actually results in depression, loss of self-esteem, ill-health, and in extreme cases, it can even result in suicide. Some of the greatest investors of our time, such as Jesse Livermore, have taken their own lives following investment failure (Wilkerson, 2011, May 25).

Private Banking Services

As a private money lender, the investor is engaged in the private banking business. In essence, the investor is the bank. There are three primary services that traditional banks provide to their customers. They provide a way for customers to save their money; they provide the means for customers to borrow money, such as a home mortgage, home repair loans, car loans, or college tuition loans. Finally, they also provide a way for customers to make educated investments in vehicles such as mutual funds, CDs, 401(Ks), IRAs, and real estate.

However, traditional banks are not the only places where a borrower can have access to borrow funds. A number of private lenders may be available to help fund the borrower's loan as well. Therefore, investors who are engaged in the private money lending (PML) business are providing at least the lending and investment aspects of the traditional banking services. Hence, private lenders are essentially private bankers.

While banks and private lenders offer some of the same services, they also have a few key differences between them. For example, there could be variations in the following underwriting guidelines:

- ❖ Interest rates
- ❖ Application process
- ❖ Loan approval process
- ❖ Loan limits

Interest rates

One of the differences between private lenders and banks is the interest rates they charge the borrowers. In most cases, banks have lower interest rates because they have a lesser cost of funds than other lenders. The bank customers, who are the depositors, keep a lot of money in their checking and savings accounts. Therefore, banks have easy access to those funds to lend out. Moreover, because banks today pay very little interest for those deposits, or none at all, then those funds are extremely inexpensive for the bank to use.

However, most borrowers who seek private lenders to borrow funds do not have the credit scores to get the lower interest rates offered by traditional banks. Therefore, these borrowers have no other alternative than to procure the money from a private lender at substantially higher interest rates.

Application Process

Another difference between private lenders and banks is the application process. Applying for a loan with a traditional bank, the borrower will have to fill out a large amount of paperwork and provide different types of documentation to the bank.

Conversely, applying for a loan with a private lender, the borrower may not need to go through all of these steps. The application process for private loans is much more relaxed when compared with banks because private lenders do not have to abide by all the lending regulations that traditional banks have to follow. However, this situation is rapidly changing because of the passage of the Dodd-Frank Act of 2010, which is requiring greater oversight after issuing several final rules in 2013 through the Consumer Financial Protection Bureau (CFPB) concerning the mortgage markets. Therefore, the private mortgage lending industry is becoming quite similar to the conventional banking industry.

Loan Approval Process

The approval process for both types of lenders is also a key difference between the two. With a traditional bank, the borrower has to meet specific guidelines, which determine whether the borrower is worthy of receiving the loan. Conversely, when applying for a loan with a private money lender, the borrower must meet the guidelines used by that lender. The guidelines for private lenders are typically more relaxed than those of traditional banks. What this means is that it will be easier for the borrower to get approved, regardless of their credit situation. However, just because private money lenders might have somewhat more relaxed lending guidelines, this does not mean that the loan is guaranteed to be issued. What it does mean is that the lender will work with the borrower to find a safe way to be able to grant the loan.

Unfortunately, this flexibility is changing somewhat because, as of 2013, under the passage of the final rules of the Dodd-Frank Act, private lenders are now required to make a reasonable, good-faith determination of the consumer's *ability-to-repay*. The lender must now determine that the consumer has the ability-to-repay any credit transaction secured by a dwelling, which excludes any open-end credit plan, timeshare plan, reverse mortgage, or temporary loan.

The final rules also establish certain protections from liability under this requirement for *"Qualified Mortgages."* The amendments also implement Section 1414 of the Dodd-Frank Act, which limits prepayment penalties. Finally, the amendments require creditors to retain evidence of compliance with the rule for three years after a covered loan is consummated. This rule is effective for transactions for which the creditor received an application on or after January 10, 2014.

Loan Limits

When borrowing money from a traditional lender, the borrower typically will only be able to borrow up to a certain limit. The limit may be based on banking regulations, or it could be based on how much money the borrower earns and their credit history. With private lenders, the borrower can often borrow more money, as the loan limits can be more flexible. However, those limits and approval are subject to the equity available in the property being used as collateral.

Achievable Returns from Private Money Lending

Private mortgage investing is probably one of the best investment vehicles to build wealth that most investors are unfamiliar with. Unlike investing in traditional investment vehicles such as mutual funds, bonds, and stocks, investing in private mortgages offers numerous benefits, which include a high return on investment with less risk and volatility.

Private mortgage investments are secured by both the strength and confidence in the borrower and on the value of the property being used as collateral. Traditionally, real estate property values are less volatile than stock market-type investments. Additionally, unlike stocks, bonds, and mutual funds, when the lender invests in a private mortgage loan, their returns equate to a fixed monthly income, just like a salary.

Furthermore, private mortgage investing can generate a consistent income stream at a predetermined interest rate. Thus, the returns that can be achieved with private mortgage loans are not subject to irregular distribution intervals and variable current market rates of returns. With investments in stocks, bonds, and mutual funds, there is no control over the market or the investments; the investors are subjected to the whims of the prevailing economic conditions and the effectiveness of the firm managing the investments.

Customarily, the average stock market return is claimed to be approximately 8% to 10% per annum. However, this fact is not entirely accurate because the stock market return largely depends on the time frame the investment was made in. Moreover, all of these proclaimed average returns are determined by computer models. *The fact is that by selecting a specific period of time, anyone can make the average stock market return be any percentage or number they want.* Therefore, there are some undeniable truths about statistics; they can be manipulated, massaged, and misstated. Additionally, if bogus statistical information is repeated often enough, it eventually is considered to be true. Stock market volatility can be a frightening and painful experience for most investors, especially for the investors who are already in retirement.

In contrast, with private mortgage lending, the investor has 100% control over the process. The investor can investigate the property being invested in, meet the borrower if they choose, and dictate the terms of the loan. Private mortgage investing as of 2019 offers a rate of return on first-lien mortgages between 7.5% and

12%. On second-lien mortgages, the rate of return can be more substantial, which can range between 12% and 18%. However, investing in second and third lien position mortgages is not a recommended practice—in the opinion of the author— unless the investor is also the holder of the other lien positions.

While no single investment vehicle is perfect, the results from the research study undertaken to evaluate the suitability of this investment vehicle confirm that investing in private mortgage loans is a sound and effective way to optimize the investors' money with a high degree of safety. According to Carney (2011), no other investment vehicle offers such a degree of control over the investments with so many mitigating hedge protection strategies. Carney further contends that it is difficult to find a business where a high and consistent income stream can be generated with such a minimal amount of work involved. In the private money lending business, the borrower is the individual who works hard; it is the person that takes the risk to build equity in the lender's collateral through the borrower's capital improvements and diligent work (Carney, 2011).

Difference between Mortgage and Trust Deed Investing

When an investor or borrower purchase a real estate property, they will need to sign either a mortgage or a deed of trust. The use of these types of security documents depends on which state the borrower lives in. Both *mortgages and deeds of trust* are considered security instruments; however, the similarities end there. A security instrument, by definition, is a generic name for something that gives a creditor rights in the property for the protection of a debt from the borrower. It may include a security agreement for personal property, which could be a mortgage or a deed of trust on real property that shows evidence that an asset or property has been pledged as security (Thelawdictionary, n. d.).

The mortgage, or deed of trust, is the security instrument or the document that pledges the property as security for the loan. It is the mortgage or deed of trust that is the legal document that permits the lender to foreclose on the property if the borrower defaults by failing to make their required monthly payments. The differences between a mortgage and a deed of trust will only affect homeowners when foreclosure becomes an issue.

A mortgage and a deed of trust are not the same type of document, even though these terms are used interchangeably quite frequently. The difference between a mortgage and a deed of trust is subtle. They both create a lien on real estate, by law they are considered evidence of a debt, and both are generally recorded in the county in which the property is located.

The difference between a mortgage and a deed of trust, which can also be called a trust deed, relates to the following:

❖ The number of parties involved in the lien transaction.

❖ The name of the security instrument or documents.

❖ The method of foreclosure to be used in the event of defaulted payments.

Customarily, it is the state law that dictates whether a mortgage or a deed of trust is used as the security instrument; however, some states permit either document to be used (see Appendices B & C). It is important to note that for states using the deed of trust security document, in the event of payment default, the foreclosure process undertaken is called a non-judicial foreclosure, which is a foreclosure that is processed without court intervention. Conversely, for states that use the mortgage security document, in the event of payment default, the foreclosure process used is a judicial foreclosure, which is a court proceeding action.

However, there is a third type of foreclosure called strict foreclosure. This type of foreclosure is the least common, and it is only allowed in six states, which are: Connecticut, Illinois, Indiana, Maine, New Hampshire, and Vermont (see Appendix B). A strict foreclosure result when a mortgage agreement containing a strict foreclosure decree is violated. The decree or order states that if the homeowner defaults on payments, the lender may file a lawsuit against the debtor with the objective of obtaining full possession of the property if the owner cannot pay the mortgage loan in full by a specific date (Twyman, n. d.).

To fully understand the difference between a mortgage and a deed of trust, the borrower must first understand the concept of promissory notes. Most homebuyers usually think of the mortgage or deed of trust as the contract they are signing with the lender to borrow money to purchase the property. However, that is not the case. It is the promissory note that is the legal instrument that contains the promise to repay the amount borrowed. The promissory note is essentially an IOU that contains the promise to repay the loan. A promissory note contains details about the loan, such as the maturity date, interest rate, payment amount, and frequency. This document is not customarily recorded.

The promissory note itself, however, is not secured by the real estate. The mortgage or deed of trust is the security instrument or document that pledges the property as security for the loan, thus creating a permanent record in the county in which the real property is located. Therefore, it is the mortgage or deed of trust that permits a lender to foreclose if the borrower defaults by failing to make the monthly mortgage payments. When these security documents are recorded, it essentially puts the public on notice and creates what is called a *"notice of the lien"* to anyone who cares or has a reason to research the title to the property. Appendix B shows a table that indicates which security instrument is used by the different states to secure the promissory note to the real property, as well as which foreclosure process is undertaken in the event of a payment default.

Therefore, there are two primary distinctions between a mortgage and a deed of trust. They are as follows:

❖ The number of parties involved in the real estate transaction.

- ❖ The type of foreclosure that will be used to enforce the lien in the event of a borrower's default, which are the following:
  - Judicial foreclosure (mortgage states)
  - Non-judicial foreclosure (trust of deed states)
  - Strict foreclosure (both mortgage and trust of deed states)

A Mortgage is a Two-Party Transaction

- ❖ The borrower (the mortgagor)
- ❖ The lender (the mortgagee)

A Trust Deed is a Three-Party Transaction

- ❖ Borrower (the trustor)
- ❖ The lender (the beneficiary)
- ❖ The title company, escrow company, or bank (the trustee) that holds title to the lien for the benefit of the lender and whose sole function is to initiate and complete the foreclosure process at the request of the lender.

Types of Foreclosures

Judicial, Non-Judicial, and Strict Foreclosures

A foreclosure is the legal process or remedy available to the mortgage holder or lender to take back the collateral or property for a promissory note that is in default. It is important for borrowers to understand that when they purchase a house and assume the responsibility of a mortgage loan, they essentially are given the privilege of using the property until the mortgage is paid off; thus, they still do not own the house.

In addressing the topic of mortgage foreclosures, the terms *"judicial"* and *"non-judicial"* are frequently mentioned, and occasionally the term *"strict foreclosures"* will be heard. These three types of foreclosures involve very different processes, which primarily refer to how each individual state handles the real estate foreclosure process. A mortgage is enforced pursuant to a court-supervised, judicial foreclosure process, while a deed of trust gives the lender the option to bypass the court system altogether by following the procedures outlined in the deed of trust and the applicable state law. This latter procedure is called a non-judicial foreclosure, or a trustee's sale. A strict foreclosure is a foreclosure proceeding in which the lender is entitled to take possession of the property directly upon default of the mortgage agreement.

Judicial Foreclosure

The Judicial Foreclosure process is required in about half of the 50 states, and it is permitted in almost all states (see Appendix B). This type of foreclosure requires the lender to file a lawsuit in order to obtain a final summary judgment. A judicial foreclosure is performed through a series of court filings, appearances before judges, and filing notices to the borrowers and junior lienholders. The lender must hire an attorney and prove in court that they have the right to take possession of a property. The foreclosure process ends in a judge giving the lender permission to proceed with a foreclosure auction or sheriff's sale, which is generally supervised by the court.

It is a time-consuming and expensive process, but it does have an added benefit for the lender. If the lender does not receive sufficient money from the foreclosure auction sale to pay off the amount owed on the promissory note, the lender can sue the borrower(s) for the remaining balance owed. This process is known as a deficiency judgment. In some non-judicial foreclosure states, where a trust deed was used as the security instrument, the lenders have the option of electing to do a judicial foreclosure in order to preserve the option to sue for a deficiency judgment.

Many states require a judicial foreclosure process, and some states allow both forms of foreclosures—either a judicial or non-judicial foreclosure process. Lenders generally prefer the faster non-judicial process if it is available, but may choose a judicial foreclosure process in special situations, especially if the foreclosure is on very large commercial properties, and when litigation is likely. That is because the judicial process gives the lender certain advantages over the non-judicial foreclosure process, such as seeking deficiency judgments, as mentioned above. However, it can also create some disadvantages, such as permitting the right of redemption, which favors the borrowers.

Non-Judicial Foreclosure

The non-judicial foreclosure is becoming the most common process for performing a foreclosure because it is a faster and less expensive way to foreclose. Many states that in the past have been mortgage states, recently have passed laws that will allow for the use of trust deeds (see Appendix B). The non-judicial foreclosure process is performed by foreclosure companies without the need to go through the court system. A lender chooses a private foreclosure company to act as a trustee and perform the foreclosure process, which can take from 30 days to a year, depending on the state laws (see Appendix B). This is a faster, more efficient, and less-expensive process for the lender than a judicial foreclosure. This is the reason many states are changing to the trust deed instrument—so they can facilitate and expedite the foreclosure process.

The non-judicial foreclosure process begins by recording a notice of default at the county recorder's office, noticing the borrower and any junior lien holders, and publishing the notice of default in local newspapers. This process is usually done several times over a period of weeks or months. There is typically a waiting period of weeks or months for the borrower to cure the default.

After that, the next step in the foreclosure process is announcing the trustee sale, or foreclosure sale, by recording a notice of sale at the recorder's office and publishing the auction sale date and property address in a local newspaper. Shortly thereafter, the trustee sale or foreclosure sale is conducted by an auctioneer, where the public is allowed to bid on the defaulted property, and it is sold to the highest bidder. If the trustee conducts a foreclosure sale, the title is conveyed from the trustee to the new owner via a document called a trustee's deed.

This auction is usually an all-cash auction sale, where bidders must qualify to bid by presenting the auctioneer with cashier's checks prior to the bidding process. The winning bidder then pays the auctioneer by cashier's check immediately afterward. If there are no bidders at the trustee sale, the property reverts back to the beneficiary (the lender), and the title is still transferred from the trustee to the lender using the trustee's deed. Finally, the foreclosure trustee prepares and delivers a trustee's deed, granting title to the winning bidder within the next few days or weeks, and it is recorded in the county recorder's office. Unlike a judicial foreclosure, once the property is sold, the borrower has no right of redemption.

While the lender or state law will ultimately determine which security instrument will be used to secure the loan, it is important for investors to understand the difference between these two security instruments. This difference should be understood because it will impact the cost and duration of the foreclosure process in the event that the borrower defaults on their mortgage obligation. This information is very significant for private money lenders to know because it can determine in which states the investors might want to invest their money—a mortgage or deed of trust state. Knowing the advantages and disadvantages of the various foreclosure proceedings in each state will reduce the risk associated with the investment.

Strict Foreclosure

It was previously mentioned that only six states would permit a strict foreclosure process. In this type of foreclosure proceeding, the lender will file a lawsuit against a homeowner who has defaulted on their mortgage payment obligation. If the borrower cannot pay the mortgage within a specific timeline ordered by the court, the property reverts back to the lender or mortgage holder. Therefore, the property is not subjected to an auction sale like in the other two types of foreclosure proceedings.

A strict foreclosure is quite similar to a deed in lieu of foreclosure, with the exception that the borrower does not have the option to refuse. Their only course of action, if they wish to fight the proceeding, is to take the matter to court. In a strict-type foreclosure, the mortgage agreement contains a strict foreclosure decree that states that the lender owns the property until the mortgage has been paid in full. If the borrower breaks any of the conditions of the mortgage before it is paid in full, they will lose any right to the property, and the lender will take possession of the asset (foreclosure-hq.com, n. d.).

Even though the laws differ between the various states that permit strict foreclosures, the customary process to initiate this type of foreclosure is for the lender to file a lawsuit and take the matter to court to prove that the borrower is in default under the terms of the mortgage agreement. The borrower is then given a length of time, determined by the court, to bring the mortgage payments up to date. If the borrower fails to repay the debt within the court-allotted time, the lender receives full title to the property as a complete settlement of the debt.

Therefore, no auction sale is required, and the borrower forfeits any equity they have built in the property either through repayment of principal or increase in property value. However, because of the apparent opportunities for abuse and the general unfairness to the borrower, strict foreclosures are uncommon in the modern marketplace. Customarily, a strict foreclosure takes place mostly on properties that are considered underwater, which is when the debt amount is higher than the value of the property.

Deficiency Judgment

A deficiency judgment may occur after a foreclosure has been completed if the lender suffers a loss on the loan and is not able to recover their original principal amount. The lender has the right to sue in court and attempt to get a judgment against the borrower for the amount of the loss or deficiency. Therefore, deficiency judgments are court orders that make the borrowers personally liable for their unpaid debt. This process is not permitted in all states and may also depend on whether a judicial or non-judicial foreclosure process was used (see Appendix B). Junior liens, such as second and third mortgage holders who were wiped off the title by a foreclosed senior lien, may be allowed deficiency judgments if the junior lien was not created at the time of purchasing the property (Legal Alerts, 2012, July 6).

Right of Redemption

The right of redemption after a trustee sale, or foreclosure sale, allows the borrower who just lost their home at the foreclosure auction sale, the opportunity to repurchase the property from the bank or the winning bidder, usually at the same price as the highest bid at the auction sale. Therefore, the right of redemption is a statutory period in which the debtor has an opportunity to satisfy their debt obligation and prevents losing their property. For example, Florida Chapter 45 Statute 45.0315 that addresses the right of redemption allows foreclosed homeowners the opportunity to cure the mortgagor's indebtedness on their property by paying the final judgment amount prior to the issuance of the certificate of sale to the new owner.

What this means is that once a final judgment amount has been entered, the lender or mortgage holder has the right to auction the property. However, it is not until sometime after the sale has been completed that the certificate of sale is issued. This provides the opportunity for the foreclosed homeowner at any time before or after the auction, and up until the certificate of sale is issued, the right to pay the final judgment amount and redeem the property, which voids the auction sale.

Moreover, in Florida, if the foreclosed homeowner is not able to pay the final judgment amount, there is another option to challenge the sale of the property. This option is called an *"equitable right of redemption"* period. The premise behind this concept is that it is only fair for the foreclosed homeowner to have a window of time to be able to redeem or save their home after the foreclosure sale has been consummated. This principle does not apply in all states; however, some state laws are more generous than others. If the foreclosed property owner can come up with the necessary funds, they may be able to get their home back even after someone else buys it at a foreclosure sale.

For example, in Florida, the *equitable right of redemption provision* will permit the foreclosed homeowner ten days after the property is sold to object to the terms of the sale. This window of opportunity is allowed if there was a violation of the court-ordered procedures or because the sale price was the result of bidder collusion or other unfair practices that led to an artificially low purchase price. This right is important because if the property is sold for less than what the foreclosed homeowner owed, then the lender may obtain a deficiency judgment against the foreclosed homeowner (Scrofano, n. d.).

The provisions of *right of redemption and equitable right of redemption*, which are allowed by some states and for a specific period of time after the auction sale, may take weeks or months (see Appendix B). This is a disadvantage for bidders and lenders because if any property improvement costs were put into the property, they would not be recoverable if the borrower exercises this right of redemption.

Deed in Lieu of Foreclosure

A *"deed in lieu of foreclosure"* (DILF) is a deed instrument in which the borrower (mortgagor) voluntarily conveys all interest in real property to the lender (mortgagee) to satisfy a loan that is in default, thus avoiding foreclosure proceedings. This process usually occurs when borrowers are cognizant of the fact that a foreclosure is inevitable, and to avoid the embarrassment and expense of having to subject themselves to a foreclosure process, the property owner will opt for a DILF to amicably end the ordeal. A deed in lieu of foreclosure is occasionally referred to as a "friendly foreclosure" (Johnson, 2014, July 22).

This process requires an agreement between both the borrower and lender, and the borrower typically is the party that initiates the agreement. Subsequently, the borrower releases the title to the lender to satisfy the loan and vacates the property. The deed in lieu of foreclosure offers several advantages to both the borrower and the lender. The principal advantage to the borrower is that it immediately releases the borrower from most or all the personal indebtedness associated with the defaulted loan. The advantages to the lender of accepting the DILF are the financial benefits of avoiding foreclosure expenses and the possibility of preventing damages to the property during the eviction process, which is a likely event.

However, there are also disadvantages associated with a deed in lieu of foreclosure for both the borrower and lender. For the borrower, a DILF can be as damaging to their credit rating as a regular foreclosure. The disadvantage for the lender is accepting a DILF without undertaking a complete title search to identify any existing liens against the property. If an adequate title search is not performed, the lender will end up being responsible for the existing debt associated with those liens. That is why it is not uncommon for a lender not to accept the DILF if they discover that there are other liens against the property. Moreover, some lenders will not consider a DILF if the property lacks equity. In a foreclosure auction, if the property sells for an amount much higher than the loan balance, the borrower may receive a portion of the sale price; however, this will be up to the lender to decide, because the borrower forfeits that right in a deed in lieu of foreclosure (Johnson, 2014, July 22).

Tax Consequences of Deed in Lieu of Foreclosure

If a borrower can get a deed in lieu of foreclosure, they might be liable for taxation on the cancellation of indebtedness, or what is classified as cancellation of debt (COD) income by the IRS. Ordinarily, when $600 or more of debt is forgiven or canceled by a creditor, the amount that has been forgiven is considered income for federal tax purposes, whether the debt is a mortgage or another kind of credit. The resultant tax liability would be based on whether the loan is classified as a non-recourse loan or a recourse-type loan. This classification is specified in the loan documents that were originally signed by the lender and borrower.

Essentially, if the lender's only option is to get back the property when the borrower defaults, then it is classified as a non-recourse type loan. Conversely, if the lender can sue for a deficiency judgment to collect any debt shortfall when the property is auctioned at the foreclosure sale, the loan is a recourse-type loan. Should a lender prevail in court and win a deficiency judgment, the lender will need to submit Form 1099-C to the IRS in the case of a shortfall in a recourse loan where a deed in lieu of foreclosure has been granted. This is known as the borrower's cancellation of debt (COD) income.

In the case of a non-recourse loan, the IRS will consider the tax consequences of the deed in lieu of foreclosure as if the borrower had sold the property. If the current market value of the property is less than what is owed on the existing mortgage, the property owner will have a personal loss that is not considered tax-deductible. Conversely, if the value of the property is higher than the outstanding loan, the property owner will have a capital gain that may not be taxed if the borrower can comply with the Internal Revenue Code (IRC) Section 121 two-year residency requirement. Essentially, IRC Section 121 provides each taxpayer who filed a federal tax return an exclusion on the capital gains tax when selling their primary residence. The exclusion entails the requirement that every two years it allows $250,000 for those filing a single return and $500,000 for those married filing a joint return, provided the following conditions exist:

❖ The property represents their principal residence.

❖ The taxpayer has lived in the home for at least two of the last five years.

In the case of a recourse loan, the situation is similar to the non-recourse loan except that the borrower will also be taxed for COD income if the value of the property is less than what is owed. If a borrower receives a COD, ordinary income rates will be applied for the cancellation of debt income.

If a debtor has received a COD, then the obligation to repay will no longer exist. However, the Internal Revenue Service customarily considers the cancellation of debt (COD) as a type of income for the debtor, although there are certain exceptions to this rule that could facilitate the elimination of the tax liability.

For example, taxpayers under certain situations, such as bankruptcy and insolvency, may be able to avoid paying taxes on the cancellation of debt. If the debt was forgiven as part of a bankruptcy proceeding, the debt is not taxable. For taxpayers with a debt that was canceled while under a period of insolvency, a portion or the entire amount of the COD may be exempt from taxation.

That is why the IRS highly recommends that taxpayers consult with a tax accountant or attorney to determine whether the debtors are truly insolvent. Otherwise, they may file their income tax return improperly, which could result in penalties and interest being owed to the IRS on an incorrectly filed tax return.

An important area where debt cancellation usually occurs is when a home has foreclosed, and the property owners receive a COD, which makes the canceled debt taxable, unbeknownst to most taxpayers. However, as previously mentioned, an exception to this rule is granted for non-recourse loans. Moreover, from 2007 to 2018, under the Mortgage Forgiveness Debt Relief Act of 2007, taxpayers were also allowed to avoid counting the debt cancellation as income when the foreclosed property was a primary residence.

The Mortgage Forgiveness Debt Relief Act (MFDRA) of 2007 was initially scheduled to sunset in 2010. Thus, the Act initially covered a three-year period between 2007 and 2010. Fortunately for property owners, it has been extended five times to 2012, 2013, 2014, 2016, 2017, and then to 2019. This last extension can also apply to debt that is discharged in 2020, provided that there was a written agreement entered into in 2019 (Mott, n. d.; Lofsgordon, n.d.).

5

Methods of Investing in
Private Mortgages

S ophisticated investors are always looking for ways to diversify
their portfolios. An increasingly popular option for these
types of investors is private mortgage investing. Private mortgage
investing is very attractive to investors seeking diversification
because they are able to generate investment income that is not
subjected to the uncertainty and volatility of traditional stock or
bond markets.

The private mortgage lending industry is not a well-publicized
economic sector. However, the practice of private or hard money
lending can be found in all fifty states (see Appendix J). The
Alternative Lending Magazine (ALM) puts out a "Hard Money
State Rankings Report" annually that lists the ranking of every
state as it relates to hard money loans. This list is compiled through
the use of accurate, real-time, Internet-based data collected from
housing funding and sales trends, and lender behaviors such as
recorded deeds and final closing statements. Appendix J shows the
most current hard money state rankings for the year 2012.

Lenders in this industry are predominantly small, highly
specialized mortgage brokers familiar with residential and
commercial real estate lending. The trend in California and other
states is towards the development of m*ortgage funds or mortgage*

pools, which are structured and operated similar to commercial banks. Private money lenders, hard money lenders, private money bankers, and real estate bankers are terms used interchangeably to mean the same thing. Mostly, they are groups, individuals, companies, or funds that pool private money and then lend those pooled funds for profit.

A private mortgage is a form of an asset-based loan—a secured debt obligation—that produces a consistent, predictable income stream or cash flow to an investor. It generates this income stream with all the securities, protections, and recourse that a mortgage lien can provide. While mortgages do not typically provide any capital appreciation, they do generate a steady stream of interest payments, which can exceed current CDs, bonds, and money-market rates. In contrast to stocks and bonds, the underlying security in private mortgage investing is a tangible, brick-and-mortar type of asset.

Mortgage investing can offer investors the same legal rights and remedies a traditional bank mortgage can provide. These are lawful protections such as title insurance, hazard insurance, and several other risk-mitigating remedies that can be employed and can ensure the enforceability of a mortgage lien and provide substantial downside protection for the investor.

Additionally, private mortgage loans are also secured by personal guarantees from the borrowers, which can provide an additional layer of legal recourse beneficial to the private lender/investor. It is important to note that when the author speaks of private mortgages, he is explicitly referring to *first-lien mortgage bridge loans* on commercial and residential real estate. For example, apartment buildings, mixed-use properties, retail properties, and non-owner occupied single-family homes, which are the properties that carry less investment and legal risk. It is recommended that lenders do not invest in mortgages in single-family, owner-occupied homes because of the legal protection afforded these types of mortgages through homestead exemption laws, and now the Dodd-Frank Act of 2010.

The Dodd-Frank Act has been fully implemented as of January 10, 2014, with some unintended consequences—some positive and some negative—as is always the case with the implementation of any new laws. The original Dodd-Frank Act provisions, as well as the newly implemented final rulings, are addressed in Chapter 6, which is the section of the book that covers the mortgage lending industry and its laws, rules, and regulations.

The reason for choosing to invest in private mortgages is often a combination of the limited downside risk of the capital invested and the attractive returns that can be generated with this type of investment vehicle. Typically, private mortgage investment participation can be done in three primary forms as follows:

❖ Sole private money investor

❖ Fractionalized mortgage investment

❖ Mortgage Fund investment

Sole Private Money Investor

This form of investing can range from private individuals investing directly under their names or through trusts, S corporations, LLCs, and pension funds, as well as self-directed IRAs. These individual investors generally have substantial knowledge and experience in real estate, mortgage, or trust deed investing. The mortgage or trust deed is written in the name of the single investor, and all interest payments go directly to the investor on a monthly basis. Investing in private mortgages in this fashion places the burden of having to perform all the work and the servicing of the loan on the individual private lender. The caveat with this style of mortgage investing is that because all the associated risks lie with the individual investor, it should only be done by experienced private mortgage lender/investors who are familiar with the entire lending process.

The motivation for investing in this way includes the simplicity of the underlying investment and a desire for the following features:

- ❖ An investment secured by real estate.

- ❖ Regular income derived from monthly interest distributions.

- ❖ Higher yields than those available from investing in CDs, money-market funds. (MMFs), savings accounts, bonds or bond funds.

- ❖ An active involvement in real estate finance.

Fractionalized Mortgage Investment

This type of investing refers to a group of investors, each funding a percentage of the total amount of the loan. For example, if a borrower required a one million dollar loan, the note may be fractionalized into ten different investors, each contributing $100,000. Therefore, each investor would own 10% of the transaction; all ten investors would be vested on the recorded security document as a first-lien position loan, and they all would share in the profits based on the percentage of their initial contribution. Monthly payments are made to a servicing agent, who then distributes the payments pro-rata (proportional) to the individual investors.

The benefit of fractionalized investing is that it can permit investors with smaller amounts of funds to participate in property investment because they are combining resources with other investors. Fractionalized mortgage, or trust of deed, investing can also provide the benefits of simplicity and transparency. Each individual investor reviews each prospective loan prior to making a decision to invest. However, one negative aspect of fractionalizing is that building each loan one investor at a time can take time, which essentially can detract from the main advantage of private money lending, which is the speed of execution.

Conversely, fractionalized investing can also present significant problems if there are disputes between multiple investors concerning the disposition of the property. Each investor is a vested partial owner of the promissory note and trust deed (or mortgage). Since they jointly own the investment, the group of investors must come to an agreement whenever there is a question of how to proceed in the event of a default. Sometimes this problem can be resolved or avoided if a mortgage servicer is used that can handle collection services and initiating foreclosure proceedings.

Mortgage Fund Investment

Mortgage Funds, or Mortgage Pools, resemble equity mutual funds, which are composed of a wide selection of stocks. These Mortgage Funds primarily operate by having investors' deposit money in the Fund, the objective of which is to invest in mortgages or deed of trust depending on the State the Fund resides in. The Fund is managed by mortgage brokers or mortgage bankers who are licensed or certified by the State. Money from the Fund is lent to borrowers and is secured by first, second, or third lien position deeds of trust or mortgages depending on the objective of the Fund. The Fund is named as the holder of the note, rather than the individual investors.

Mortgage Fund investments, or Mortgage Pools, are real estate partnerships that offer investors participation as limited partners in a pool of trust deeds or mortgages. The partners receive income generated from mortgage interest, which is typically distributed monthly or quarterly. Mortgage Funds allow investors greater diversification through the ability to participate in a larger number of trust deeds or mortgages, rather than a select few as in single or fractionalized mortgages or deeds of trust.

When an investor purchases shares of the Mortgage Fund, they obtain a proportionate interest of all the loans in the Fund. Interest earnings from the loans in the Fund are passed directly to investors, who can choose to receive distribution checks or reinvest the earned interest stream back into the Fund to create a compounding effect. Therefore, unlike in single mortgage or fractionalized pools investing in a mortgage Fund, compound interest can be achieved.

The investor yields are similar to those obtained through fractionalized investments. The primary difference between these two types of investment lies in their degree of diversification. With Fund investment, the risk is spread across a portfolio of many loans, not centered on a single loan as with fractionalized investments. Thus, the risk with Fund investing is spread across the entire pool of borrowers and the various types of properties within the Fund in a variety of locations. As a result of this diversification, in the event of late payments or defaults, there is minimal to no impact on the investors' returns. These risks are mitigated by the reserve accounts that are established by the Funds and by each Fund's manager that would compensate for any shortfall.

Another difference with Fund investing is liquidity. If an investor in a fractionalized investment wishes to cash in his position, he must either be replaced with another investor, or the investor must wait for the loan to be paid off by the borrower. Because many private money loans take the form of short-term bridge loans lasting on average between one and three years, this waiting period is generally limited.

Mortgage Fund investing can generally offer quick, and sometimes immediate, repayment of principal. This prompt reimbursement is facilitated because:

❖ The Funds have established reserve accounts for that purpose.

❖ Funds are generally oversubscribed, which means that there are more investors wanting to get into the Fund than those wanting out. Thus, providing a degree of liquidity for Fund investors.

A final difference with Fund investing is that of control. The situation is similar to the equity markets where investors have the choice of selecting single stocks in which to invest or investing in a mutual fund. With mortgage or trust deed investing, the sole mortgage investors and the fractionalized investors are inclined to make their investment decisions on each property, which is akin to selecting individual stocks. The Fund investors who delegate this duty to the Fund manager is similar to mutual fund investing.

Besides the benefits of diversification and ease of entry, many investors prefer the Fund, or Mortgage Pool investing, because of the ability to fund the investment through a variety of sources. For example, in addition to investing with personal funds, these Mortgage Funds will allow investors to invest through other accounts and entities, such as an investor's self-directed IRA, trusts, pension plans, LLCs, and corporations (see Chapter 10, Legal Ways of Holding Title).

As mentioned in the introduction to this chapter, sophisticated investors are always searching for ways to instill diversification into their portfolios to mitigate investment risk. An increasingly popular option for these types of investors is to use Private Mortgage Funds or Mortgage Investment Pools. Private Mortgage Funds and Pools are attractive to investors seeking diversification because they can generate investment income from a non-market correlated investment vehicle that is not subjected to the market volatility of traditional stocks or bonds. The premise behind choosing to invest in a Private Mortgage Fund is often a combination of the limited downside risk of the capital invested, attractive returns on investment (ROI), and trusting experienced professionals to manage the Fund according to the prescribed investment criteria.

Notwithstanding all the positive attributes of Fund and fractionalized pools investing, one negative consequence that should be considered by investors for these types of investments is the passing away of the Fund or pool manager. The manager plays the most crucial role in the success of these Funds. The reason being it's that these individuals have highly specialized investment knowledge; thus, they are difficult to replace. This type of scenario has not occurred yet; therefore, it is hard to gauge what would happen to the Fund or pool if this situation occurred.

The concept of Mortgage Fund investing is neither new nor difficult to understand. For investors who have been fortunate enough to have discovered this investment vehicle, the reward has been a consistent high return on investment. The primary objective of this type of Mortgage Fund is to simply aggregate or pool investors' capital, underwriting, originating, and managing of a portfolio of private mortgages with the goal of paying the generated interest to the Fund's investors minus the fund management fee, without the need to participate in the uncertainty and volatility of the stock market.

At this juncture, it is important for the reading audience to be aware of the fact that there is a publicly-traded investment vehicle that essentially mimics the same investment philosophy as that of private mortgage investing. This investment vehicle is called a mortgage real estate investment trust, or mREIT, which was briefly discussed in Chapter 3. Notwithstanding that brief discussion, it is appropriate to provide a more detailed explanation of this investment because of the similarity to direct private mortgage investing, which is the topic of this chapter.

The Mortgage REITs

As previously explained in Chapter 3, in the 1960s, under the Eisenhower administration, Congress created a new type of security called a real estate investment trust (REIT) that allowed real estate investments to be traded in a manner similar to stocks. The objective of this legislation was to facilitate a way for the small investor to participate in the income potential associated with large-scale real estate projects.

Therefore, a REIT is a company that specializes in real estate, either through the purchases of properties, mortgages, or both. Essentially, there are two major types of REITs:

❖ Equity REITs, or eREITs, which purchase and operate real estate properties with the objective of generating a passive income stream from the collection of rents and leases.

❖ Mortgage REITs, or mREITs, which conversely invest in mortgages and mortgage bonds such as mortgage-backed securities (MBSs), with the objective of generating a passive income stream from the interest that is earned from the portfolio of mortgage loans the fund owns.

The mREITs have been attracting investor interest since the yields on CDs, bonds, and money-market accounts have substantially been reduced by the Federal Reserve policy of maintaining a low-interest-rate environment. It is not uncommon for mREITs to pay dividend yields of 10% or higher, with the potential for some capital appreciation as well.

Although the objective of mREITs is the same as private mortgage investing (PMI), which is to generate a high-income stream, the risks associated with mREITs are similar to any market-correlated investment. Thus, they will be subjected to the volatility of the market, just like any other type of stock. Moreover, mREITs will also be subjected to numerous additional risks; such as interest-rate risk, portfolio quality risk, dividend cut risk, mortgage default risk, refinancing risk, operating loss risk, quantitative easing (QE) risk, prepayment risk, and limited capital risk.

While investing directly in private mortgages will have some similar risks; ultimately, the investor will have more control over the investment, which will help mitigate the investment risk. With direct private mortgage investing, the ultimate risk is a foreclosure, which can be a positive event for the investor if the proper due diligence process and loan structure arrangement have been performed.

Another new way to invest in real estate private mortgages is through the concept of Crowdfunding. This funding vehicle is essentially quite similar to the fractionalized mortgage investment concept previously described, except that the Internet is the mechanism used to procure the funds or pledges. The following section is intended to provide a brief description of the concept of

Crowdfunding as well as the historical origins and future potential of this fundraising concept.

The Crowdfunding Concept

Crowdfunding is a financing method that involves funding a project with relatively modest contributions from a large group of individuals, rather than seeking substantial sums from a small number of investors. Today many people erroneously believe that crowdfunding is a new phenomenon. However, the novelty of the concept lies in the technologies and the mindset that is giving it a new momentum. The Internet is the technology that has made it possible for anyone and everyone to participate in crowdfunding.

Thus, crowdfunding is a term used to describe an evolving method of raising money through the Internet. Furthermore, crowdfunding, as a concept pre-dates the Internet and projects like the renovation of the Statue of Liberty, raised the required funds from donations pledged from a large number of donors, in essence, the crowd.

Therefore, crowdfunding is not as new as people might think. In fact, the concept has a long and rich history with roots going back to the 1700s. For example, in the 1700s, Jonathan Swift—the famed author of Gulliver's Travels—started the *Irish Loan Fund* to provide small loans to low-income families in rural areas. Swift recognized that said individuals had no experience with credit and held little collateral but could still be considered creditworthy.

This concept of microlending became popular, and by the 1800s, more than 300 programs throughout Ireland were loaning small amounts of money for short periods of time. It was estimated that at the peak of the program, 20% of the households of that period were utilizing the program (Clark, 2011, September 15).

Thus this form of lending, in essence, is the precursor of the popular concept of microfinance popularized by Dr. Mohammad Yunus. Professor Yunus is a Bangladeshi social entrepreneur, banker, economist, and civil society leader who was awarded the Nobel Peace Prize. He received the award for founding the Grameen Bank and pioneering the concepts of microcredit and microfinance in the mid-1970s (Clark, 2011, September 15; Nobelprize.org, 2006).

Crowdfunding is defined or described as the practice of funding a project or venture by raising monetary contributions from a large number of people, typically via the Internet. Other experts described it as; the practice of raising funds from two or more people over the Internet towards the purpose of a common Service, Project, Product, Investment, Cause, and Experience (SPPICE) (Oxford Dictionaries, n. d.; Drake, n. d.). Therefore, there are two essential components for crowdfunding to work:

- ❖ Solicitation from the "crowd" to raise funds.
- ❖ Using the Internet or web as the community.

The SPPICE definition, as proposed by David Drake of *Crowdsourcing.org*, significantly improves the description because it takes into account the involvement of the crowd to achieve the overall success of the venture. It is not just about injecting the investor's money into a project. Instead, it is eliciting crowd collaboration to ensure the success of the project.

The first successful recorded project using the crowdfunding financing method occurred in 1997 when the British rock band *Marillion* funded their reunion tour by raising $ 60,000 through small online donations from their fans (Giveforward.com, n. d.). Subsequently, inspired by this innovative method of financing, Brian Carmelio founded ArtistShare (a record label and business model for creative artists) became the first dedicated crowdfunding platform in 2001. Shortly after that, more crowdfunding platforms such as Sellaband (2006), IndieGoGo (2008), and Kickstarter (2009) began to emerge, and the crowdfunding industry has grown each year consistently.

Entrepreneur Michael Sullivan is the individual credited with coining the term crowdfunding back in 2006 with the launch of *Fundavlog*, which was a failed attempt at creating an incubator for video blog-related projects and events that included a simple funding functionality. The Fundavlog model launched by Sullivan was *based on the principles of reciprocity, transparency, shared interests, and funding from the crowd.*

However, the term crowdfunding began to be used more frequently in 2009 with the lunched of the Kickstarter platform as a way to fund creativity. Kickstarter took this concept and built a model that helps creative minds get the funding necessary from their peers. Kickstarter's Projects range from documentaries to iPod wristwatches (Clark, 2011, September 15).

Different Types of Crowdfunding

Essentially there are four different types of crowdfunding as briefly explain below. They are as follows:

- ❖ Donation-Based Crowdfunding
- ❖ Reward-Based Crowdfunding
- ❖ Equity-Based Crowdfunding
- ❖ Debt or Lending Based Crowdfunding

Donation-Based Crowdfunding

In this type of funding, the crowd gives or pledges money or some other resource for the purpose of supporting a cause they believe in. The funds are provided with no expectation of receiving a return except for the feeling of goodwill. In essence, contributions are geared towards a charitable cause of interest to the donor.

Reward-Based Crowdfunding

In this type of funding, the crowd or pledger receives a tangible item or service in return for their pledged funds. This is a popular way of crowdfunding. Donations and rewards crowdfunding has been used as a strategy for fundraising prior to the passage of the JOBS Act of 2012.

Equity-Based Crowdfunding

Equity crowdfunding has received enormous interest after the passage of the JOBS Act of 2012. In this type of crowdfunding, the crowd/investors receive a proportionate piece of equity or an ownership stake in a specific property or portfolio of properties. The investor subsequently will share in the profits as the property is developed and sold or managed for rental income. In equity-based crowdfunding, the company seeking the funds is selling its shares to the crowd pledging the funds.

Debt or Lending Based Crowdfunding

In this final type of crowdfunding, the crowd/investors are repaid for their investment over a period of time. In this type of crowdfunding, the company is borrowing money from the crowd in exchange for interest payments. When investing in debt instruments, the crowd/investor is acting as the lender to the property owner or the deal sponsor. This type of crowdfunding is quite suitable for investors interested in private mortgage lending, which is the focus of this book. In fact, this form of real estate crowdfunding has been receiving an increasing amount of interest lately because of the potential for generating a consistent and significant passive income stream.

One of the newer real estate crowdfunding platforms that are pursuing the private mortgage lending model is *Zeus Crowdfunding*. Launched in 2016, the objective of this new real estate crowdfunding lending platform is to empower accredited investors to take real estate investing into their own hands while giving borrowers a brand-new avenue from which to fund the projects that they believe in. Zeus Crowdfunding, through its proprietary product, Z-Crowd™ is offering investors attractive risk-adjusted returns in semi-liquid investments while providing guarantees for the preservation of capital (Kaufman, 2019). Moreover, according to

Zeus Crowdfunding, investors can earn up to 14% in semi-liquid, passive investments in real estate notes.

The real estate industry is one of the most recent entries to crowdfunding. Numerous platforms have sprung up over the past couple of years to enable investors from around the world to invest in real estate. Some of the real estate crowdfunding platforms that have come to the market place are:

❖ Crowdbaron

❖ CrowdStreet

❖ Fundrise

❖ Groundbreaker

❖ Groundfloor

❖ iFunding

❖ Patch of Land

❖ Realcrowd

❖ Realty Mogul

❖ Realty Shares

❖ Zeus Crowdfunding

It is important for investors to understand that not all real estate crowdfunding sites are created equal. Some real estate crowdfunding platforms make direct investments in real estate; others buy mortgages, and others make peer to peer (P2P) loans. In essence, each of these platforms has its own niche and strategy, with various minimum amounts of investment. Needless to say that the contract law principle of *"Caveat Emptor"* or let the buyer beware applies, and a thorough due diligence process is warranted before investing in any of these crowdfunding sites (Miller, n. d.). Investors should understand that real estate crowdfunded investments are generally unsecured investments, which means that if the platform were to go under, investors could lose their capital.

The reason for the proliferation of these crowdfunding sites is attributed to the opportunity created by the passage of the landmark legislation known as the *Jumpstart Our Business Startups (JOBS) Act*. This Act was signed into law on April 5, 2012, by President Barrack Obama for the purpose of supporting entrepreneurship and small business growth. The JOBS Act, composed of seven titles, is designed to encourage small business and startup funding by easing federal regulations and allowing individuals to become investors.

The goal of the Jobs Act is to reduce some strict securities regulations with regards to advertising and solicitation of funds. An additional goal is to open up the general public as an emerging capital market, allowing Emerging Growth Companies (EGCs) as well as smaller startup businesses to go directly to the general public to raise funds. The JOBS Act will achieve these goals using two distinct sections or titles of the legislation, specifically Title II and Title III, which are considered the two most important provisions affecting the equity crowdfunding and startup community. Title II is called *"The Access to Capital for Job Creation,"* and Title III is called *"Crowdfunding."*

Title II of the JOBS Act went into effect on September 23, 2013. The implementation of this title essentially legalized the public solicitation of accredited investors in the United States. It did this by removing a prohibition ban on the mass marketing of private securities offerings—meaning those securities not formally registered with the Securities and Exchange Commission (SEC).

In other words, Title II dramatically changed the way investment capital can be raised. This change was accomplished by modifying existing Regulation D rules, specifically those rules pertaining to how companies can offer and sell their securities without having to register the securities with the SEC (Sec.org, 2013, September 23).

Essentially, what Title II did was to modified Rule 506 of Regulation D. Historically, Regulation D of Rule 506 offerings have been exempted from SEC registration provided that the offering is not publicly advertised and that the purchasers are largely qualified institutions or accredited investors.

The modification to Title II was to adopt paragraph (c) to Rule 506. Under the new Rule 506(c), issuers can now offer securities through means of general solicitation, provided that:

- ❖ All purchasers in the offering are accredited investors. Accredited investors are those whose net worth is greater than $1 million—excluding a primary residence—or whose individual income exceeded $200,000 or $300,000 for couples for the past two years with the expectation to continue to generate that level of income in the current year.

- ❖ The issuer takes reasonable steps to verify their accredited investor status.

- ❖ Certain other conditions in Regulation D are satisfied.

In essence, Rule 506(c) allows issuers, sponsors, syndicators, and others who are raising capital from private investors to advertise those private-investment opportunities to accredited investors under certain conditions. Title II essentially gives crowdfunding firms the green light to access a direct market of a large pool of prospective investors via the Internet and social media outlets, such as Facebook and Twitter. Moreover, it has opened up a new investment vehicle for potential investors to access direct real estate investment opportunities with ease (O'Connell, n. d.).

Before the passage of the JOBS Act, the crowdfunding funding method had been used to generate financial support for such projects as artistic endeavors like films and music recordings, typically through small individual contributions (donations) from a large number of people—in essence, the crowd.

While this funding method can be used to raise funds for many things, it generally had not been used as a means to offer and sell securities. That is because offering a share of the financial returns or profits from business activities—before the passage of the JOBS

Act—could have triggered the application of the federal securities laws. These laws would be triggered because an offer or sale of securities was required to be registered with the SEC unless an exemption was available.

Title III of the JOBS Act—Crowdfunding—is the provision that created an exemption under the securities laws so that this type of funding method can be easily used to offer and sell securities—in essence, legalizing *securities crowd investing.* The Act accomplished this objective by amending the *Securities Act of 1933* by adding two new Sections, 4(6) and 4A. Together, these new sections exempt crowdfunding transactions from the registration requirements of the Securities Act. Prior to the passage of the Act, the SEC already permitted crowdfunding-type offerings to accredited investors. However, now, after the passage of the legislature, offerings under the JOBS Act Title III and Regulation Crowdfunding anyone can invest, not just the accredited investors (sec.org, 2013, September 15; Noked, 2013, December 6).

Additionally, Title III further established the foundation for a regulatory structure that would permit these entities to use crowdfunding, as well as directing the SEC to write the rules to implement the exemptions. It also created a new entity—a funding portal—to allow Internet-based platforms or intermediaries to facilitate the offer and sale of securities without having to register with the SEC as brokers (Sec.org, 2013, October 23).

In conjunction, all these measures were intended to facilitate the small business to raise capital while providing significant investor protections. Since the passage of the JOBS Act, there has been a substantial increase in the use of crowdfunding services and even the launch of new crowdfunding platforms. This legislation passed with bipartisan support in the House with a vote of 390 to 23, and in the Senate with a vote of 73 to 26. This Act has garnered many accolades from the venture capital and startup communities.

field of private mortgage investing to become familiar with the laws and regulations that could affect this endeavor.

It is imperative for private money lenders to understand that these regulations and laws are always in flux (continuously changing). Therefore, cultivating a continuous education seeking frame of mind is an essential and safe practice to follow. Every investor who is involved in the private money lending industry should develop the habit of keeping abreast of any potential changes in the law to avoid any unintended consequences that could lead to legal ramifications. The use of a knowledgeable and competent attorney familiar with the field of private mortgage lending is an essential and worthwhile investment, especially for investors with time constraints that impede their ability to keep current regarding all the new laws and regulations that seem to be always forthcoming.

The United States Federal Government has passed a series of loan laws intended to provide parity among the mortgage banking and lending industry. The purpose of these laws passed by Congress is to attempt to provide a uniform set of standards so a borrower in one state will not be subjected to different lending practices than a borrower in another State.

Ultimately, the decision to lend money is left up to the banks or lending institutions. However, a potential borrower can now file a report if they feel these laws were compromised in their particular case. The laws and regulations that will be presented in this chapter are what the author considers to be the most relevant to the mortgage lending industry and the private money lender investor.

The Dodd-Frank Wall Street Reform and Consumer Protection Act

The Dodd-Frank Act was signed into law on July 21, 2010, and presently is the source of all the financial changes taking place in the lending industry as it became effective on July 21, 2011, one year after its enactment. The Dodd-Frank Act is a massive piece of legislation intended to address countless problem areas that are believed to have caused the financial crisis of 2008. The Act is more than 2,300 pages long and includes 16 titles (see Appendix D). Therefore, a detailed explanation of the entire Act is beyond the scope or intent of this chapter.

Notwithstanding the intended scope of the chapter, the author will present a short overview of the key provisions of the Dodd-Frank Act, with a brief summary of the regulations that are particularly pertinent to the content and objectives of this book. Hence, the emphasis will be on the provisions that should be of particular interest to mortgage lenders, as well as the regulations that will impact the mortgage lending industry the most. Thus, this emphasis will continue to be mentioned throughout the book to ensure its importance. It is incumbent upon and even crucial for all individuals reading this publication to seek the expertise of competent professionals to mitigate investment risk. While concomitantly, the novice investors acquire their own level of expertise with the subject.

Key Provisions of the Dodd-Frank Act

The Dodd-Frank Act seeks to achieve the following:

❖ Establish the Financial Stability Oversight Council (FSOC) to address systemic risks.

❖ Provide liquidation authority to permit an orderly liquidation of systemically risky companies.

❖ Revise bank and bank holding company regulatory regimes by transferring the Office of Thrift Supervision (OTS) functions to the Office of Comptroller of Currency (OCC), and clarifying the regulatory functions of the Federal Deposit Insurance Corporation (FDIC) and Board of Governors of Federal Reserve (FRB).

❖ To establish the regulation of investment advisers to hedge funds.

- ❖ Establish a new Federal Insurance Office (FIO) to monitor the insurance industry, including any regulatory gaps that could contribute to systemic risk.

- ❖ To restrict banks, bank affiliates, and bank holding companies from proprietary trading or investing in a hedge fund or private-equity fund.

- ❖ To increase the regulation and transparency of over-the-counter (OTC) derivatives (options) markets.

- ❖ Establish new regulation of credit-rating agencies.

- ❖ To establish new requirements regarding executive compensation, including shareholder say on pay. The term *"say on pay"* is used for a rule in corporate law whereby a firm's shareholders have the right to vote on the remuneration of executives.

- ❖ It will require that securitizers retain an economic interest in assets they securitize.

- ❖ To empower the new Consumer Financial Protection Bureau (CFPB) as an independent office in the Federal Reserve Board (FRB) with broad new authorities, functions, and responsibilities under a wide range of current consumer financial protection laws.

- ❖ To establish extensive requirements applicable to the mortgage lending industry, including detailed requirements concerning mortgage originator compensation and underwriting, high-cost mortgages, servicing, appraisals, counseling, and other matters.

- ❖ To preserve enforcement powers of states with respect to financial institutions and restricting preemption of state laws by federal banking regulators.

Essentially, these are the key provisions that the Dodd–Frank Wall Street Reform and Consumer Protection Act (Dodd-Frank

Act) seeks to enforce *Public Law 111–203; H.R. 4173*. This Act was signed into federal law by President Barack Obama on July 21, 2010, at the Ronald Reagan Building in Washington, D.C. The Act made some significant changes to the American financial regulatory environment that affect all federal financial regulatory agencies and impact almost every part of the nation's financial services industry (see Appendix D).

Title XIV, called the *"Mortgage Reform and Anti-Predatory Lending Act,(MRAPLA)"* is the part of the Dodd-Frank Act that is replete (loaded) with provisions or regulations that will affect the mortgage lending industry. This Act adds disclosures and substantive rules relating to mortgage lending that will affect mortgage brokers, lenders, appraisers, settlement services providers, and others participating in any mortgage lending activity. Therefore, it is a significant title of the Dodd-Frank Act that all mortgage lenders should be very familiar with.

This title was introduced into the Dodd-Frank Act as a result of the 2008 economic great recession, as it has been called. This recession was triggered in part by the *bursting of the real estate bubble*, which resulted in what is now known as the housing crisis.

During that time, due to the prevailing low-interest-rate environment, mortgages became extremely easy to obtain. Many of those mortgages had been predatory in nature, with provisions that made it difficult for borrowers to pay off the mortgages in the event that their real estate value decreased. What follows below is a brief summary of all the provisions from the Dodd-Frank Act that are pertinent to the mortgage lending industry.

Provisions of the Act Pertinent to the Mortgage Lending Industry

As previously mentioned, the Dodd-Frank Act of 2010 was a massive legislative undertaking that addressed numerous components of the entire financial services industry. The brief summary that follows will highlight the provisions or regulations of Dodd-Frank that should be of particular interest to all mortgage lenders.

Credit Risk Retention

This Dodd-Frank Act provision requires the federal banking agencies and the Securities and Exchange Commission (SEC) to issue rules to require securitizers to retain an economic interest of at least 5% of the credit risk in the assets they securitize. *"Securitize"* essentially means a pooled group of financial assets, such as mortgages, that together create a new security, which is then marketed and sold to investors, for example, mortgage-backed securities (MBS).

Moreover, the provision requires regulators to establish and define a specific exemption for qualified residential mortgages (QRMs), taking into consideration the underwriting and product features that historical loan performance data indicate result in a lower risk of default. Furthermore, it authorizes alternative forms of risk retention for commercial mortgage-backed securities.

Office of Credit Ratings

This provision created the Office of Credit Ratings (OCR) in the SEC to monitor and enforce the credit-rating agency (CRA) rules, including rules designed to increase transparency and reduce conflicts of interest.

Consumer Financial Protection Bureau (CFPB)

Dodd-Frank also establishes the Consumer Financial Protection Bureau (CFPB) as an independent entity housed within the FRB. It assigns the CFPB broad authority to write rules to protect consumers from unfair or deceptive financial products, acts, or practices, and reassigns to CFPB responsibility for major consumer protection laws, including RESPA, TILA, HOEPA, HMDA, and more. Moreover, it assigns the CFPB new responsibilities under RESPA to develop RESPA/TILA disclosures, and it establishes several new

Home Mortgage Disclosure Act (HMDA) data requirements to be implemented by CFPB.

Consumer Financial Protection Bureau (CFPB) Authority

Additionally, this provision assigns the CFPB regulatory and supervisory authority to examine and enforce consumer protection regulations with respect to all mortgage-related businesses, large non-bank financial companies, and banks and credit unions with greater than $10 billion in assets. It makes the CFPB the primary regulator for non-depository lenders. *The exclusions* from CFPB authority are real estate brokers, persons regulated by state insurance regulators, auto dealers, accountants, tax preparers, and others.

Consumer Financial Protection Bureau (CFPB) Transfer Date

Dodd-Frank requires the treasury, in consultation with FRB, FDIC, FTC, NCUA, OCC, OTS, HUD, and OMB to designate the date for the transfer of functions to the CFPB within 60 days after enactment. The dates must generally be between 180 days and 12 months of enactment. Furthermore, it authorizes the treasury to revise the date after further consultation with agencies. If it is determined that the transfer of functions is not feasible within 12 months, the treasury must report to Congress.

All of the provisions that follow are part of *Title XIV, or the Mortgage Reform and Anti-Predatory Lending Act*, whose subtitles A, B, C, D, E, F, G, and H are designated as *Enumerated Consumer Laws*, which will be administered by the new Bureau of Consumer Financial Protection (CFPB).

The section focuses on standardizing data collection for underwriting and imposes obligations on mortgage originators to only lend to borrowers who are likely to repay their loans (see Appendix D for all titles that encompass the Dodd-Frank Act of 2010).

Residential Mortgage Loan Origination Standards (Subtitle A)

This provision of Title XIV involves mortgage originators who take or assist with applications and negotiate terms of mortgages. It excludes from originator definition creditors (except creditors in table-funded transactions for anti-steering provisions), servicer employees, agents, contractors, persons or entities performing real estate brokerage activities, and certain employees of manufactured home retailers.

Duty of Care (Subtitle A)

Title XIV amends the Truth in Lending Act (TILA) to establish a *"duty of care,"* which requires all loan (mortgage) originators to be properly qualified, registered and licensed as needed. Moreover, they also have to comply with any regulations designed by the Federal Reserve Board (FRB) to monitor their operations. Originators are also required to include on all loan documents the unique identifier of the mortgage originator provided by the Nationwide Mortgage Licensing System and Registry (NMLS).

Compensation of Mortgage Originators and Anti-Steering Provisions (Subtitle A)

This Title XIV provision establishes that mortgage (loan) originators are prohibited from receiving compensation that is correlated to the face amount of the loan, which should diminish incentives for such originators to steer borrowers towards residential mortgage loans that the borrower cannot repay.

However, it would allow compensation to originators under the following conditions:

- ❖ To be based on the principal amount of loan.

- ❖ To be financed through the loan's rate as long as it is not based on the loan's rate and terms. The originator does not receive any other form of compensation, such as discount points, origination points, or fees, however denominated other than third-party charges from the consumer or anyone else.

❖ As a form of incentive payments based on the number of loans originated within a specified period of time. It expressly permits compensation to be received by the creditor upon the sale of the consummated loan to a subsequent purchaser, i.e., compensation to a lender from the secondary market for the sale of the consummated loan. However, creditors in table-funded transactions are subjected to the anti-steering compensation restrictions.

This rule is intended to prevent unethical behavior and predatory lending, but it also means that brokers will not have the incentives to work with imperfect borrowers who have more difficulty qualifying for a loan because brokers will not be compensated for the additional work of closing such a loan.

As with any new regulations, there are always consequences to their implementation. The complaint by mortgage brokers regarding this brand-new provision of Title XIV of the Dodd-Frank Act is that the rules are out of sync with how the mortgage industry operates. The consequence resulting from the implementation of this provision is that under certain situations, mortgage originators must be paid a salary or hourly wage instead of a commission only. This change places an enormous burden on small, regional lenders who cannot handle the extraordinary overhead of a salary or wage structure for all their employees in an industry that is set up for commission-based compensation.

The new rule also says that mortgage originators cannot steer potential borrowers to the loan that will result in the highest payment for the mortgage originator. Instead, they must present borrowers with options containing different fees and interest rate structures so borrowers can choose the option that is in their best interests. The rule prohibits originators from steering any consumer to a residential mortgage loan for which the consumer lacks a reasonable *ability-to-repay (ATR)*, or that has predatory characteristics or effects.

Minimum Standards for Mortgages (Subtitle B)

Title XIV establishes minimum standards for all mortgage products. Creditors may not make a home mortgage loan unless they reasonably determine that the borrower can repay the loan. This assessment is based on the borrower's credit history, current income, expected future income, current obligations, debt-to-income ratio (the residual income the consumer will have after paying non-mortgage debt and mortgage-related obligations), employment status, and other financial resources other than the consumer's equity in the dwelling or real property that secures repayment of the loan.

Ability to Repay (Subtitle B)

For certain types of mortgages, there is a presumption of *ability-to-repay, as enumerated in Title XIV and as determined by the Federal Reserve Board (FRB)*. On January 10, 2013, the CFPB adopted final rules implementing the requirements of the Dodd-Frank Wall Street Reform and Consumer Protection Act of 2010 for residential mortgage lenders to consider borrowers' ability-to-repay before extending credit. This rule is now fully implemented and, in effect, as of January 10, 2014.

Section 129C of the Truth in Lending Act (TILA), as added by Sections 1411 and 1412 of the Dodd-Frank Act, requires a residential mortgage lender to make a reasonable and good faith determination based on verified and documented information that the borrower has a reasonable ability-to-repay their loan according to its terms.

The rules mandate that lenders have to consider eight factors when underwriting a mortgage loan and to determine the borrower's ability-to-repay:

❖ The current or reasonably expected income or assets.

❖ The current employment status.

- ❖ The monthly payment on the loan.

- ❖ The monthly payment on any other loan obligation being paid simultaneously.

- ❖ The monthly payment for mortgage-related obligations.

- ❖ The current debt obligations, such as alimony and child support.

- ❖ The monthly debt-to-income ratio or residual income.

- ❖ Determination and assessment of the borrower's credit history.

Although the lender determines all these factors, it does not stipulate or mandate how this assessment should be done, as long as the process employed leads to a determination that is reasonable and made in good faith. The rules also take into account certain types of prepayment penalties that are considered prohibited. Moreover, Title XIV establishes that any violation of these minimum standards by a creditor can be used as a defense by a borrower to set off or recoup damages. Therefore, since this provision grants borrowers the legal right to sue for damages, the determination that borrowers have the ability-to-repay their loan is crucial for creditors to assess.

Of course, if a borrower commits fraud in obtaining the mortgage, the creditor will not be held liable. Moreover, there must be additional disclosures given to borrowers for home mortgages, both at the time the mortgage is made, as well as in the monthly loan statements.

Safe Harbor and Rebuttable Presumption (Subtitle B)

This provision allows any creditor, assignee, or securitizer of a qualified mortgage (QM) to be presumed to meet the ability-to-repay requirements. However, this presumption may be rebuttable by the borrower. Under a safe harbor, a borrower is unable to challenge whether the lender met its ability-to-repay obligations. Under a rebuttable presumption, the borrower has the ability to raise a legal challenge but must overcome the legal presumption that the lender complied with this obligation.

Qualified Mortgages (QM) (Subtitle B)

The term *"qualified mortgage (QM)"* means any residential mortgage loan, including loans that meet several requirements, such as ascertaining that the income relied on to qualify borrowers, has been verified and documented. In addition to determining that underwriting guidelines and ratios are consistent with statutory and regulatory requirements, and total points and fees payable in connection with the loan do not exceed 3% of the total loan amount.

It is important at this time to address a source of confusion in the mortgage lending industry regarding two terms that have similar names and origins but do not mean the same thing. These terms are *"qualified mortgage"* (QM) and *"qualified residential mortgage"* (QRM). The Dodd-Frank Act contains these two terms that will have a significant future impact on traditional elements of the mortgage lending industry.

This legislation is designed to prevent certain high-risk activities from occurring within the financial sector—the kinds of activities that fueled the housing collapse and the subsequent economic meltdown. The Dodd-Frank Act aims to reduce the number of borrower defaults and foreclosures in the area of mortgages. It seeks to do this by imposing certain guidelines on the mortgage lending industry and providing the lenders with strong incentives to follow those guidelines.

The first term, *qualified mortgage (QM),* is contained within section B of Title XIV of the Dodd-Frank Act, in the recently issued ability-to-repay (ATR) rule. Its purpose is to ensure that mortgage lenders extend credit based on a reasonable *"good faith determination"* of a consumer's ability-to-repay. If a mortgage is deemed to be a qualified mortgage, the lender—by following the designated provisions and guidelines—receives certain protection from liability.

The second term, *qualified residential mortgage (QRM)*, relates to the proposed risk retention rule under the Securities Exchange Act of 1934. Its purpose is to require securitizers to retain no less than 5% of the credit risk when they create, sell, or transfer asset-backed securities to third parties, except for securities wholly comprised of QRMs.

The CFPB has defined QM in connection with its final ATR rules. However, the lending industry and its lenders had to wait for a final rule defining the term *"qualified residential mortgage."* The CFPB is not writing the QRM definition. Instead, this task was assigned to the following six federal agencies that will be the ones responsible for jointly approving the QRM definition. They are the Federal Reserve Board (FRB), the Office of the Comptroller of the Currency (OCC), the Federal Deposit Insurance Corporation (FDIC), the Securities and Exchange Commission (SEC), the Federal Housing Finance Agency (FHFA), and the Department of Housing and Urban Development (HUD).

Thus, they have collectively been designated the QRM agencies responsible for writing and issuing the final rules. The objective of the QRM final rules definition is intended to determine which loans are exempt from the risk retention requirements of the Dodd-Frank Wall Street Reform and Consumer Protection Act.

Initially, the final rule defining QM differed from the proposed rule defining QRM. This difference posed a problem because the Dodd-Frank Act mandates that the QRM definition be no broader than the definition of QM in both the law and the regulation. As noted by the CFPB in its release on the ATR rule, while the QM definition will set the outer boundary of a QRM, the QRM agencies have discretion under the Dodd-Frank Act to define QRM in a way that is stricter than the QM definition.

However, as noted at Senate Banking Committee hearings, regulators with the responsibility for writing final risk retention rules recognize that different definitions for QM and QRM could impact the housing recovery and increase compliance costs. That was the reason why regulators admitted the benefit of creating a congruent definition for both QM and QRM. Regulators also acknowledged that they purposely delayed the final rulemaking to define QRM until the CFPB conclusively issued their final rule defining QM. It is important to note that as of January 10, 2014, the CFPB final rule defining QM and QRM went into effect. Thus, the definition of these two terms—QM and QRM—are now congruent, mirror images of each other after considerable debate.

At this juncture, the author believes that a brief description of the *law of unintended consequences* is entirely appropriate. The concept of unintended consequences is one of the building blocks of economics. The term was coined and popularized in the 20th century. The law of unintended consequences implies that the actions of people—and especially of government—always have effects that are unanticipated or unintended. These effects could either be positive or negative.

Economists and other social scientists have warned about this power for centuries. However, for just as long, politicians and popular opinion have mostly ignored its effects. Most often, the law of unintended consequences can be seen in the unanticipated effects the passage of new legislation and regulation can produce, as we have observed with the Dodd-Frank Act. Thus, the law of unintended consequences provides the basis for many criticisms of government programs. In fact, it is crucial to understand that the law of unintended consequences is at work always and everywhere (Norton, n.d.).

It is expected that the mortgage lending market or industry will continue to undergo many changes going forward. As the CFPB continues to exert its power, it will modify and impose new mortgage regulations that will fundamentally change all aspects of the mortgage lending industry, from loan origination to mortgage servicing processes. Unfortunately, while the CFPB had been hard at work implementing all the new Dodd-Frank Act regulations, President Trump signed into law a new bill that undoubtedly will create additional unintended consequences.

On May 24, 2018, President Trump signed into law the Economic Growth, Regulatory Relief and Consumer Protection Act (Economic Growth Act) or Public Law 115-174, S.2155. This Act was bipartisan legislation passed as Senate bill 2155 in the U.S. Senate on March 14, 2018, and the same version was approved by the U.S. House of Representatives on May 22, 2018. The purpose of the Economic Growth Act was to ease the regulatory burden imposed by the Dodd-Frank Act of 2010.

The Economic Growth Act essentially modifies some provisions of the Dodd-Frank Act. This new law neither repeals nor replaces Dodd-Frank; it merely rollback or restore some of its provisions. It provides regulatory relief for smaller banks with less than $10 billion in assets by exempting them from complying with the Volcker Rule, which is a ban on proprietary trading and certain relationships with investment funds. Additionally, it provides an exemption for banks that meet a new Community Bank Leverage Ratio and other risk-based capital ratio and leverage ratio requirements.

Another modification of the new Economic Growth Act is to increase, from $50 billion to $250 billion, the asset threshold at which enhanced prudential standards apply to a bank holding company. The bill also amends the Truth in Lending Act (TILA) to allow a depository institution or credit union with assets below a specified threshold to forgo certain ability-to-pay (ATR) requirements regarding qualified mortgage (QM) loans (CRS.Gov, June 6, 2018; Congress.Gov, 2018).

Most changes made by the Economic Growth Act can be grouped into one of five issue areas, which are:

1. Mortgage lending
2. Regulatory relief for community banks

3. Consumer protection

4. Regulatory relief for large banks

5. Regulatory relief for capital formation

All these new regulations force banks and broker lending businesses to refine their loan products, their underwriting requirements, and other aspects of their mortgage operations to ensure compliance with the newly passed regulations.

All these industry changes confirm the contention of the author that becoming a perpetual student will be a prudent and safe habit to cultivate in order to keep abreast of the many changes the Dodd-Frank Act is imposing on the mortgage lending industry. Because all aspects of the mortgage lending industry are fundamentally being changed by all these new—and at times conflicting—laws, the author will continue to update the information herein, retaining the original language of the rules and regulations to keep a historical perspective of the transformation and evolution of this industry.

Qualified Mortgages (QM) Guidelines

On January 10, 2013, the CFPB adopted final rules implementing the requirements of the Dodd-Frank Act of 2010 that mandated that residential mortgage lenders consider the borrower's ability-to-repay before extending credit. Therefore, now that the long-anticipated clarification between qualified mortgages (QMs) and qualified residential mortgages (QRMs) has been completed and adopted henceforth, these two terms can finally enjoy the presumption of compliance with the ability-to-repay (ATR) rules. It can now specify when that presumption is conclusive or rebuttable. Thus, a qualified mortgage is a loan that satisfies all the qualified mortgage (QM) requirements of Section 129C of TILA, in addition to adhering to certain additional requirements imposed by the CFPB.

The CFPB ability-to-repay rule established three categories of qualified mortgages (QMs); they are:

1) General qualified mortgages.

2) Balloon-payment qualified mortgages made by certain lenders.

3) Transitional qualified mortgages.

The ability-to-repay rule provides that general QMs, among other requirements, may not:

❖ Have a term of more than 30 years.

❖ Include points and fees equal to more than 3%.

❖ Be granted to a borrower with a debt-to-income ratio greater than 43%.

❖ Include "no-doc" loans where the lender does not verify income.

❖ Include certain characteristics of non-traditional mortgages, including interest-only and negative amortization loans.

While loans with balloon payments generally do not qualify as QMs, the CFPB provides an exception for loans made by small lenders (defined initially as having less than $2 billion in assets) in rural areas. The CFPB also established a transitional qualified mortgage category for a covered transaction where a borrower has a debt-to-income ratio above 43%. However, it has to also satisfy all other criteria of the general qualified mortgage, as well as the underwriting criteria of government-sponsored enterprises (GSEs) such as Fannie Mae and Freddie Mac, the FHA, VA, USDA or the Rural Housing Service (RHS). This transitional QM category expires on January 10, 2021.

Qualified Residential Mortgages (QRMs)

Under the Dodd-Frank Act, securitizers of asset-backed securities are required to retain an economic risk of no less than 5% in the assets collateralizing the asset-backed securities. However, among the exceptions in the newly adopted rule is that the risk retention requirements do not apply if all the assets collateralizing the securities are qualified residential mortgages. The Dodd-Frank Act further requires that the definition of QRM be no broader than the definition of QM adopted by CFPB. The proposed rule to define both QM and QRM as congruent definitions was issued on April 29, 2011. This proposal was finally adopted on January 10, 2013, and it was fully implemented as of January 10, 2014. Currently, for a loan to be considered a qualified mortgage (QM), it generally should include the following:

- ❖ The amortization term cannot exceed 30 years.

- ❖ It must fully amortize over its term, so it cannot feature negative amortization, interest-only, or graduated payments or balloon payments.

- ❖ Underwriting must take into account all mortgage-related obligations, must be based on the maximum rate permitted during the first five years, and must be on a fully amortized basis.

- ❖ The lender must consider and verify the borrower's current or reasonably expected income or assets and current debt obligations, alimony, and child support, and it cannot be a *"no-doc"* loan. A *no-doc or low-doc* loan refers to loans that do not require borrowers to provide documentation of their income to lenders or do not require much documentation.

- ❖ It cannot require points or fees in excess of 3% of the loan amount, other than bona fide discount points on prime loans, with higher thresholds for smaller loans.

The passage and adoption of the new rules and definitions of QMs and QRMs were excellent responses by the CFPB. It was an outstanding response because if the six agencies responsible for coordinating the definition clarification and congruency process had adopted some but not all of QM as the definition of QRM. Then mortgage lenders and securitizers may have had to consider two underwriting standards to satisfy the ability-to-repay and credit risk retention rules of Dodd-Frank (Gustini, Spencer, & Butcher, 2013, February 26; Coronet, 2012, 2013). The final definitions creating congruency between the terms QM and QRM were forthcoming for a long time with many delays from the CFPB; however, finally, congruency of the definitions for the two terms has been achieved.

Critics of Qualified Residential Mortgages (QRMs)

Studies show that low down payments are by far the best predictor of mortgage defaults. Because of this finding, regulators want to establish a standard minimum down payment of 20% for qualified residential mortgages (QRMs). However, this was only a proposal—not an implementation—and because of the lobbying efforts by critics, this proposal was not adopted in the newly passed rules (Coronet, 2014, January 6).

According to the American Bankers Association (ABA), a 20% down payment would have resulted in a QRM loan ineligibility of 14.5% to 20% for borrowers of this type of loan. The objective of the proposed final rule for QRMs was intended to decrease borrower default risk by establishing high lending standards for down payments, borrower debt-to-income ratios, and borrower income documentation.

Although consumer protection is a good thing, some industry players were critical of the proposed rule. They claimed that the 20% down payment standard would make it more difficult for the average person to buy a home, requiring them to save longer for a down payment or to seek a higher-interest, non-QRM loan. The critics also believe that the rule would push more borrowers into government-subsidized mortgages like the FHA loan.

Moreover, critics contended that higher down payments would create a minimal decrease in default rates. If it becomes more difficult to borrow, then it also becomes harder for existing homeowners to sell or move. Thus, such changes would affect everyone in the housing market, not just potential new borrowers.

However, fortunately for the critics, this proposal was not included in the new rules, now fully implemented.

Refinancing Process in QRMs

The critics further argued that refinancing would have also been affected by the proposed QRM rule because it would have also increased the home-equity requirements for refinancing. Homeowners would need 25% or 30% equity to refinance. Moreover, the rule would have required borrowers to have a lower percentage of debt (including the proposed mortgage debt) relative to their incomes. Borrowers would thus have qualified for smaller mortgages than they would have normally had qualified for, and borrowers at the margin would not be able to qualify for enough of a loan to purchase a home. Again, fortunately, the proposed rule was not adopted in the new rule.

The QRM proposal only applies to private mortgages that are not government-subsidized or guaranteed by the Federal National Mortgage Association (Fannie Mae) or the Federal Home Loan Corporation (Freddie Mac). Fannie Mae and Freddie Mac are entities known as government-sponsored enterprises or GSEs. GSEs are quasi-governmental entities established by acts of Congress to enhance the flow of credit to specific sectors of the American economy. The purpose of these GSE agencies—though privately held—provide public financial services. In essence, GSEs help to facilitate borrowing for all sorts of individuals, from students to farmers to homeowners.

Private mortgages currently represent approximately 10% of the market, which is considered a very small market share. However, since Fannie Mae and Freddie Mac have been under government conservatorship since 2008, their future role in facilitating housing finance is uncertain. In fact, the current director of the FHFA, Mark Calabria, says that it is possible the GSEs could remain in conservatorship at least until 2024. The uncertainty of GSEs to come out of their conservatorship could limit their ability to provide house financing services. This situation could be a positive event for the private lender investor that could fill the void.

However, one thing is certain; these troubled, government-controlled mortgage finance companies will continue to shrink their monopoly by forming a joint firm to securitize future mortgages. According to former acting director of the FHFA, Edward J. DeMarco, who acted as the first conservator for the troubled agencies Fannie Mae and Freddie Mac during the financial crisis from 2009 to 2014. He claimed that the overarching goal of these institutions is to create something of value that could either be sold or used by policymakers as a foundational element of the mortgage market of the future (Martel, 2013, March 5).

In theory, the new rules mean greater protection for consumers in the form of mortgages that they can afford to repay. In reality, as previously mentioned, new regulations always have unintended consequences that often lead to further problems and even more regulations. The results from all of these new regulations are that consumers may see higher fees and decreased loan availability.

Three Percent (3%) Limit—Calculation of Points and Fees—Qualified Mortgages (QMs)

This provision applies definition from section 103 (aa) of the Truth in Lending Act (TILA) for the purposes of calculating points and fees subject to 3% of the loan amount limit for qualified mortgages (QMs), with the following exclusions:

❖ Up to and including two bona fide discount points if the interest rate from which the mortgage's interest rate will be discounted does not exceed the average *prime offer rate* (APOR) by more than 1%. Or one bona fide discount point, if the interest rate from which the mortgage's interest rate will be discounted does not exceed the APOR by greater than two percentage points.

- ❖ Any government insurance premium and any private insurance premium up to the amount of FHA insurance premiums provided PMI premium is refundable on a pro-rata basis.
- ❖ Any premium paid by the consumer after closing. Such as monthly mortgage insurance (MMI).

Liability for Mortgage Originators (Subtitle B)

This provision establishes that mortgage originators are liable for violations of the *duty of care and anti-steering* prohibitions. The liability is up to the greater amount of actual damages or an amount equal to three times the total amount of direct and indirect compensation or gains accruing to mortgage originator for the loan involved, plus costs and reasonable attorney's fees.

Discretionary Regulatory Authority (Subtitle B)

This provision grants broad discretionary regulatory authority to the CFPB to prohibit or condition terms, acts, or practices relating to residential mortgage loans. This regulatory authority applies to practices the Board finds to be abusive, unfair, deceptive, predatory, necessary, or proper to ensure that responsible, affordable mortgage credit remains available to consumers.

Prepayment Penalties (Subtitle B)

This provision prohibits prepayment penalties for non-qualified mortgages. It restricts prepayment penalties to loans that are not adjustable and do not have an APR that exceeds the average prime offer rate (APOR) by 1.5 or more percentage points for first-lien loans. Moreover, it further restricts prepayment penalties for Jumbo loans that exceed 2.5 or more percentage points, or 3.5 or more percentage points for subordinate lien loans.

Furthermore, it requires a three-year phase-out of prepayment penalties for qualified mortgages (QMs). It prohibits the provision of offering a loan with a prepayment penalty without offering a loan that does not have a prepayment penalty.

Average Prime Offer Rate (APOR) (Subtitle B)

This refers to the average prime offer rate (APOR) for a comparable transaction as of the date on which the interest rate for the transaction is set, as published by the FRB. The APOR is an annual percentage rate that is derived from average interest rates, points, and other loan pricing terms currently offered to consumers by a representative sample of creditors for mortgage transactions that have low-risk pricing characteristics.

The Federal Reserve Board publishes average prime offer rates for a broad range of types of transactions in a table updated at least weekly, as well as the methodology the Board uses to derive these rates.

Limitation on Arbitration (Subtitle B)

This provision of the Act establishes that no residential mortgage loan and no extension of credit under an open-end consumer credit plan secured by the principal dwelling of the consumer may include terms that require arbitration—or any other nonjudicial procedure—as the method for resolving any controversy or for settling any claims arising out of the transaction, except on reverse mortgages.

High-Cost Mortgages (Subtitle C)

The *Home Ownership and Equity Protection Act (HOEPA)* is a bill written by U.S. Representative Joseph P. Kennedy (D-Mass). It was subsequently signed by President Clinton and enacted in September of 1994 as an amendment to the Truth in Lending Act (TILA). The purpose of this bill was to address abusive practices in refinancing and home-equity mortgage loans with high-interest rates or high fees. The law requires certain disclosures and clamps restrictions on lenders of high-cost loans.

Loans that meet HOEPA's high-cost coverage tests are subject to special disclosure requirements and restrictions on loan terms.

Furthermore, borrowers in high-cost mortgages have enhanced remedies for violations of the law.

The provisions of TILA, including HOEPA, are implemented in the Bureau's Regulation Z. In essence, Regulation Z is the regulation that started the Truth in Lending Act (TILA). Moreover, Regulation Z is a Federal Reserve regulation that helps consumers in credit and other financial transactions.

In response to the recent mortgage crisis, Congress amended HOEPA through the Dodd-Frank Act in order to expand the coverage of HOEPA and add protections for high-cost mortgages and purchase-money mortgages. This provision also includes a requirement that borrowers receive homeownership counseling before obtaining a high-cost mortgage. In addition, several provisions of the Dodd-Frank Act also require or encourage consumers to obtain homeownership counseling for other types of loans.

Scope of HOEPA Coverage

The final rule implements the Dodd-Frank Act's amendments that expanded the universe of loans potentially covered by HOEPA. Under the final rule, most types of mortgage loans secured by a consumer's principal dwelling are potentially subject to HOEPA coverage. This also includes purchase-money mortgages (seller-financed mortgages), refinances, closed-end home-equity loans, and open-end credit plans (e.g., home equity lines of credit or HELOCs).

The final rule retains the exemption from HOEPA coverage for reverse mortgages. In addition, the final rule adds an exemption from HOEPA coverage for three types of loans that the Bureau beliefs do not present the same risk of abuse as other mortgage loans:

❖ Loans to finance the initial construction of a dwelling.

❖ Loans originated and financed by the Housing Finance Agency.

❖ Loans originated through the United States Department of Agriculture's (USDA) Rural Housing Service section 502, Direct Loan Program.

Revised HOEPA Coverage Tests

The final rule implements the Dodd-Frank Act's revisions to HOEPA's coverage tests by providing that a transaction is a high-cost mortgage if any of the following tests are met:

❖ The transaction's annual percentage rate (APR) exceeds the applicable average prime offer rate (APOR) by more than 6.5 percentage points for most first-lien mortgages. Or by more than 8.5 percentage points for a first mortgage if the dwelling is personal property, and the transaction is for less than $50,000.

❖ The transaction's APR exceeds the applicable average prime offer rate by more than 8.5 percentage points for subordinate or junior mortgages.

❖ The transaction's points and fees exceed 5% of the total transaction amount, or for loans below $20,000, the lesser of 8% of the total transaction amount, or $1,000, with the dollar figures also adjusted annually for inflation.

❖ The credit transaction documents permit the creditor to charge or collect a prepayment penalty more than 36 months after transaction closing or allow such fees or penalties to exceed, in the aggregate, more than 2% of the amount prepaid.

The final rule also provides guidance on how to apply the various coverage tests, such as how to determine the applicable average prime offer rate (APOR) and how to calculate points and fees.

Restrictions on Loan Terms

The final rule also implements the new Dodd-Frank Act (DFA) restrictions and requirements concerning loan terms and origination practices for mortgages that fall within the Home Ownership and Equity Protection Act (HOEPA) coverage test. For example:

- ❖ Balloon payments are generally banned, unless:
  - They are to account for the seasonal or irregular income of the borrower.
  - They are part of a short-term bridge loan.
  - They are made by creditors meeting specified criteria, including operating predominantly in rural or underserved areas.
- ❖ Creditors are prohibited from charging prepayment penalties and financing points and fees.
- ❖ Late fees are restricted to 4% of the payment that is past due, fees for providing payoff statements are restricted, and fees for a loan modification or payment deferral are banned.
- ❖ Creditors originating HELOCs are required to assess consumers' ability-to-repay (ATR).

Office of Housing Counseling Services (Subtitle D)

Subtitle D, known as the *"Expand and Preserve Home Ownership Through Counseling Act,"* through Title XIV, establishes the Office of Housing Counseling (OHC) within the Department of Housing and Urban Development (HUD). The OHC is headed by the Director to carry out a wide range of counseling-related activities, including research, public outreach, and policy development, as well as coordinating and administering HUD counseling-related programs.

This office is responsible for providing information, educational programs, and assistance to borrowers during the mortgage application process. HUD, of which the Office of Housing Counseling is a part, is also responsible for conducting a study of defaults and foreclosures and maintaining a database of all foreclosures and defaults for all one-to-four unit residential properties.

Additionally, the Secretary of Housing and Urban Development (HUD) is also responsible for informing potential homebuyers about home inspection counseling services and warning them about foreclosure rescue scams.

Mortgage Servicing (Subtitle E)

This provision requires that creditors first establish a five-year escrow or impound accounts to pay taxes, hazard insurance, and any other necessary insurance in most situations. For consumers who waive escrow services, the creditor must provide the consumer with disclosures that clearly explain the consumers' responsibilities.

The mortgage servicing providers or servicers are prohibited from obtaining force-placed insurance without a reasonable basis to believe the borrower has not maintained property insurance. Furthermore, they are prohibited from charging fees for responding to valid written requests, for failing to respond within a logical amount of time to requests about errors in payment allocation, for failing to respond within ten (10) business days to a request to provide information about the mortgage (loan) owner, or for failing to comply with any other obligations.

Appraisals Activities, Appraisal Management Companies (AMCs) and Automated Valuation Models (AVMs) (Subtitle F)

This provision prohibits appraiser coercion and requires rulemaking by the FRB, OCC, FDIC, NCUA, FHFA, and CFPB on appraiser independence. The provision requires the following:

❖ The interim rules by CFPB within 90 days of enactment on appraiser independence to replace Home Valuation Code of Conduct (HVCC).

❖ The physical appraisal for every subprime mortgage and two appraisals for subprime mortgage when there has been a purchase or an acquisition of the property at a lower price within 180 days.

❖ Requires that the appraisal subcommittee of the Federal Financial Institutions Examination Council (FFIEC) must monitor state and federal efforts to protect consumers from improper appraisal practices and unlicensed appraisers. It also requires the FRB, OCC, FDIC, NCUA, FHFA, and CFPB to prescribe minimum requirements for appraisers, appraisal management companies, and standards for Automated Valuation Models (AVMs).

Mortgage Resolution and Modification (Subtitle G)

Title XIV also creates a program to help protect current and future residential tenants by making sure the property owner has sustainable financing, funds for rehabilitation of the property, and an easy way to transfer the property to responsible new owners, if necessary.

Additionally, the Home Affordable Modification Program established under the Emergency Economic Stabilization Act (EESA) of 2008 will be modified to give more information to the public, as well as borrowers, whose requests for a mortgage modification are denied. Furthermore, this provision also extends the Protecting Tenants at Foreclosure Act (PTFA) through 2014.

Miscellaneous Provisions (Subtitle H)

Congress first states that the effort to reform residential mortgage credit practices and protections should include meaningful structural reforms of the Federal National Mortgage Association (Fannie Mae) and the Federal Home Loan Mortgage Corporation (Freddie Mac). Moreover, this provision of Title XIV commissions the Government Accounting Office (GAO) to perform a study on government efforts to catch mortgage foreclosure rescue scams and loan modification fraud, and a Housing and Urban Development (HUD) study on drywall presence in foreclosures.

The Emergency Homeowners' Relief Fund (EHRF) was made available to the public on October 1, 2010, concomitantly with additional funding for neighborhood stabilization programs. Finally, this provision establishes a program to provide foreclosure legal assistance to low and moderate-income homeowners and tenants.

Extent of the Bill's Reach

This bill directs certain provisions to all residential mortgage loans and other provisions to specified categories of mortgages, which include qualified mortgages (QMs), non-qualified mortgages, higher-risk mortgages, and high-cost, or HOEPA, mortgages.

Regulatory Authority

This provision assigns regulatory authority to the FRB, CFPB, and federal banking agencies, such as the FRB, OCC, FDIC, and the NCUA and other agencies under various sections of the Act. The provisions assigned to the FRB under title XIV are reassigned to CFPB, except for provisions relating to housing counseling and certain appraisal-related matters. The provision assigns HUD regulatory responsibility for the housing counseling provisions.

Implementation of the Act

Title XIV of the Dodd-Frank Act of 2010, the Mortgage Reform and Anti-Predatory Lending Act, was implemented in order to provide standards for the level of disclosure required for borrowers so that individuals getting a mortgage would be aware of the obligations and the risks. This title prohibits certain predatory lending tactics that were used frequently during the real estate bubble and also establishes certain provisions for loan modifications, which will help to change and reduce mortgages that are completely out of the borrower's ability-to-repay (ATR).

In essence, the ATR rule requires mortgage lenders to make a good-faith effort to determine that borrowers are likely to be able to pay back their loans. This determination of ability-to-repay is essential because, during the financial crisis, many lenders made loans without making sure borrowers had enough income to repay their mortgage loans. As a result, many borrowers ended up in risky loans that they should not have had.

In practice, this ATR rule means that lenders must find out, consider, and document a borrower's income, assets, employment, credit history, and monthly expenses. One way a lender can follow the ability-to-repay rule is by making a qualified residential mortgage (QRM). The importance of following the ATR rule is demonstrated by Fannie Mae's insistence that underwriters evaluate the homeowner's ability and willingness to repay as a primary condition of approving loans. All debts, including the proposed loan, must be disclosed and considered in awarding a loan. If there are changes that occur during loan origination, Fannie Mae expects underwriters to find out about it.

These criteria are so crucial that Fannie Mae insists that a fresh underwriting evaluation be performed if unknown information from the borrower is discovered that makes the debt-to-income ratio go above 45% or to increase by 3% or more. According to Fannie Mae executives, following these new guidelines has resulted in lower default rates.

Other Federal Laws that Affect the Mortgage Lending Industry

There are other major federal laws that affect the mortgage lending industry. Each one of these laws or acts impacts a different area of the mortgage lending process and protects the borrower as a mortgage loan consumer. These federal laws are the Truth in Lending Act (TILA), Fair Housing Act, Real Estate Settlement Procedures Act, Equal Credit Opportunity Act, Home Mortgage Disclosure Act, Fair Credit Reporting Act, Community Reinvestment Act, New Homeowner's Protection Act, Fair Debt Collection Practices Act, and the Gramm-Leach-Bliley Act (GLBA).

Truth in Lending Act (TILA)

The TILA was enacted in 1968 as part of the Consumer Credit Protection Act (CCPA). This law lays out written disclosure requirements, including finance charges, annual percentage rates, the amount financed, total number of payments, and total sales price. The TILA also sets rescission rights that allow consumers three days to rescind on a loan transaction.

Fair Housing Act

This 1968 law forbids discrimination in housing transactions based upon race, color, sex, religion, national origin, familial status, or handicap. Discrimination can include refusal to rent or sell, setting different terms or conditions, refusing to make a mortgage loan, discriminating in appraising the property, and advertising or making statements that indicate limitations or preference. There is also additional protection for those with a disability.

Real Estate Settlement Procedures Act

The RESPA was adopted in 1974 and protects consumers by requiring disclosures to borrowers and prohibiting practices that can increase closing costs on a loan. This act requires that disclosures include the Good Faith Estimate of settlement costs, an Affiliated Business Arrangement Disclosure, a HUD-1 Settlement Statement, an Initial Escrow Statement, an Annual Escrow Statement, and a Servicing Transfer Statement.

Equal Credit Opportunity Act

The ECOA was adopted in 1975 and prohibits credit discrimination based on sex, race, marital status, national origin, age, religion, or receipt of public assistance. This act covers application content, the acceptability of questions, and the verbal/written discouragement of an application.

Home Mortgage Disclosure Act

The HMDA was signed in 1975 and set forth the requirement that all lenders report public loan data. This information helps to determine if financial institutions are serving the housing needs of their communities and identify possible cases of lending discrimination.

Fair Credit Reporting Act

This 1978 act promotes the accuracy and privacy of consumer credit information from consumer reporting agencies. Consumers have the right to view everything in their report. The credit agency must also supply a list of those who have requested an individual's credit report.

Community Reinvestment Act

The CRA was enacted in 1977 to encourage lenders to meet the credit needs of the people in their communities, including those in low to moderate-income brackets. The act requires that the lenders' records be evaluated periodically to ensure compliance.

New Homeowner's Protection Act

The HPA was adopted in 1988 and established homeowners' rights and rules for private mortgage insurance (PMI) cancellation. This act protects the homeowner from paying unnecessarily for PMI.

Fair Debt Collection Practices Act

This act, adopted in 1977, prohibits certain practices of debt collection. It disallows unfair, deceptive, or abusive practices, and protects consumers' debt information from public disclosure.

Gramm-Leach-Bliley Act (GLBA)

The Gramm-Leach-Bliley Act (GLBA), also known as the Financial Services Modernization Act of 1999, was enacted on November 12, 1999, and signed into law by President Bill Clinton. This act specifically protects the financial information of consumers. The Financial Privacy Rule requires notification from the lender to the borrower regarding their practices of collection and sharing information. The Safeguards Rule requires security measures on the part of the lenders to protect the sensitive information of its consumers. The Pretexting Rule prohibits fraudulent statements and impersonation to obtain confidential financial information.

Passage of this bill repealed part of the Glass-Steagall Act of 1933, removing barriers in the market among banking companies, securities companies, and insurance companies that prohibited any one institution from acting as any combination of an investment bank, a commercial bank, and an insurance company. With the passage of the Gramm-Leach-Bliley Act, commercial banks, investment banks, securities firms, and insurance companies were again allowed to consolidate. Some economists believe that the removal of essential elements of the *Glass-Steagall Act* was the cause of the financial crisis of 2008.

The Housing and Economic Recovery Act (HERA) of 2008

The Housing and Economic Recovery Act (HERA) of 2008 was signed into law on July 30, 2008, by way of Public Law 110-289. This act constitutes a significant new housing law that is designed to assist with the recovery and the revitalization of America's residential housing market to encompass the modernization of the Federal Housing Administration (FHA), foreclosure prevention, and enhance the protection to consumers. A key component of HERA, which is an essential law for private mortgage lenders to understand, is the Secure and Fair Enforcement for Mortgage Licensing Act (SAFE Act) of 2008.

The Secure and Fair Enforcement for Mortgage Licensing Act (SAFE Act) of 2008

The Secure and Fair Enforcement for Mortgage Licensing Act (SAFE Act) of 2008 was also enacted on July 30, 2008, as part of HERA, which mandates a nationwide licensing and registration system for residential mortgage loan originators (MLOs). The SAFE Act is designed to enhance consumer protection and reduce fraud by encouraging states to establish minimum standards for the licensing and registration of state-licensed mortgage loan originators. Thus, the Act is the federal response to the mortgage meltdown of 2008, the financial crisis (USA.gov, n. d.).

The SAFE Act prohibits individuals from engaging in the business of a residential mortgage loan origination without first obtaining and maintaining annually:

- ❖ For individuals who are employees of covered financial institutions, registration as a registered mortgage loan originator (MLOs) and a unique identifier (federal registration), or

- ❖ For all other individuals, a state license and registration as a state-licensed mortgage loan originator, and a unique identifier (state licensing/registration).

The SAFE Act requires that federal registration and state licensing and registration be accomplished through the same online registration system, the *Nationwide Mortgage Licensing System (NMLS) and Registry*. The NMLS Federal Registry was created at the direction of federal banking regulators to fulfill the registration requirement of federally chartered or insured institutions and their mortgage loan originators (MLOs) in compliance with the Consumer Financial Protection Bureau's rules and the SAFE Act.

The NMLS Federal Registry Resource Center provides institutions and mortgage loan originators with tools and guidelines for completing the mandated registration process in NMLS. The objectives of the SAFE Act include aggregating and improving the flow of information to and between regulators, providing increased accountability and tracking of MLOs, enhancing consumer protections, supporting anti-fraud measures, and providing consumers with easily accessible information at no charge regarding the employment history of, and publicly adjudicated disciplinary and enforcement actions against, MLOs (USA.gov, n. d.).

On July 28, 2010, the OCC, FRB, FDIC, OTS, NCUA, and FCA, collectively known as the "agencies," published substantively similar regulations implementing the SAFE Act's federal registration requirements for the institutions they supervise and the institutions' MLO employees (SAFE Act regulation). Moreover, on July 21, 2011, Title X of the Dodd-Frank Act transferred rulemaking authority for the SAFE Act from the agencies to the Consumer Financial Protection Bureau (see Appendix D). On December 19, 2011, the CFPB restated the implementation of the SAFE Act regulations to 12 CFR 1007 (76 Federal Register 78483), establishing a new Regulation G, the SAFE Mortgage Licensing Act–Federal Registration of Residential Mortgage Loan Originators.

In this chapter, the author has covered the laws that have a direct impact on the mortgage lending industry. Needless to say, the passage of all these lending and consumer protection laws leads to confusion and creates the potential for legal dangers, resulting from the difficulty of just keeping abreast of all the changes in these laws.

It was previously mentioned that the SAFE Act requires that individuals engaged in the business of residential mortgage origination must have federal registration and state licensing to perform those duties while working for a lending institution. This provision poses a dilemma for the private mortgage investor who is also in the business of originating residential mortgages but is not an employee of a lending institution.

The question that arises is this: does an independent private money lender who engages in residential mortgage origination need to be licensed by the state in order to be able to originate residential loans? The reason for this confusion surface because the SAFE Act does not provide a definition of what an employee is.

However, the regulation's preamble explains that the meaning of "employee" under the SAFE Act regulation is consistent with the common-law, right-to-control test. Under the common-law test, the employer has the right to tell the employee what to do, how, when, and where to do the job. Thus, the results of this test generally determine whether an institution files an Internal Revenue Service Form W-2 or Form 1099 for an individual (CFPB Consumer Laws and Regulations, n .d.).

The regulation does provide a definition of what a mortgage loan originator (MLO), means, which is an individual who:

❖ Takes a residential mortgage loan application, and

❖ Offers or negotiates the terms of a residential mortgage loan for compensation or gain.

This definition clearly encompasses the function of a private mortgage lender, which leads to the dilemma of whether a private mortgage investor needs a state license to engage in this endeavor. The answer to this dilemma is addressed by the *"de minimis exception"* provision of the SAFE Act, Section 1007.101 (c) (2), which is as follows: the SAFE Act regulation provides an exception to the MLO registration requirements for any employee of a covered financial institution. This exception applies if the MLO has never been registered or licensed through the Registry if, during the past 12 months, the employee acted as an MLO for five or fewer residential mortgage loans.

When an institution relies on the *de minimis exception* in lieu of registration, the MLO employee must register prior to *originating the sixth residential mortgage loan* within 12 months. Covered financial institutions are prohibited from engaging in any acts or practices to evade the registration requirement.

This licensing issue was further addressed by Representative Frank (of the Dodd-Frank Act) and Senator Bacchus in a letter to then HUD Secretary Shaun Donavan. The objective of the letter was to encourage HUD to allow *de minimis exemption* of five transactions per 12 months, from MLO licensing in situations of seller financing. However, Donavan's response to their letter was a request for new requirements that all loan activity should be registered regardless of MLO licensing requirements with the NMLS registry. Thus, requesting that all private loans be registered.

Based on this response from HUD, it would be safe to say that a private mortgage lender/investor should originate up to five loans per annum without a license. Any additional loans beyond five should be placed through a licensed lender, or the investor should become a licensed mortgage originator (USA.gov, n. d.). Moreover, the final rules implemented under the Dodd-Frank Act, as of January 10, 2014, have imposed new restrictions and exemptions for owner-seller financing. These brand-new rules are very important to understand because they can also determine whether a private lender will be required to have a mortgage lending license or not (see Chapter 7).

Private mortgage investors (lenders) not only have to abide by federal laws, but also by the state laws in which they would like to invest. In the state of Florida, for example, the statute that addresses the lending activities of private money lenders is *Chapter 494.* According to Section 494.00115, which is the Florida statute that addresses the licensing exemptions of Chapter 494, it specifically states under exemption 494.00115(2)(e) that an individual making or acquiring a mortgage loan using his or her own funds for his or her own investment, and who does not hold himself or herself out to the public as being in the mortgage lending business, is exempt from having a license.

Additionally, the private money lender should also be aware of exemption 494.00115(2)(f) that states that an individual selling a mortgage that was made or purchased with that individual's funds for his or her own investment, and who does not hold himself or herself out to the public as being in the mortgage lending business, is also exempt from having a license. In essence, if the individual does not advertise that he or she is in the mortgage lending business, then a license is not required.

Regarding the term or description of "holding himself or herself out to the public as being in the mortgage lending business" is clarified by statute 494.00115(5)(a, b, c, and d). For example, statute 494.00115(5)(a), as used in this section, includes any of the following descriptions. Representing oneself to the public, through advertising or other means of communicating or providing information, including the use of business cards, stationery, brochures, signs, rate lists, or promotional items, by any method, that such individual can or will perform the activities described. Private money lenders should be very familiar with statutes 494.00115(2)(f) and 494.00115(5) (a, b, c, and d) if doing business in the state of Florida.

Moreover, private or hard money lenders do not have to be licensed in most states, unless they are lending money on owner-occupied residential real estate. Therefore, if the lending activity is geared to the commercial and non-owner occupied residential real estate market, a license should not be required. However, because the mortgage industry continues to evolve and change in the quest to instill fairness and protection for the consumer, anyone involved with the private mortgage lending industry should develop the safe habit of always verifying all regulatory information pertaining to this market. The mortgage lending industry is one where it pays to be a perpetual student in addition to having a competent attorney that is familiar with the industry.

7

The Private Money Lending Industry

T he private money lending industry is not well publicized and is mostly concentrated in large states like California and New York (Private Money, n. d.). However, every state will have private and hard money lenders who engage in this type of investing vehicle, either as a part-time investor or full-time private money operations. The industry is made up of predominantly small lenders who have discovered the alternative investment vehicle of private mortgage investing. Furthermore, besides these small lenders, there are also some highly specialized mortgage brokers/lenders who are familiar with residential and commercial real estate lending, as well as real estate rehabbing. Appendix J shows a list of the hard money lending activity ranking for all 50 states, which is compiled by the *Alternative Lending Magazine* (ALM).

A private money lender originates loans ranging from thousands to millions of dollars every year to both public and private individuals and businesses. They have no connections to the government in their lending practices and are free from the politics of large lending institutions. The investors involved in this industry range from private individuals, trusts, S corporations, LLCs, self-directed IRAs, hedge funds, and some pension funds. The individual investors, who participate in this market or industry, typically have substantial knowledge and experience in real estate as well as mortgage and trust deed investing.

Most recently, there has been an inclination in the industry for individual investors to pool their money with other sophisticated investors through Mortgage Investing Funds. These Funds are managed by private money bankers, real estate bankers, or private real estate bankers, which are terms that essentially mean the same thing. Private money bankers are groups, individuals, companies, or Funds that pool private money for the purpose of lending those pooled funds for profit.

The health of real estate lending has been a closely watched concern since 2008 as the residential sub-prime mortgage market collapsed, and the credit markets essentially dissipated or dried-up for this type of lending practice. However, it is no longer only brokers, builders, and potential borrowers who are paying attention to this industry; it has also become a hot topic for individual investors looking for a safer place than the stock market to invest their money.

The motivation for investing in private mortgages, either through a pooled-type Fund or as a sole individual investor is because of the simplicity of the underlying investment and the investor's desire to seek the following features:

❖ An investment that is secured by real estate without being exposed to the uncertainty and risky volatility of the stock market.

❖ An investment that can consistently generate a passive income stream derived from monthly interest payments or dividend distributions.

❖ An investment vehicle that can generate higher rates of return than the current yields garnered from money-market funds, savings accounts, CDs, and bonds.

❖ An investment where the investor can have an active involvement in real estate financing rather than direct property ownership.

Participants in the Private Money Lending Industry

Private or hard money lending plays a crucial role in the business of many real estate investors. To thrive in this industry, it is essential for the mortgage lending investor to be familiar with the role of the individuals behind the private money lending process. Additionally, the mortgage investor should also understand, and be well versed in, all the functions that entail the loan application approval and the loan processing as well as the funding process.

Essentially, there are six participants in the private money lending industry whose functions are important for the mortgage investor to understand. These are:

❖ The hard money lender or hard money lending company.

❖ The private money lending source.

❖ The title insurance company.

❖ The escrow or settlement service provider.

❖ The property appraiser.

❖ The hard money loan servicing company.

The Hard Money Lender or Hard Money Lending Company

Traditionally, decades ago, when a borrower needed a loan, they would go see a loan officer at a local bank, customarily the same place where the borrower had their checking, savings, and possibly their investment accounts. Today, borrowers have access to a greater range of borrowing options to meet their needs for required funds. In the current market environment, the borrower can apply for a loan with private mortgage lenders, hard mortgage brokers, credit unions, conventional or traditional banks, state and regional housing agencies, or get a purchase-money mortgage from the seller (seller-financing) of the property being purchased.

Seller-Financing Restrictions under the Dodd-Frank Act

It is crucial to know that private property owners who want to offer seller-financing to facilitate the sale of their property have been swept into the regulations of the Dodd-Frank Act (DFA). This change in the regulations means that seller-financing is now regulated by Title XIV Section 1401(2) (e), the mortgage loan origination standards. Under Dodd-Frank, the Consumer Financial Protection Bureau (CFPB) was created. The CFPB, together with other laws, has expanded previous regulations as it relates to the requirements of licensing, training, screening, and compensation practices of loan originators, mortgage brokers, bank officers, and lenders in general, in consumer loan transactions. On January 10, 2014, the *Loan Originator Rule* came into effect to implement the new Dodd-Frank requirements. This Rule was expanded to include specific restrictions on seller-financing in owner-occupied residential real estate transactions where the dwelling is secured by a mortgage unless the seller is entitled to certain exclusions or exemptions.

Essentially, the law requires the seller-financer to be licensed as a mortgage loan originator (MLO) to be able to execute the loan transaction. Thus, restricting private property owners who want to sell their property using owner financing. The Dodd-Frank Act, however, does provide some exemptions or exclusions to property owners who offer seller-financing from having to become a licensed mortgage loan originator (MLO). In spite of the available exemption, the act subjects the property owner (seller-financer) to the same legal liability as an MLO.

The Dodd-Frank Act defines mortgage loan originators (MLOs) as *"any person who for direct or indirect compensation or gain or in the expectation of direct or indirect compensation or gain takes a residential mortgage loan application or offers or negotiates terms of a residential mortgage loan."* Hence, the loan originator rules under the Dodd-Frank Act, as just mentioned, requires that said persons be licensed, are subject to certain restrictions on compensation, and must comply with vague guidelines on proving the borrower's ability-to-repay (ATR). Therefore, under the Dodd-Frank Act, any person who offers and negotiates terms of a residential mortgage loan is deemed to be a *"mortgage loan originator."* Consequently, they must be a licensed mortgage broker in compliance with all laws, unless one of the seller-financing exceptions apply.

There is no exemption for a person who is not a seller who wishes to make a loan secured by a residential mortgage. Lenders must be licensed mortgage brokers or use the services of a licensed mortgage broker in connection with the loan. This license requirement only applies to mortgages that secure loans on residential dwellings containing one to four units and includes houses, apartments, townhouses, condominium units, cooperative units, mobile homes, trailers, and boats used as residences. The rules apply whether the individual is purchasing a primary residence, second home, or vacation residence.

Non-Applicability of the Dodd-Frank Act

As indicated above, the Dodd-Frank Act (DFA) applies only to *residential mortgage loans, a very significant distinction to understand.* However, there are situations where the DFA is not applicable. For example, DFA does not apply to the following conditions:

1. DFA does not apply to loans secured by vacant land, commercial properties, rental properties, or properties used for investment purposes. The rules also do not apply to residential properties on which the buyer does not intend to reside—non-owner occupied.

2. DFA does not apply to *non-consumer buyers*, even if the property being purchased is a residential property. Examples of non-consumer buyers are:

- Corporations
- Limited liability companies (LLCs)
- Partnerships, etc.

Therefore, if Dodd-Frank does not apply as set forth above, the seller does not have to analyze whether the transaction meets one of the two seller-financing exceptions discussed below.

Even if the transaction involves property being purchased by a consumer for their residence (owner-occupied), the Dodd-Frank Act provides certain exceptions for sellers who wish to sell their property and take back a mortgage (seller-financing). Under these exceptions, the seller-financer will not fall under the definition of a "mortgage loan originator (MLO)" if the seller and the financing terms meet specific criteria.

Seller-Financing Exceptions of the Dodd-Frank Act

There are two exceptions from the requirements of the *loan originator rule*, which means that a lender's license is not required under the Dodd-Frank Act for owner-seller financing, irrespective of whether the property owner is a person, estate, trust, corporation, partnership, or LLCs.

Under the first exception, there is a one (1) property exclusion. Under this exception, a seller-financer who extends credit to a buyer secured by a mortgage encumbering a residential dwelling is not considered a "mortgage loan originator (MLO)" and thus not require a license, if the following conditions apply:

- ❖ The seller is a natural person, estate, or trust.
- ❖ The seller provides financing for only one (1) property in any 12 months period.
- ❖ The seller owns the property securing the financing.
- ❖ The owner/seller did not construct or act as the builder for the construction of the property.

Moreover, to comply with the law, the financing activity must also meet the following criteria:

- ❖ The seller financing must have a repayment schedule that does not result in negative amortization.

- ❖ Balloon payments are allowed. However, it is recommended they should not be less than five (5) years conservatively. But apparently, there is a two-year window, and after two years, this allowance may terminate.

- ❖ The seller financing must have a fixed rate or an adjustable-rate that resets after five or more years. The rate-adjustments can be made annually as long as they are reasonable, with a lifetime limit of 2% per annum and 6% lifetime cap as mandated by the Dodd-Frank Act.

- ❖ The seller does not have to vet the borrowers or determine the borrower's ability to repay.

Under the second exception, *there is a three (3) property exception.* Under this exception, a seller-financer who extends credit to a buyer secured by a mortgage encumbering a residential dwelling is not considered a "mortgage loan originator (MLO)" and thus not require a license, if the following conditions apply:

- ❖ The seller is a natural person, estate, trust, or an entity.

- ❖ The seller provides financing for three (3) properties or less in any 12 months period.

- ❖ The seller owns the property securing the financing;

- ❖ The owner/seller did not construct or act as the contractor for the builder of the property.

Moreover, to comply with the law, the financing activity must also meet the following criteria:

- ❖ The seller financing must be fully amortizing, and there must be no balloon payments or structures allowed.

- ❖ The seller financing must have a fixed rate or an adjustable-rate that resets after five or more years, and must have caps on rate changes, and also lifetime caps.

172

❖ *The seller must determine, in good faith, that the consumer has a reasonable ability-to- repay* even though the seller is not required to formally document how they made their good faith determination that the buyer had the ability-to-repay. However, a prudent seller should keep records in case the analysis is ever called into question. Some of the documents that should be kept include current or reasonably expected income or assets, income tax returns, employment, monthly payments, debt obligations, debt to income ratios, credit history, etc.

For both exceptions, as mentioned above, adjustable interest rates must have reasonable annual and lifetime limits on rate increases. Additionally, it must provide for the rate to be determined by the addition of a margin to an index rate based on a widely available index such as indices for U.S. Treasury securities or LIBOR. CFPB's Official Interpretations note that an annual rate increase of up to 2 percentage points is reasonable. A lifetime rate cap or ceiling of 6 percentage points, up to any applicable usury limit, subject to a minimum floor, is reasonable. These *"safe harbors"* are not mandatory, but sellers would be wise to adopt them.

It is crucial to note that a corporation, partnership, or LLC can never avail itself of the one (1) property exception and may only use the three (3) property exception. A potential loophole would allow for a corporation to convey the property in question to its individual owner(s), who could, in turn, provide seller-financing under the terms of the one (1) property exception. However, taking advantage of such a loophole under the new laws is very risky, and not recommended at this point.

Aside from the imposition created by all the new restrictions that Dodd-Frank and the SAFE Act have imposed on the mortgage lending industry, essentially, there are no prohibitions on any type of loan a creditor can still originate. The lender simply has to follow the mandates of the Act, which is to make a *reasonable or good faith determination* that the borrower possesses *the ability-to-repay* the loan (Callahan, 2014, June 29).

It is important for lenders to understand that Dodd-Frank applies to loans of residential, owner-occupied properties. Therefore, lenders can still originate any other type of mortgage loan, such as loans for vacant land, commercial property, and investment property, since nothing has changed for these types of loans. Additionally, certain types of loans are specifically excluded from the Dodd-Frank Act. For example, even if you do lend money to a person who is going to occupy a residence, if the residential loan to the owner-occupant is for a home-equity line of credit (HELOC), a timeshare, a reverse mortgage, bridge loans with terms of less than 12 months, or for manufactured housing, nothing has changed regarding these types of loans (Callahan, 2014, June 29).

It is a fact that any newly implemented law will have unintended consequences that everyone must live with until those effects are resolved, and the Dodd-Frank Act is no exception. Rather than fearing the consequences of the law, lenders should become well informed about the provisions of the law and follow its mandates. Everything in life is about changes and adjustments—causes and effects if you will. It is also a continuous troubleshooting session that has to be mastered if success is the ultimate goal.

In the private money lending industry, the lender can be an individual or a company that is responsible for processing a loan for a borrower from beginning to end. In essence, the lender would be involved from the taking of the application to the mortgage closing process. What this means is that the individual or firm is usually an entrepreneur managing the entire business operation and not just processing the loan, as would be the case with a mortgage loan originator.

The Private Money Lending Source

The private money investors are the most important individuals in the private money lending industry. Without these investors, there would be no money to initiate the hard money loans because these are the individuals who provide the funding for the private loans. The individual private money investor could have a dual lending function. These individuals can act as the hard money lenders, providing their funds directly to the borrower. Conversely, they can be the investors who provide the money/funding sources for the hard money broker business, or they could even be engaged in both types of funding activities—direct or indirect.

However, most private investors are outside entities or individuals who have established a beneficial business relationship with the private or hard broker/lender business. *A vital caveat for all private money lenders who provide the funds to hard money broker who also participates in lending their own money is to make sure that the loan opportunities being provided are of good investment quality.* When the broker/lender is also a participant in his own lending business by providing his funds for lending, it can create a potential conflict of interest because the broker can very easily keep the best-quality loan opportunities for himself. To understand the concept of conflict of interest, the reader should read the conflict of interest section in Chapter 3.

This information is significant to keep in mind because the broker/lender will always be in a position to review all the deals first because he is the one performing the underwriting evaluation. Therefore, it would be very easy for the broker to keep the safest and best-quality loans. Needless to say, this situation will not occur if the private money investor is doing business with an honest broker/lender who understands the importance of embracing the policies of business ethics and transparency to the ultimate success of his business endeavors.

The Title Insurance Company

The title insurance company is an auxiliary or supporting service for the processing of a borrower's loan. The title insurance company is responsible for furnishing a title report on the subject property that serves as collateral for the loan. To complete this report, the title insurance company will search county records for all information, judgments, liens, and easements as they relate to the real estate and to the borrower's historical personal and financial records. This report will be needed by the hard money lender to determine if the property can be insured. If the property is insurable, the transaction proceeds and the title company will release a title insurance policy.

Title insurance is a form of indemnity insurance, principally available in the United States and Canada. The purpose of title insurance is to insure against financial loss from defects in the title to real property. It could also be from the invalidity or unenforceability of mortgage loans. Title insurance is essentially a product developed and sold in the United States as a result of an alleged comparative deficiency of the U.S. land records laws. It is meant to protect an owner's or lender's financial interest in real property against loss due to title defects, liens, or other matters that are specified in the insurance policy.

Moreover, title insurance will defend against a lawsuit attacking the title, as it is insured, or reimburses the insured for the actual monetary loss incurred, up to the dollar amount of insurance provided by the policy. Title insurance differs from other forms of insurance, such as car, life, and health insurance, in that these types of insurance coverage protect against potential future events and is paid for with monthly or annual premiums. A title insurance policy insures against events that occurred in the real estate property's past and the people who owned it for a one-time premium paid at the close of the escrow.

The first known title insurance company in the United States was The Law Property Assurance and Trust Society, which was founded in 1853 in Pennsylvania (Burke, 1986, § 1.1 P.2). The vast majority of title insurance policies are written on land within the United States. It is essential that any known title defects be divulged to the title company to ensure a clean title.

The Escrow or Settlement Services Companies

An escrow or settlement services company is an independent third party that collects and pays out the funds under the instructions of the private lender/investor. These companies are tasked with the supervision of the final signing of all applicable deeds, mortgages, and loan documents, and the subsequent recordings of all pertinent documents with the appropriate county office. Generally, the escrow company is an impartial party that facilitates the real estate sales transaction. The escrow company holds the buyer's funds or the title of the seller. It does not release the escrowed funds or the title until all specific conditions of the sale are met. Once the conditions have been met, the company may prepare closing documents and transfer the property to the buyer or the funds to the seller (Wisegeek, n. d.). These services can also be provided by an attorney specializing in real estate. However, there are many states that are considered escrow states that are required by law to use the services of an escrow company.

There are essentially two types of real estate closings to facilitate the loan and the purchase of real estate properties. There is the traditional-type closing, and the other is an escrow closing. In the traditional type of closing, there is one closing and funds disbursement process, which essentially finalizes the transaction. This process customarily is referred to as the closing.

Conversely, in escrow states like California, all the stipulations for the transfer of the property and funds are cleared before the day of the closing. All essential documents and funds are held *"in escrow"* by the assigned escrow or settlement agent until the time of the closing. If all the stipulations between the seller, buyer, and lender have been met according to the escrow instructions, then the closing can proceed; all funds are disbursed, and the sale is final. This type of closing is typically referred to as the closing of escrow.

The Property Appraiser

The property appraiser is a licensed professional who is entrusted to furnish an appraisal report that states an opinion of value on the property. A real estate appraiser's job is to interpret the market to estimate a property's value. The appraiser's function is to compile data and conduct a meticulous examination of the property, and the stability of the neighborhood. For example, property amenities such as pools, upgraded kitchens, and baths, and the overall physical condition of the property being appraised. Furthermore, the appraisers will also make sketches, take photographs, and make a detailed report about the positive and negative points of the property. These professional appraisers customarily possess both real estate and lending experience.

The appraisal report is not a matter of public record, but it is an essential report that is compiled for the exclusive use of the private money or conventional lender. However, the borrower is also entitled to request a copy of the report for his own perusal. An appraisal is essentially an estimation of the market value of a home performed by licensed professional appraisers employing specialized real estate assessment methodologies.

Appraisers should always be objective third parties in the mortgage process and not work directly for the lender or real estate company. Their objective is to supply a realistic judgment about a property's actual value at the time of the appraisal evaluation. It is customary for an appraiser to review a minimum of three other comparable properties that have recently been sold within the neighborhood. Property values can frequently fluctuate because of economic conditions within a town, county, city, or nationally; therefore, comparing relevant sales is a vital function for the validity of the appraisal.

Thus, the appraisal report's primary role is to act as a safeguard or protection for both the homebuyers and the lenders. The appraisal essentially protects the homebuyer against paying too much for a home, and it safeguards the lender from issuing a loan for more than the property is worth. Private money lenders retain the services of appraisers to determine the value of a home rather than the sale price.

As stated above, appraisers should be objective, independent contractors whose sole function is to provide protection for both the borrowers and the lenders. However, there can be fraud in any industry, and the lending industry is no exception. It is common knowledge that in the mortgage lending industry, appraisal fraud is quite common. The way appraisal fraud work is rather simple. For example, when a borrower approaches a mortgage lender about refinancing their home, they will receive a good faith estimate for the loan. This estimate includes the market value for the home, which is typically the minimum value amount needed to complete the loan.

Appraisers are hired by the very lenders who need a specific property market value to facilitate the loan. Rather than being independent in doing their jobs, appraisers are really in a situation where they work for the lender, which essentially is an inherent conflict of interest (see Chapter 3). Therefore, if a lender needs the value to be higher to facilitate a loan, there will always be appraisers willing to tweak the numbers to facilitate the transaction.

As a result of fraudulent appraiser practices, appraisers, tired of being pressured into inflating home values, are leading the charge for reform in their industry. Appraisers blame mortgage brokers and lenders for the prevalence of this appraisal fraud epidemic (Mortgage Scams: Appraisal Fraud, n. d.).

However, before real reforms are instituted in the real estate appraisal industry, there are certain mitigating strategies that can be employed to avoid this issue that include the following:

❖ **The borrower or homeowner can hire their own appraiser.**

Since the borrower has to pay for the appraisal when buying or refinancing a home anyway; it would be prudent for the homeowner or investor to select the appraiser to ensure the risk they are taking is legitimate.

❖ **Use an ethical appraiser.**

Make sure that the selected appraiser is state-certified and get referrals from persons who have used ethical appraisers in the past. A good practice could be to look for an appraiser that works for banks rather than one who works for mortgage brokers. Banks will be more likely to hire competent and ethical appraisers.

Property Assessments vs. Property Appraisals

At this juncture, it is important to clarify the two common methods that are used in determining property values that tend to create a certain degree of confusion among some real estate investors. Property values are customarily determined by conducting either a property assessment or a property appraisal.

A property tax assessment is a process performed by municipal governments to calculate the value of every property within a municipality, township, or county to determine the amount of property taxes. Whatever value the county property appraiser estimate is the value that will be used to assess property taxes. Thus, the primary function of the assessor is to gather or collect research data from public records about every single property.

There is no national standard, so educational requirements for assessors differ considerably depending upon the state or locality. The county assessor is not required to have an appraiser's license, although most property assessors are licensed appraisers. The challenge that county assessors face during the undertaking of the data-gathering process is that county records and the available information to determine the taxable assessed values are mostly outdated and, at times, are entirely incorrect. Therefore, the propensity for making calculation errors during the property assessment process is so great that property values are either overpriced or underpriced. These property assessment mistakes will result in tax iniquities that will impact the property owners, either positively or negatively.

That is why it is highly recommended that homeowners contract with a property tax consultant to file an appeal to contest the property assessment value each year. These companies typically work on a contingency basis, which means that if they do not save the property owner's some taxes, there is no charge, except for the non-refundable application filing fee. The typical filing fee for this appeal is $15.00, and the contingency fee for a successful appeal is customarily 25% to 35% of the tax amount saved.

According to the National Taxpayers Union (NTU), it is estimated that over 60% of properties in the United States are currently over-assessed. Furthermore, *Consumer Reports* has published a report that claims that property tax records have demonstrated the existence of a 40% error rate with property tax estimates (Evergeht, 2007, January 17; Consumer reports, 1992, November v57 nil p.723). This statistic should be sufficient evidence for the need to file a yearly property tax review appeal.

Appraisals are given preference over property assessments because of their more broad-based spectrum and timely nature. The appraisal's report is an essential tool used by both the private and conventional money lenders to determine the amount, terms, and conditions for the granting of a mortgage loan. It is also an important report for property sellers to assess the value of their property. This process enables them to get an idea of the amount of money that would be logical to ask for a particular property. The appraisal value, undoubtedly, is the most accurate and current value of the property for buyers as well as sellers

The Hard Money Loan Servicing Company

Private mortgage investors typically do not service their mortgage loan investments. The reason could be that they prefer to delegate this function to a mortgage servicing company because of lack oftime, or they might not possess the expertise to perform the day-to-day administrative tasks of handling their own mortgage servicing functions. Therefore, many lenders' contract with third-party companies, called servicers, to handle the managerial duties related to loans that the lender owns.

Essentially, loan servicing is the process by which a mortgage servicing company collects the monthly mortgage payments from the borrowers, which is composed of interest, principal, late fees, and other incidentals, if applicable. This servicer also keeps and maintains the funds in escrow and makes required payments as they become due, such as the payments for taxes and insurance. Another function of the mortgage servicing process is to submit to investors their financial statements and the collection of monthly payments as well as providing investors their year-end tax reports on the interest paid by borrowers for tax reporting purposes.

This service can be provided by companies whose sole function is to provide mortgage servicing. Conversely, this service can also be performed by the hard money lending company (the mortgage broker) that facilitates the loan opportunities for private lenders. These mortgage brokers customarily like to keep these mortgage servicing functions as an additional source of revenue for their business. In fact, they are very reluctant to part with this added benefit even when some private mortgage investors would prefer to perform their own mortgage servicing function.

Customarily, the level of service provided by mortgage servicing companies or by the hard money broker/lenders varies depending on the type of loan and the terms negotiated between the servicer and the investor seeking their services. Additionally, mortgage servicing companies, as well as mortgage broker/lenders providing the mortgage servicing function, also like to include other service activities such as monitoring delinquencies, workouts/restructuring, and executing foreclosures in the event the loan is in default. All these mortgage servicers want to perform all these other servicing activities described above because the servicer generally receives contractually specified servicing fees and other ancillary sources of income, such as float and late charges. The typical mortgage servicing fee charged by these mortgage servicing providers is between 1% and 2% of the monthly mortgage payment. However, these fees could be negotiated depending on the volume of business the private lender is generating for the servicer.

At this juncture, it should be emphasized that the mortgage lending industry, in all its facets, is riddled with fraudulent practices by all the industry participants, including mortgage servicers. Therefore, the private mortgage lending investor should be aware of the misdeeds perpetrated by the individuals that operate in this industry. The private lending investors who provide the funding source for many of the loans originated by hard money lenders/brokers that also provide the mortgage servicing function should be very careful with these individuals. They should take their time to carefully read the mortgage servicing agreements these individuals use since they always want to involve themselves in providing additional administrative services to increase their revenue stream.

The mortgage lending industry in all its ramifications is all about money; thus, there is an inherent conflict of interest. Moreover, the private investor should be wary of the hard money lenders who sell mortgage notes to investors with the condition that they must retain the loan servicing function. It is a quid pro quo, and if the investor does not agree to this condition, then they won't be allowed to invest in loans from these brokers. In essence, these mortgage brokers want to retain control of their borrowers for potential future services that generate additional fees.

Therefore, it is crucial for private mortgage investors to educate themselves and become familiar with the laws and regulations of the industry. Moreover, they should also understand the various roles of the participants who make up the private money lending industry. This education is essential so that private money lenders understand how their loans are processed. Remember that acquiring a complete education in the field the investor wants to invest, is in itself the best risk-mitigating strategy that ensures their safety.

The Future Growth of Private Money Lending

Glenn Fydenkevez (n. d.), president of Master Plan Capital LLC, a commercial real estate investment banker, contends that in today's real estate market, it is not difficult to discover good deals in commercial real estate. What is challenging for the investor is finding the money to finance the transaction because securing a mortgage loan is a harder task than uncovering excellent real estate opportunities. The task of finding the financing is especially difficult for the novice or younger investors who do not possess an extensive track record.

The reason for this difficulty is that traditional funding sources such as banks, money lending brokers, and insurance companies are not lending as readily as before the financial housing crisis. In essence, banks are not lending the way they used to, and the loans they make are being underwritten with more stringent qualifying guidelines. The resulting consequence of these banking changes is that investors without perfect credit scores or large amounts of available capital have been left without reliable funding sources. Thousands of potentially good borrowers with excellent loan proposals are being rejected by traditional lenders, which has created an excellent opportunity for the private money lender to fill the vacuum.

Moreover, for a growing number of these borrowers, the answer has been to seek private mortgage lenders (PMLs) or hard money lenders (HMLs). Even though private mortgage lenders charge higher interest rates and origination points, these hard money lenders can be more flexible in their lending decisions. They can close and fund multi-million-dollar deals in a shorter period of time. Henceforth, the private money lender—as an alternative lender—has been filling the financial vacuum that was created by the credit crisis.

Therefore, the private lending sector is a thriving industry, while the traditional institutional lenders are struggling alone. The large volume of loan applications flooding into the offices of private mortgage lenders is allowing these lenders to be more selective in choosing their clientele. Moreover, the agony of borrowers who face the prospect of losing their properties or projects, makes this situation a lenders market. As the credit market remains stagnant, the growth in private lending is projected to continue to increase significantly (Fydenkevez, n. d.).

Difference between the Subprime and Hard Money Lender

It is appropriate at this point to clarify the distinction between the subprime lender and a private or hard money lender. The subprime lender was a resource for those who had poor credit scores with a FICO below 640, an inadequate credit history, insufficient funds for an adequate down payment, or were unable to prove their sources of income. These borrowers did not meet traditional industry standards to qualify for a loan. They were considered high-risk borrowers and thus were subjected to higher interest rates than were available from conventional lenders. Research has shown that 96% of the operating subprime lenders that opened their doors in 2005 are now out of business (PRWeb, n. d.).

In the past, the differences between subprime lenders and hard money lenders were often confusing. Contrary to popular belief, these two lending sources are different. They both serve as lenders for people who do not qualify for traditional loans through mortgage companies, credit unions, and banks.

However, hard money lenders typically lend to borrowers who other lenders do not lend to. For example, a hard money lender will usually consider a borrower who might be facing foreclosure. That is why hard money lenders are considered the loan of last resource. The private or hard money lender customarily does not base their loans on the borrower's credit history, but rather they emphasize the equity in the homeowner's property, which is evaluated by the loan-to-value (LTV) ratio. However, in the new lending market environment, this is not always the case anymore. Although the LTVs continue to be the primary tool used to evaluate hard money loans, most private mortgage lenders are also reviewing the credit scores, credit history, and the borrower's ability-to-repay (ATR). Customarily, these types of loans are meant to be short-term bridge loans.

Presently, due to the increasing number of individuals with poor credit, there is a growing demand for this subprime type of lending, but with no actual subprime lender available to fill this vacuum, the hard money lenders are the ones meeting this demand. Consequently, today 3.7% of all newly originated loans are hard money loans (PRWeb, n. d.).

Why the Need for Private Mortgage Lending?

Private mortgage lending involves loans secured by real estate and made by a private lender instead of a bank, lending institution, or government agency. These types of mortgage loans are hard money or asset-based loans, which are short-term bridge loans, typically six-months to three-years in duration.

Customarily, they are made to the professional real estate investor for the purchase, rehabilitation, or equity cash out of real property. However, the reasons for these types of loans could also be multifactorial, and since every deal could be different, every loan opportunity is considered.

As previously explained, the decision to make this type of loan is primarily based on the equity and value of the property being considered as collateral. However, the borrower's credit and ability-to-repay currently are very important elements in the underwriting process because of the corruptive economic climate prevailing in the lending industry today. The security for the loan is further enhanced by requiring that LTVs represent a maximum of 65% to 70% of the appraised value of the property. On non-income producing property, such as raw land, lots, and construction money, a maximum of 55% LTV is required to initiate the loan.

Hard or private money loans are expensive loans on which investors are willing to pay interest rates of 7.5% to 12% on first-liens, and 12% to 18% on second-lien mortgages or deeds of trust in this current, low-interest-rate environment. In addition to these high-interest rates, historically first-lien yields of six points or 6% over prime have also been obtainable.

It should be evident to the reader why these loans are a good investment for the private mortgage lender, which is the focus of the research study undertaken for this book. However, the question that arises is this: why should real estate investors—or any borrower—be willing to pay these high rates when conventional mortgage money is less expensive? There is a multitude of reasons why borrowers or real estate investors are agreeable to paying these higher interest rates.

No matter the reasons for paying these higher interest rates, they all fall into four categories, which are:

- ❖ Not meeting conventional bank qualifying guidelines
- ❖ The need for a quick decision
- ❖ Financial information privacy concerns
- ❖ Possibility of greater borrowing capacity

Not Meeting Bank Qualifying Guidelines

There are situations where a real estate investor or borrower or the real estate property itself does not qualify for a conventional mortgage loan. This situation can arise as the result of a low borrower credit score, too much borrower debt, or simply that the borrower's income-producing property does not generate sufficient income to cover the property's debt service.

Moreover, the property itself may not support the type of loan the borrower wants. Many institutional lenders will not make loans in amounts under half a million dollars. Others will not lend on a second lien position in spite of the availability of significant protective equity in the property. Conventional lenders will also not lend in situations where major repairs or extensive rehabilitations are necessary unless the project is sufficiently big, and the borrower has substantial experience undertaking such a large development.

In these cases, the private mortgage lender may be the only funding resource available for the real estate investor/borrower. Institutional lenders are concerned with both the appraised value of the property and the borrower's creditworthiness. Private mortgage lenders are mostly concerned with the estimated value and LTV as long as the appraised value represents a fair market price.

Hence, if a property is producing or can produce adequate income to cover the note payment, and the value of the property will fully secure the mortgage and provide sufficient protective equity, then the borrower's credit is not an issue for the private mortgage lender. However, in today's overregulated market, the ability-to-repay (ATR) rule under the Dodd-Frank Act has become a very important guideline to follow for every lender.

The Need for a Quick Decision

Mortgage money obtained from banking or institutional sources, called conventional mortgage money, will typically take between 60 and 90 days to be processed. Moreover, traditional lenders will also require a property appraisal and a detailed examination of the borrower's credit history and current financial status. Additionally, it will need the financial statements and tax returns, not only for the property securing the loan but for all real property and any business interests owned by the borrowing entity, as well as the personal financial information about the borrower himself. Suffice it to say, this is a labor-intensive and stress-producing endeavor for the borrowers.

In contrast, private mortgage lenders can generally complete a lending transaction within seven to ten days. Since the property that will be used as collateral is customarily the main criterion evaluated to determine loan eligibility, less information on the borrower and the borrower's other properties are required. This assessment typically results in a quicker approval process. The private mortgage lender can frequently decide to lend within 24 hours of receiving the property and borrower's information. Conversely, institutional mortgage funding must be approved by a loan committee that may only meet infrequently at specific times—possibly once or twice per month.

This cumbersome and inconvenient process could delay the lending process for a long time, usually 60 to 90 days without any assurance that the loan will be approved. This process does not take into account that many of these loan requests will have to go back to the loan officer repeatedly for additional information, which will delay the borrowing process even further.

These delays from conventional banks can result in investors losing their deal opportunities. That is one of the reasons why many real estate investors will choose to pursue private money funding in spite of it being more costly. However, for the real estate investor, the cost of missing out on the buying opportunity is more expensive than paying the higher interest rates charged by the private lender.

Financial Information Privacy Concerns

Some borrowers may not be inclined to divulge—or to be able to provide—the personal financial information being requested by the lending institution. Other borrowers might not want to go through the time-consuming and uncertain application process associated with obtaining an institutional mortgage loan. Furthermore, borrowers could be undergoing some legal issues that prevent them from revealing such information, or simply do not want to provide the information being requested for whatever reason. For example, the borrower might be going through a divorce, a lawsuit, or a business separation, and has decided not to furnish any information that could be detrimental. The reasons could be multifactorial.

Furthermore, the borrower could be an ineffective manager that may not have all of their financial records updated, or the investor's accountant may be delayed with the preparation of financial statements or have filed a request for a tax extension. All these situations can affect a traditional loan application. However, it should have no impact on the decision of the private lender who is considering granting the loan, as long as the property location, the amount of protective equity in the collateral, and exit strategy meet the requirements of the private or hard money lender.

Possibility of Greater Borrowing Capacity

Every loan that is made by a private money lender is specific to the opportunity being presented by the borrower. The borrower may be able to borrow a greater amount of funds from a private or hard money lender than from a conventional lender because of the flexibility with this type of loan. For example, through the process of cross-collateralization, a borrower could receive the funds necessary for the specific deal the investor wants to make.

A cross-collateralized loan is a way for a borrower or investor to generate funds for a project or business opportunity that may not be possible with traditional lenders. Therefore, cross- collateralization is a method used by private money lenders to facilitate the granting of a loan when there is insufficient collateral in a property to meet the underwriting guideline to issue the loan.

When applying this method of cross-collateralizing, two or more different properties are offered as collateral to procure the loan. Cross-collateralization is also known as a blanket loan, where one loan covers several properties. Cross-collateralization will be employed by hard or private money lenders who want to approve a loan request but have determined that the subject property been offered as the collateral does not provide adequate security to approve the loan.

Thus, the benefit for the lender in accepting additional properties to increase the collateral amount is that it will mitigate the lender's level of risk. Conversely, the benefit of cross-collateralization is that the borrowers are able to receive the loan because of the increased level of protective equity provided. However, there can be negative unintended consequences when using cross-collateralization to procure a loan because the borrower incurs the risk of losing all the properties that were offered as collateral in the event of a default on the loan agreement.

Therefore, putting up two or more properties as collateral can be a risky strategy for borrowers if they do not possess the wherewithal or the financial resources to make the loan payments. Before cross-collateralization is contemplated, borrowers must be confident that they have the means to maintain payments on the loan. A foreclosure in dual or multiple property situations will show up as two or more foreclosures in public records, as well as the borrower's credit report.

In closing this chapter, it is essential to state that the material appearing herein is meant to provide an educational foundation for the reader. It is not, therefore, a substitute for legal advice. Concerning any specific law issues, readers of this book should seek advice from a competent attorney with expertise on this confusing and, at times, conflicting topic. The mortgage lending industry continues to be in flux, as well as the laws, rules, and regulations. Moreover, these laws, rules, and regulations are still untested by the courts, and governmental agencies have not provided sufficient clarity on some of the inconsistencies and vague requirements. Therefore, a private money investor should be cautious in this environment. Always seek the counsel of competent and knowledgeable individuals and attorneys; you do not want to be a "test case" against the federal government (Barnes & Walker, n.d.).

8

The Borrower and Loan Opportunity Vetting Process

A t the commencement of any investment endeavor, there is a vetting process that takes place to mitigate investment risks. This discovery process, in essence, is the due diligence process. Due diligence in a broad sense refers to the level of judgment, care, prudence, determination, and activity that an investor would reasonably be expected to undertake in evaluating a potential borrower and the loan opportunity associated with that borrower. Therefore, due diligence is a program of critical analysis that private mortgage investors undertake prior to making any business decisions, which, in this case, is committing to a lending opportunity.

The majority of real estate investors subscribe to the common belief that real estate investing means adopting the time-consuming strategy of buying, fixing, selling, or flipping. It could also mean that the traditional landlord-type strategy of "buy and hold" that entails long holding periods while waiting for the properties to appreciate in value. While these two views of real estate investing have been the traditionally accepted strategies of investing in real estate, there are other ways that might be more appealing to investors.

Another way of investing in real estate is through private mortgage lending. Although not a mainstream investment model, it is a strategy that can help further diversify an investment portfolio.

While concomitantly garnering a higher return on investment as compared to bank CDs, bonds, and money-market accounts, as well as avoiding stock market volatility and uncertainty.

Private mortgage lending is the focus of the qualitative research study undertaken to write this book. The study demonstrated that private mortgage lending is a real estate investment strategy that allows the participant to make money just like the banks do. Because the investor acts as the bank in the transaction, they are subjected to the same protections the banks would receive. The research study further demonstrated that private mortgage investing possesses numerous beneficial hedging strategies that help mitigate investment risks with more control than other investment vehicles.

It is also essential for private mortgage investors interested in this investment vehicle to understand that typically, private mortgages do not provide any capital appreciation. However, there are situations in which capital appreciation can be achieved, which will be explained in another section. This investment vehicle is primarily suitable for those individuals who are seeking to generate a consistent passive income stream of fixed interest payments, which in today's market, exceed current money-market, savings, and bank CD rates.

In this chapter, the author will address the steps involved in the due diligence or vetting process that will help evaluate the borrowers and the loan opportunities associated with these real estate investments.

Private Money and Conventional Loans Comparison

There are two types of loans available to all real estate investors: private (hard money) or traditional (conventional) loans. However, before explaining the differences between these two types of loans, it is important to define the terminology used to describe private money lending. The following terms, private money lending, private mortgage investing, private money lender, hard money loan, hard loan, private investors loan, equity loan, trust deed investment loan, and any derivation thereof; are all synonymous terms that are used to describe the same thing.

As previously mentioned, a private money lender is a non-institutional (non-bank) individual, company, or group of individuals who loan money secured by a promissory note and mortgage, or deed of trust, for funding a real estate transaction. These entities make mortgage loans secured or collateralized by the real estate property with a 30% to 35% protective equity cushion to mitigate investment risk. In essence, a loan-to-value (LTV) of 65% to 70%. Conversely, conventional loans require more paperwork and must follow certain traditional lending guidelines.

Private money lenders are not required to follow the same lending guidelines that conventional lenders have to adhere to. They can select who they want to do business with and are more concerned about the property appraisal value and the available protective equity in the property, as determined by the property's loan-to-value (LTV) ratio. Private lenders are also focused on the interest rate to be charged and usually are not as concerned with the personal credit history of the borrower. However, in today's overregulated lending industry, lenders have to be additionally concerned with the borrower's ability-to-repay (ATR), especially for qualified residential mortgages (QRMs) as mandated by the Dodd-Frank Act.

However, the guidelines private lenders follow will depend on the lenders' due diligence experience and their risk aversion style. A caveat is appropriate to mention at this point: the author strongly contends that in today's market, every detail should be checked thoroughly, including the creditworthiness and ability-to-repay of the borrower. Risk mitigation is the key to success in any investment field.

Therefore, it is a wise practice to perform a comprehensive evaluation on all borrowers, both individual and corporate, before committing to the loan opportunity that is being presented.

Furthermore, keeping abreast of property values and changing market conditions is also essential to further mitigate investment risk for the lenders.

Essentially there are three main differences between conventional lending and private money lending. They are as follows:

- ❖ The underwriting considerations.
- ❖ The lenders' and investors' relationship.
- ❖ The loan structure, the interest rate, and the terms of the loans.

Underwriting Considerations

Mortgage underwriting is the process a lender uses to determine if the risk of offering a mortgage loan to a borrower under certain parameters is acceptable. Therefore, the underwriting process is an essential lending function, which is performed by both private and conventional lenders. To help the underwriter assess the quality of the loan, banks and lenders create guidelines and even computer models that analyze the various aspects of the mortgage and provide recommendations regarding the risks involved. However, it is always up to the underwriter to make the final decision on whether to approve or decline a loan.

Conventional lending underwriting is based on credit, income, and equity evaluation. In contrast, in private money lending, the emphasis has been mainly based on how much equity the property has and the borrower exit strategy. Regarding the LTV ratio, traditionally, the standard that has been applied is that as long as there is sufficient protective equity in the property, which means the LTV ratio is 65% to 70%, and then the hard money loan could be done. However, as the result of the 2008 real estate financial crisis and the increased amount of corruption prevalent in the mortgage lending industry, this is no longer the sole consideration for making private loans. Today many private money lenders are following more traditional underwriting guidelines and looking at ability-to-repay, character or willingness to pay, as well as the debt-to-income ratio.

Underwriting includes all the analysis necessary to confirm valuation, income, property condition, and the borrower's capacity to execute on repayment or exit strategy. This process might sound similar to the underwriting process employed by a conventional bank in evaluating a traditional loan, but the reality is that underwriting private money loans are a completely different process than underwriting traditional loans.

In the private money industry, no two transactions or investors are alike. Most hard money mortgage loans are made by private, non-institutional investors, which predominantly are individuals who retain the loan and service the note or mortgage themselves, unless they prefer to use a loan servicing company to avoid the extra work involved. Each individual private lender sets their own economic, demographic, and geographic criteria, which typically means lending in their local area. The loans private individuals are willing to invest in will vary based on what they are comfortable with. Because each investor and each mortgage or deed of trust transaction is different, the underwriting process for hard money loans is highly individualized and flexible.

Perhaps the most unique characteristic of private money lending is the methodology used for underwriting the loans. Underwriting private money loans are performed by a sole mortgage investor who will typically use a manual underwriting process as compared to an automated process for traditional lending institutions. Mainstream-type loans can be easily processed in assembly-line fashion because conventional lenders use automated underwriting systems. Therefore, they shift most of the responsibility for lending decisions to the secondary marketing agencies, such as Fannie Mae, Freddie Mac, and Ginnie Mae.

In contrast, private money lending is person-oriented, not process-oriented, which requires a manual approach to loan underwriting. This is a human touch element that cannot be easily automated. Unlike the conventional mortgage industry, there is no formalized private mortgage marketplace, no secondary market, no securitization, and there are no governmental organizations such as FNMA, FHA, and VA that have established uniform underwriting guidelines. In essence, private money lending lacks uniform underwriting guidelines. However, this does not mean the industry is devoid of guidelines; it just means that the underwriting processes the industry implements are as individual as the loans that are being made.

Because there is no official governmental entity to establish specific guidelines for private or hard money lenders to follow, there is much more flexibility in the process. However, that does not mean there aren't certain core factors that each private lender follows to satisfy the underwriting of their loans. Despite the lack of specific guidelines for the individual lenders to follow, in today's overregulated mortgage industry, it is a wise practice to be well informed about the laws and regulations that could possibly affect this area of the lending industry. Especially now that the Dodd-Frank Act is regulating the mortgage lending industry through Title XIV. It has been strongly recommended that it would be a prudent practice to invest some financial resources in working with a knowledgeable and competent attorney that is familiar with the private mortgage investing process.

Regardless of the lack of a standardized underwriting process, private money underwriting typically attempts to satisfy the following criteria to mitigate the risks of lending when considering a loan opportunity:

❖ **Collateral Evaluation**

The property or properties being used as collateral to secure the loan.

❖ **Creditworthiness Assessment**

- Capacity of the borrower's ability to pay the loan obligation (ability-to-repay)

- Character (willingness to pay the loan obligation)
- Credit score and credit history

❖ The Reason for the Loan Request

It is important to understand the reason why the loan is being pursued through a private lender. Essentially, this is what's known as the *"story behind the loan"*—a critical element in private money lending.

❖ A Realistic Exit Strategy

It is crucial for the borrower(s) to provide a believable, detailed plan of how the loan will be repaid. The borrower's exit strategy is the key to whether or not the property being offered as collateral is a viable investment option.

Collateral Evaluation

The collateral refers to the type of property, its value, the property use, and everything else that is attributed to all of these aspects of the property. The different types of properties used as collateral intrinsically possess distinct levels of risks. These levels of risks can be hierarchically classified in order of degree of risk as follows: single-family residence, planned unit development (PUD), duplex, townhouse, low-rise condominium, high-rise condominium, triplexes and fourplexes, and condotels (condominium-hotels).

Occupancy is also considered part of the collateral. A home can be owner-occupied or used as a second home or investment. Owner-occupied and second homes have the least amount of default, while investment properties have higher occurrences of default. Analyzing and evaluating the collateral as it relates to the combination of occupancy and the type of collateral, the lender can determine the amount of risk they are willing to absorb with any loan opportunity they might be contemplating.

For example, even though an owner-occupied property has the least occurrence of default, which should translate to less risk, this is not always the case. The reason this is not always the case; it's because some states have what are called homestead exemptions laws. A homestead exemption law is an established allowance set up by each state to protect the homeowners from high property tax bills, the creditors, and from situations where a spouse dies. This exemption is only valid on a homeowner's primary residence and not on any other type of property.

Homestead exemption laws possess three main features, which are designed to protect the homeowners from the following:

❖ They prevent a forced sale on a home to pay off creditors.

❖ In the event that a spouse dies, the laws give a homeowner the right to stay in the home.

❖ The exemption reduces the assessed value of the home, which in turn decreases the homeowner's tax liability.

Therefore, private money lenders must understand that the homestead exemption laws that prevent a forced sale of a home, to pay the creditors will actually make an owner-occupied home a riskier type investment even though these properties have a lower occurrence of defaults. Conversely, this situation does not happen with investment-type properties because they do not have homestead exemption protection. Hence, although these properties have a greater occurrence of default, they are much easier to foreclose in the event of a default. Consequently, they are less risky investments to be used as collateral for the private mortgage lender.

Traditionally, private money investors considered the underlying collateral securing the loan as the primary and most important factor for granting the loan. However, in view of the inherent corruption that permeates the marketplace today, all the other underwriting criteria are also evaluated, such as creditworthiness, character, the reason for the loan, and exit strategy.

Elements of the Collateral that Should be Evaluated

In reviewing and evaluating the collateral, the private mortgage lender should analyze the following elements of the property or asset that will be used in securing the loan:

❖ Protective equity

❖ Loan-to-value (LTV) ratio

❖ Property marketability

❖ Property salability

❖ Physical condition of the property

❖ Property location

❖ Quality control

Protective Equity

In any investment, intrinsic hedging strategies help to mitigate investment risk. Protective equity serves as a hedge within a mortgage or trust deed investment that provides the cushion for the risk taken in facilitating or providing the loan. The amount of protective equity in the property protects the investor against the following types of risks:

❖ Payment defaults risk

❖ Market fluctuations risk

❖ Property devaluation risk

Edward J. Pinto (2011, February 5) of the American Enterprise Institute, stated that forensic studies undertaken regarding the housing crisis showed that government housing policies and low down payments were the primary causative factors, which resulted in the housing crisis of 2008. These studies also showed that low down payments are the best predictor of mortgage defaults. Furthermore, Pinto contends that the major cause of the financial crisis in the United States was the collapse of housing and mortgage markets, which resulted from the accumulation of an unprecedented number of weak and risky non-traditional mortgages (NTMs).

These NTMs began to default in record numbers commencing in early 2006, triggering the collapse of the worldwide market for mortgage-backed securities (MBSs), which subsequently triggered the instability and insolvency of financial institutions. In essence, this situation is what has been called the financial crisis. Many people believe that the crisis was attributed to governmental policies that forced a systematic, industry-wide loosening of the mortgage underwriting standards in an effort to promote affordable housing to everyone (Pinto, 2011). This crisis is evidence of the unintended consequences that typically result from the intervention of well-intentioned government policies attempting to instill fairness in the system.

Because of these findings, industry regulators of traditional mortgages want to establish a standard minimum down payment of 20% for qualified residential mortgages (QRMs). QRMs are supposed to decrease a borrower's default risk by establishing high lending standards for down payments, the borrower debt-to-income ratios, and borrower income documentation.

In the private money lending industry, the standard criterion is maintaining the LTV ratios in the range of 65% to 70%, which means that there is a 30% to 35% cushion of protective equity in the property, which essentially prevents the possibility of defaults. However, in the event of a foreclosure, the protective equity available from the loan ensures that there are sufficient resources to pay the total costs of the foreclosure process and recover the investor's principal. It is also not uncommon that on some occasions, there will be excess equity that can be earned by the investor, making the foreclosure default a positive event.

Protective equity is calculated by taking the liquidated value of the property or quick sale value (the price at which the property could be sold quickly) and then subtracting any outstanding debt related to the property, such as any existing loans and tax liens. Since the amount of protective equity directly relates to the security of the mortgage or the trust deed, it is fair to assume that the primary risk to the investor lies in the amount of protective equity available in the property that will be used as collateral.

The Loan-to-Value (LTV) ratio

The loan-to-value (LTV) ratio is a financial term used by lenders to express the ratio of a loan to the value of a property being purchased. The loan-to-value ratio is an important underwriting criterion use by private lenders in determining whether to extend credit or not. The LTV ratio is expressed as a percentage of the appraisal value of the property or quick sale value to the amount being loaned. It represents the maximum loan amount the lender will consider and determines how risky it makes the loan.

For example, if a buyer borrows $100,000 to purchase a property worth $125,000, the LTV ratio would be $100,000/$125,000, or 80%. The remaining 20% will have to come from the borrower as a down payment, which represents the borrower's equity. In contrast, this 20% also represents the private lender's protective equity. There is an inverse relationship between risk and the amount of protective equity, which means that the higher the LTV ratio, the riskier the loan, and the lower the LTV ratio, the less risky the loan opportunity. Thus, a 95% LTV ratio is much riskier than a 65% LTV ratio. The LTV ratio, as has been stated many times before, used to be the most important evaluating criterion for a private mortgage lender. However, with all the corruption that permeates the lending industry at all levels, the LTV ratio, although still an important risk-mitigating criterion, is no longer sufficient to mitigate investment risk. Therefore, a more complete assessment of risk mitigation is currently absolutely necessary.

One of the primary causes of default in mortgage payments is an inadequate vetting of the creditworthiness of the borrower. The borrower's creditworthiness is analyzed based on the ability or capacity to repay, which means evaluating net income, employment status, and overall borrower financial health. Furthermore, the borrower's desire to repay must also be assessed, which can be evaluated by a review of the borrower's credit and repayment history (Abbott, 2012).

Obviously, the lower the loan amount is compared with the value of the property, the more equity there is to protect the lender in the event of a default. Thus, the availability of sufficient protective equity can result in a favorable loan determination. Each private lender typically adheres to an LTV limit that they feel will garner the safest loan opportunity, which, as previously mentioned, is usually approximately 65% to 70%; however, the lower, the better.

In finalizing this section, it is important to again remind readers of the author's intentional use of a certain degree of repetition throughout some chapters of the book. This repetitiveness has been deliberate. The objective of any learning endeavor, such as a book, is to teach the reader something of value—hopefully. It is with this objective in mind that the author decided to use some repetition to emphasized specific points he considered crucial. The author, again, reminds the readers of the old philosophical Latin phrase that states, ***"Repetitio est mater studiorum."*** What this means is that repetition is the mother of all learning.

Property Marketability

Lenders also review the marketability of the property to determine how marketable the property is. Marketability is defined in the International Glossary of Business Valuation of Terms as "the ability to quickly convert the property to cash at a minimal cost." Moreover, some texts go on to add, "With a high degree of certainty of realizing the anticipated amount of the proceeds (Pratt & Niculita, 2008, p.39). Because the possibility of default is always present in the private mortgage lending business, evaluating property marketability as part of the underwriting process helps determine how probable it is that the property can sell based on its location, size, and physical condition.

Property Salability

Salability is the subjective quality representing the likelihood of purchase. When a property is determined to be salable, it indicates that the property has the potential of being marketed or sold. In other words, a property is considered to be salable when there is a high probability of selling the property within a specific time frame, price range, and acceptable terms.

Before any property is purchased, or it is considered as a loan opportunity, it is always a wise practice to evaluate the likelihood of how easily the property would sell to the next buyer when the time comes. Therefore, private lenders should cultivate the habit of inspecting the properties they intend to lend to. They should familiarize themselves with the neighborhoods and property locations for their lending preferences. Moreover, the private lender should also be well versed in the assessment process of the following physical attributes of the real estate property.

Physical Condition of the Collateral (Property)

❖ **New Property**

This is the type of property that is in a new or unused condition and can be inhabited immediately without modifications or repairs.

❖ **Usable Property**

This is the type of property that shows some wear and tear but is habitable without the need for a significant degree of repair.

❖ **Repairable Property**

This is the type of property that is unusable in its current condition. However, it can be economically repaired. It is the type of property that can be purchased for rehabbing and flipping.

❖ Salvage Property

This is the type of property that has value in excess of its basic material content, but repairing or rehabilitation is considered impractical and uneconomical.

❖ Scrap Property

This is the type of property that has no value except for its basic material content.

Property Location

Some investors like to physically inspect the properties they are lending against and will typically lend in the areas they are personally familiar with. This practice is a good habit to cultivate. In essence, in the field of private money lending, looking over the assessment of the area or location where the lender is contemplating investing is crucial to mitigate risk. For example, locations that private mortgage lenders should be familiar with are the major markets and *metropolitan statistical areas (MSAs)*, which are geographical regions with a relatively high population density with close economic ties to the surrounding area.

Typically, MSAs are not incorporated legally as a city or town would be, and neither are they structured as legal administrative divisions like counties and states. Private mortgage lenders should also be cognizant of metropolitan infill areas or land-recycling, which essentially is renewing or redeveloping blighted neighborhoods with the goal of integrating these communities back into more prosperous communities. Investing in urban locations is always preferable than investing in rural or remote locations. The best investments are in prime locations such as waterfront, resorts, middle of a major city, and in a high-end neighborhood (Metropolitan Statistical Area, n. d.)

A good and safe rule to follow is to lend only on properties the lender would not mind owning, and only in areas in which the lender would not mind living. As a matter of practice, in determining whether to lend or not once the due diligence process has been satisfactorily completed, should be to ask yourself a final question, and that is: would I love to own this property?

Quality Control

To ensure safety and to mitigate risk in any program, there should be a quality control (QC) component in place to make sure that the quality of all the factors involved in that process is analyzed and evaluated for accuracy. It is essential to have a QC process in place when engaging in private mortgage investing. For example, analyzing and evaluating the location where the collateral resides is important to ensure that mortgage investments are made only in high-quality locations.

A private mortgage investor QC program should make sure that the collateral being contemplated for a loan is not located within an area that has been designated as a significantly blighted area. Additionally, it should be determined that the property is not located within an area that is considered to be a high-crime neighborhood, where the likelihood of vandalism to the collateral would be greater compared to a more stable, lower crime area. The collateral should also be evaluated for past environmental or structural integrity issues.

Creditworthiness Assessment

The mortgage lending business inherently is not a complicated business. Whether the lending process is performed by traditional banks or by private money lenders (PMLs), the goal is essentially the same: to provide funds for people that must subsequently be repaid and generate a profit for the lender. Historically, well-functioning banks, as well as private mortgage lenders, typically granted their loans to borrowers according to four principles of lending. However, currently, a greater number of lenders, both traditional and private, are evaluating additional lending parameters of risk because of the riskier lending environment the industry is experiencing.

When lenders assess the creditworthiness of any potential client, it is done by determining what the industry has termed the *"four Cs"* of lending, and in some cases the *"five Cs,"* which are:

- ❖ Credit scores and payment history
- ❖ Character (commitment)
- ❖ Capacity
- ❖ Collateral
- ❖ Capital

Credit Scores and Payment History

The credit scores provide the lender the confidence of the borrower's ability or intention to fulfill their financial obligations. The credit report is analyzed to make this determination. The borrower needs to show a historical track record of having met their past financial obligations.

Character (Commitment)

The character will be determined by the overall impression the borrower makes on the private or hard money lender or the bank loan officer. Typically, the lender will formulate a subjective opinion as to whether or not the borrower is sufficiently trustworthy to repay the loan. The borrower has to be considered trustworthy before any lender takes a chance on them.

Capacity

This is the borrower's ability-to-repay (ATR) the mortgage loan based on their income and work history. The borrower must demonstrate that they are able to pay their debt from their existing salary. Ability-to-repay is a very important criterion, which is part of the Dodd-Frank Act of 2010, especially for qualified mortgages (QMs).

Collateral

The collateral is a question of whether the property is acceptable as security for the loan being requested. In essence, this is the property that's being purchased or refinance. The value of the collateral has to exceed the loan balance.

Capital

The capital is the wealth the borrower has, which includes the money or property accumulated that demonstrates the resources available to cover the down payment or closing costs. The source of this capital can be verified by assessing the borrower's checking accounts, savings accounts, insurance policies, gifts, IRAs or Keogh accounts, 401(K), stocks, bonds, and any proceeds from the sale of an existing property, real or personal.

The four or the five Cs of lending is the structure or the foundation that ensures that the lending process is as safe as it can possibly be. The four Cs criteria are customarily applied by private and hard money lenders, and the five Cs are used by conventional banks, which also evaluate the borrower's available capital. Any deviation from these guidelines will violate the risk mitigation requirements necessary for an adequate underwriting process. However, there is usually more elasticity in the way these evaluating criteria are used by private mortgage lenders than by conventional banks. The reason for this higher degree of flexibility is that the private or hard money lenders are not constrained by governmental rules and regulations as much as traditional loan officers (Segal, 2019).

The financial housing crisis of 2008 was a crisis of structured loans that violated, to varying degrees, all of the above lending principles—particularly the third principle, that of capacity or ability-to-repay. That is why the Dodd-Frank Act of 2010 emphasizes evaluating the ability-to-repay of borrowers in its new guidelines. The end result of violating the principle of capacity or ability-to-repay is that the United States and foreign financial institutions now hold large portfolios of promises that can no longer be credibly valued.

Private money lending employs the same rigorous credit assessment principles that traditional banks use but applies them to situations in which the lender must rely on borrower's character and capacity. The first step in the underwriting process is for the borrower to be vetted, which, in essence, is to perform a background check. The loan application and the initial meeting with the borrower are the first assessments made to determine if a borrower qualifies as a potential candidate for a private money loan.

Beginning with the first meeting, the lender must evaluate the quality of the lending opportunity, the fit with the borrower's experience and capacity, and whether the financing amount and the deal structure are appropriate. Initially, the lender will review the borrower's income history and assets to determine if the borrower is capable of meeting the terms of the loan and making the payments. This is typically the capital evaluation process traditional lenders assess in their five C's, and although this is not a customary evaluating step for private mortgage lenders, it does not mean it is not looked at. Next, the borrower's debts and credit report will be reviewed. As previously mentioned, private money lenders place a higher risk-hedging value on the protective equity in the property than the financial resources of the borrower (Seagal, 2019).

However, it has always been a wise and prudent practice to determine if the borrower has the income to be able to repay the loan. The objective of private money lenders is to generate cash flow, not foreclose on defaulted properties. Thus, determining ability-to-repay has always been an essential consideration. It is also important to understand that for certain types of mortgage loans, it is unlawful to lend money on a real estate transaction to someone who does not demonstrate the ability-to-repay the loan. For example, in primary residences, it is illegal to make a loan to someone who cannot demonstrate the ability or capacity to make their mortgage payments.

Currently, after the passage of the final rules of the Dodd-Frank Act, determining ability-to-repay (ATR) is actually mandatory. The ATR rule, which went into effect on January 10, 2014, essentially requires a lender to determine—based on documented and verifiable information—that at the time a mortgage loan is made, the borrower has the ability-to-repay the loan. Failure to make such a determination could result in a lender having to pay damages to a borrower who brings a lawsuit claiming that the lender did not follow the ATR rule.

Reason for the Loan Request

There is always a reason why a borrower is seeking financing through a private money lender rather than a conventional lending institution. To determine the reason for the loan request, the private lender needs to perform a detailed due diligence or vetting process to ensure the safety and quality of the loan opportunity.

The Vetting Process

The following list shows some of the information that should be determined before granting a loan to a borrower:

- ❖ Background assessment on the principal(s) in the transaction.
- ❖ Borrower's life events that have resulted in both successes and failures.
- ❖ What led to the borrower's current financial situation?
- ❖ Location, physical condition, and character of the property being used as collateral.
- ❖ Current status of the real estate or project.
- ❖ How long will the borrower need the funds.
- ❖ How quickly will the funds be required.

- Are there any issues with credit, bankruptcies, cash flow of the property, title, etc.?
- Are there any liens attached to the property that need to be removed?
- Is the borrower's exit strategy realistic?

This due diligence process to determine the reason(s) for the loan may uncover information that could be beneficial to the loan request. For example, the loan officer or investor could discover that there are more equity, income, assets, and collateral. The discovery of this increased financial viability makes for a stronger and less risky loan opportunity. Conversely, the vetting process may reveal a worse and riskier financial situation, which could expose the investor to potential financial loss or may result in other adverse consequences. It is essential to invest the necessary vetting (due diligence) time to determine if the reason(s) for the loan is justified.

A Realistic Exit Strategy

The borrower's exit strategy is the key to whether or not the property being offered as collateral is a viable investment option. Thus, a private funding exit strategy for a hard money mortgage loan is basically a clear and defined plan for the repayment of the mortgage at the end of the interest term. For many private lenders, the exit strategy is just as important as the collateral itself. However, it is one thing for the borrower to say he has a plan for exiting the loan, and another to be able to show the viability of the exit plan. Therefore, a sound and credible exit strategy is an essential component of the due diligence or vetting process that will facilitate the funding of the loan opportunity.

Therefore, a sound and credible exit strategy must have the following elements:

- Realistic
- Viable

- ❖ Verifiable

- ❖ Multi-faceted

In essence, the borrower must have a plan for paying off the loan to be able to qualify for the funds. Because it is harder to refinance now than it once was, each borrower needs to present a well-thought-out plan for exiting the loan obligation.

The goal of most private mortgage lenders is to stay in the loan from a minimum of six months to a maximum of two or three years. Therefore, an exit strategy that can prove that the borrower has a sound plan for paying off the loan is essential to be able to be considered for the loan.

Most private money lending standards begin with an evaluation of the protective equity available in the property to be used as collateral for the loan. However, although assessing the amount of equity is a significant element in the lending decision, it is not the only parameter that is relevant to the hard mortgage lender. There are other important standards that are evaluated besides the equity of the collateral. For example, also assessed are the quality of the collateral, the borrower's ability-to-repay, and the overall viability of the project. Additionally, the reputation of the borrower and the potential rental income the property could generate in the event that it needs to be taken back after a default is equally important. Moreover, having a realistic exit strategy is a crucial requirement to ensure that there is a plausible repayment plan to meet the loan obligation, such as resale or refinance of the property.

The Lenders' and Investors' Relationship

There is a fundamental difference in philosophy between the lender and the investor. The goal of the investor is to maximize the return on his investment or equity. The investor can attempt to accomplish this goal by using leverage borrowing, adding value to the property by making improvements, or by adding value by increasing the property's cash flow by way of rent adjustments.

Therefore, for the investor, the attained return on investment (ROI) is directly proportionate or commensurate with the risk and effort taken with the invested funds.

Conversely, the private or hard money lender plays the dual role of being an investor and lender. This individual is an investor who is engaged in the business of lending money to borrowers who may or may not qualify for conventional bank financing. The property that the investor views as a potentially appreciating asset, the private lender views as both an investment to create cash flow and as security for the loan.

The private money lender is primarily concerned with two objectives: generating an income stream much like a bank certificate of deposit (CD), but with a higher interest rate, and the return of the borrowed money as per the terms of the mortgage and promissory note agreement. Therefore, a private money lender (PML) approaches the loan opportunity as a lender and as an investor, hence the reason for the dual role as described above.

In contrast to the lender, the investor approaches the investment from the vantage point of managing the investment risks in the hopes of generating an acceptable ROI. Therefore, the property that the investor views as a potentially appreciating asset, the lender views solely as security or collateral for the loan and as an income stream.

In summary, as previously mentioned, the lender is behaving like a bank, and just like a bank, the objective is not in acquiring real estate by way of default and its subsequent foreclosure action. The goal is simply to generate an income stream for a prescribed period of time and get the loaned money back as per the terms of the promissory note agreement.

The Loan Structure, Interest Rate, and the Terms of the Loan

The qualifying criteria for a private money loan can vary widely between lenders and the loan purpose. Traditionally, in the hard money lending industry, the borrower's credit scores, income, and other conventional lending criteria may or may not be analyzed. As frequently mentioned throughout this book, for most private money lenders, the primary qualifying criterion for the obtainment of a loan is based on the value of the real estate being used as collateral, the amount of available protective equity, or LTV ratio, and the exit strategy proposed by the borrower.

However, in today's lending environment, evaluation of the creditworthiness of the borrower has become important to analyze as well. Private or hard money lenders structure their loans based on a percentage of the quick-sale value of the subject property. The term quick-sale value essentially means that the property value is based on the price of what the market will bear and not what is owed on the property.

Customarily, the largest loan a borrower can expect to obtain would be between 65% and 70% of the loan-to-value (LTV). What this means is that if the property's quick-sale value is $200,000, the lender will only consider lending $130,000 to $140,000. This low LTV ratio provides $60,000 to $70,000 of what is called protective equity, which, in essence, helps mitigate the risk of default and provide security for the lender if the borrower defaults on the mortgage payments and needs to be foreclosed.

The importance of having a low LTV ratio for the lender is because this is the amount a lender could reasonably expect to realize from the quick-sale of the property. Typically, a quick-sale will take one to four months. The quick-sale value differs from a market value appraisal, which assumes an arms-length transaction in which neither buyer nor seller is acting under any duress.

Private money mortgage loans are generally more expensive than traditional bank loans. Hard money lenders customarily lend money at 9% to 14% interest, but it can be higher depending on the risk involved with the deal. The interest rate that is charged by private money lenders is not dependent on the rates banks charge their customers. For the traditional bank, the interest charged is typically contingent on the borrower's ability to qualify for conventional bank loans, the type of real estate being purchased, the privacy requirements of the borrowers, and the creditworthiness of the borrowers, just to name a few.

In addition to high-interest rates, private money loans can have what is called origination points, which typically fluctuate between one and three points or 1% to 3%. These origination points can sometimes be eliminated if the loan is issued directly from a solo private lender/investor. However, if the loan was issued by a hard money broker/lender business, then these points are the commission earned by these individuals for brokering the loan for the borrowers.

Private money loans are short-term bridge-type loans that customarily last from six months to two or three years. However, the term of duration for these loans can be negotiable, but it will never be for more than five years. Therefore, having an exit strategy as part of one's plan to repay the loan is crucial in getting the loan. The lender needs to know the borrower has a plan for either selling or refinancing the property before the term is up.

Most private money lenders will charge a prepayment penalty if the loan is repaid before six months. In other words, the money will not be lent for less than six months, unless there is an inducement for the lender. A borrower can repay the loan before the six months period is over, but they will have to pay a prepayment for any difference in the time left in the six months. For example, if the money is repaid in two months, there will be a prepayment penalty of four months.

Another way of structuring a private mortgage loan is through cross-collateralization, which is a method used by lenders to provide additional protective equity to add more security to a loan transaction. This strategy is implemented by the lender by placing a lien on another property in addition to the property that is the subject of the loan. Technically, taking out a second mortgage on a property is considered to be cross-collateralization.

This approach is used when the subject property does not have sufficient equity to qualify for the loan by itself. Therefore, the additional property's equity is used to reduce the risk of the loan and achieve the LTV ratio required by the lender. In the event the borrower defaults on the loan and foreclosure action is pursued, the lender can foreclose on both properties. This strategy is beneficial for the borrower because combining the equity in two properties will facilitate the granting of the loan. It is also advantageous for the lender because it can achieve the LTV ratio required to facilitate the loan.

However, there are some negative implications when using this strategy that borrowers should understand before committing to this approach to qualify for the potential loan. With this cross-collateralization approach, the loan closing costs will become more expensive, because, with cross-collateralization, the lender will require an appraisal, title searches, and title insurance on both properties. The lender customarily will also require a physical inspection of both properties, which could result in some repairs being needed prior to closing that will result in additional expenses.

Another negative factor associated with the process of cross-collateralization is the fact that if the borrower decides to sell one of the properties, it would be impossible because both properties are now attached to the liens created by the loan. However, this problem can be remedied if there is additional collateral acceptable to the lender that can be used to replace the existing, released cross-collateral.

9

Minimizing Private Mortgage Investment Risk

I t is a traditional belief that achieving higher returns on investments are equated with taking on a greater degree of risk. However, that belief is not entirely accurate because attractive yields can be achieved by investing in private mortgage loans, which are backed by a hard or tangible asset like real estate.

The problem associated with most Wall Street-type investments such as stocks, bonds, and mortgage-backed securities (MBSs)—to name just a few—is that there are no limits as to how much principal an investor can lose on any of these investments. In order to make these Wall Street types of investments more acceptable to potential investors, brokerage houses customarily tout them as being guaranteed and insured, or even that they are backed by the full faith and credit of the United States government. For example, MBSs are backed by Fannie Mae (FNMA) or Freddie Mac (FHLMC), which are quasi-governmental agencies. These quasi-governmental agencies are known as government-sponsored enterprises or GSEs. They were created by acts of Congress to enhance the flow of credit to specific sectors of the American economy, such as individuals, students, farmers, and homeowners.

In contrast, a private mortgage loan investment is backed by the amount of protective equity available from the property being used as collateral. These other government-backed investments are only guarantees that are based on the credit risk and financial wherewithal of the entity guaranteeing the loan. Therefore, Wall Street-type investments are not similarly protected by a tangible asset, as is the case with a private mortgage loan. Furthermore, the rate of return generated by these investments, which are backed by the full faith and credit of the U.S. government, currently is minimal. The typical returns garnered from these investments range from less than 1% to 2.40% in the current low-interest-rate economic environment in comparison to a 7.5% to 12% for a private mortgage investment.

Investing in private mortgage loans is an alternative investment vehicle that should be considered by an investor seeking a consistent income stream with a high degree of risk mitigation potential. Private mortgage investing is a growing industry because of the ever-increasing number of real estate investors and business owners who need access to capital but are unable to obtain funding through conventional banks for a variety of reasons. Some examples of the types of properties that can be used as collateral for a private loan are income-producing commercial properties, multi-family homes, condominiums, new construction developments, and renovation or rehab projects.

There are many opportunities present in today's private lending market. These loans are usually approved at no more than 60% to 70% of LTV of the appraised market value of the commercial or residential property. The duration of these loans—because they are considered to be a bridge or transitional-type loan—is customarily six months to two or three-year terms, and on rare occasions, five years. These loans provide the borrower the opportunity to increase the income generated from the property until subsequently qualifying for a lower-cost traditional mortgage loan.

A private mortgage is an asset-based loan—a secured debt obligation—that produces a regular, predictable income stream to an investor, with all the security, protections, and recourse that a mortgage lien can provide (Winter, 2012).

The list below shows some of the investment advantages that private mortgage loans can offer an investor. They include the following:

- ❖ Reduced investment volatility
- ❖ Security of the investment
- ❖ Asset-specific investment
- ❖ Income-generating asset
- ❖ Protective equity value
- ❖ Short-term investment cycle

Reduced Investment Volatility

In contrast to the stock or bond market, private mortgage loans are classified as non-correlated investments that tend to change in value independently of the core financial markets such as stocks and bonds. Consequently, these investments are less volatile than Wall Street-type investments. Moreover, there are no real-time dynamic financial changes that affect the yield on private mortgage loans. The interest yield is fixed throughout the mortgage time duration. These loans are typically consistently paid as agreed by borrowers because of the amount of protective equity in the property.

However, if the monthly interest payments are not made, then a default will occur, which, if not corrected, will lead to a foreclosure. Should the property be foreclosed, there should be enough protective equity in the property to recover the principal invested, cover the foreclosure legal expenses, and possibly earn some additional profits if there is equity remaining following the foreclosure action.

Security of the Investment

Private mortgages are investments that are backed by a tangible hard asset, such as real estate, which, if underwritten appropriately, should have sufficient protective equity to minimize the investment risk if the borrower defaults on the loan.

Asset-Specific Investment

When investing in private mortgage loans, the debt is secured by a specific asset, such as a commercial building or investment property. Because of the specificity of the investment, it gives investors greater control to safeguard the original principal invested.

Income Generating Asset

Most traditional investments are primarily valued in relation to their liquidity and ability to provide an income stream in the form of dividends or interest payments, and in the case of stocks, the potential for equity appreciation. Regarding private mortgage loans, the amount of rent and expenses for the property are known and taken into account during the loan underwriting process. For example, in a hypothetical mortgage financing scenario where the investor funded a $65,000 loan on a $100,000 single-family, non-owner occupied investment property, the exposure on this loan is a 65% LTV ratio with a $35,000 protective equity stake. Hence, this loan has been underwritten adhering to the recommended risk-mitigating guidelines for private mortgage investing. However, the property also generates $15,000 in annual net rental income, which is sufficient to cover the loan payment and expenses for the property.

Therefore, in the event the borrower defaults on the loan payments and the property undergo a foreclosure action proceeding, once the foreclosure takes place (assuming $4,500 of legal cost to complete the foreclosure); the total investment cost for the property is now $69,500. This total amount is comprised of the original $65,000 in loans plus the cost incurred in the foreclosure of $4,500. If the property continues to generate the $15,000 of rental income, this investment will generate a return of 21.58% ($69,500/$15,000) based upon the amount of capital invested from the rental income alone. If the property is sold at its current appraised value of

$100,000, with the present investor funded financing of $ 69,500, to account for the cost of foreclosure. The return on investment would be 30.5% ($69,500/$100,000). It is obvious that these returns would more than make up for the lost time of interest income while the property was undergoing the foreclosure process.

Protective Equity Value

Customarily, when buying Wall Street-type investments like stocks, bonds, and other investments, the investor will purchase these investments at the current market value. In contrast, private mortgage loans are made at LTV ratios of no greater than 65% to 70% of the appraised value of the property. These LTV ratios mean that there is a significant amount of protective equity built-in from the inception of the loan deal that will act as a hedge against any potential property default.

In the event of a default, the discounted value of the property becomes the investment basis by the investor who executed the private mortgage loan. This built-in protective equity allows the private mortgage loan investor to inadvertently acquire the asset at a fraction of the actual market value. The built-in protective equity in the property could be realized as a potential gain from the sale of the property after foreclosure.

Short-Term Investment Cycle

Private mortgage investments are customarily short-term bridge loans ranging from six months to three years. The main goal of this type of investment vehicle is to generate a consistently high-income stream, typically in the range of 7.5% to 12%. The research undertaken for this book demonstrated that private mortgage investing could be a suitable investment vehicle for generating a passive income stream for investors who are retired or contemplating retirement. In contrast to the traditional mortgage-backed securities (MBSs) being offered by Fannie Mae and Freddie Mac that only pay 2.25% to 3.0% on their 30-year notes, private mortgage investing can easily surpass those returns with less risk (Mortgagenewsdaily. com, 2014, August).

This artificially low-interest-rate environment, which is intentionally being created by the Federal Reserve to stimulate the economy and bolster the stock market, is specifically hurting the retired individual. It is very difficult for a retired individual to sustain an adequate lifestyle with the minuscule returns traditional Wall Street-type investments are currently providing to the retired investor.

Moreover, the investors owning MBSs, which are bond-type investments, are exposed to interest rate risks because of the inherent inverse relationship bonds have with the interest rate (i.e., if interest rates increase, the bond prices decrease, and vice-versa). Therefore, in an already low-interest-rate environment, the likelihood that interest rates will increase is substantially greater than the probability of being reduced any further. If savings account rates increase to 5%, the investor will be selling a 2.25% to 3.0%, 30-year fixed mortgage-backed security at a steep discount from its face value, resulting in a loss of principal to the investor unless the investment is held to maturity. There is no U.S. governmental subsidy to recuperate this loss.

In contrast, private mortgage loans are less than five years in duration (maturity) and carry a 7.5% to 12 % rate of return with built-in natural hedges, which are the tangible properties used as collateral and the amount of protective equity. This investment is considered illiquid because there is no readily available secondary market to sell private mortgage loans. Therefore, an investor should plan to hold the loan investment until maturity. However, in the unlikely event that the mortgage note needs to be sold, there is an unregulated market to sell these notes, albeit at a discount. In fact, *"mortgage notes and the unregulated marketplace"* is another facet of the private mortgage business industry that could be the subject matter for another research study and book.

Selling private mortgage notes to a mortgage note buyer is one of the largest growing financial trends in the United States today (amerinotexchange.com, n. d.). However, delving into a complete explanation of this growing industry is beyond the scope of the study undertaken for this book project. Suffice it to say that this is a thriving industry with many participants, and like private mortgage investing, it has a steep learning curve that should be obtained before attempting to participate. Nevertheless, the author contends that this other facet of mortgage investing could be a complementary strategy with potentially synergistic effects for the private mortgage lender/investor.

The Risk Mitigation Process

Private mortgage loan investing has the potential to generate a higher rate of return than traditional investment vehicles. Investors can even achieve this goal with a higher degree of safety (as discussed throughout the book). However, it has also been mentioned that there are no 100% risk-free investments, and private mortgage lending is no exception. Hence, there are some investment risks associated with this type of investing.

The risks associated with private mortgage lending can be avoided by effectively and thoroughly performing the due diligence on the investment by following the vetting and underwriting guidelines, such as the following risk-mitigating steps. The investor should assess the following:

❖ Consider the property market.

❖ Request an appraisal report on the property.

❖ Perform a title search.

❖ Verify the lien position.

❖ Require hazard insurance to protect the collateral.

❖ Make sure an attorney reviews all of the closing documents.

Consider the Property Market

Choose properties with resale prices or value in a market segment that possesses the largest pool of potential buyers. For example, properties that have very high values relative to the rest of the market have a smaller pool of potential buyers willing to purchase the property for the appraised price. In the eventuality that a default occurs, the investor should not end up holding a property that might be difficult to sell. In other words, the investor should select properties where high demand exists for those types of properties.

Request an Appraisal Report on the Property

The goal of the private mortgage investor should be to ensure that they have more than enough protective equity to justify the loan opportunity. While an appraisal is just an opinion of value and not a guarantee of value, it should always be done with a trusted and reliable appraiser (see Chapter 7). If the loan opportunity has been referred by a hard money broker/lender who is also providing the appraisal, it might be prudent to request another appraiser unless the private money lender knows and trusts the source of the referral. It is vital for all investors to understand that ethics and integrity are voluntary choices that people make. Thus, the practice of the contract law principle of *caveat emptor*, which means *"buyers beware,"* will always apply to any commercial sales transaction.

Perform a Title Search

A title search will reveal whether land ownership is fee simple (freehold) or leasehold-type ownership. It is important to know the difference between fee simple and leasehold. The difference in these two types of land tenure is very different and affects the value of the real estate. When an investor purchases a fee simple property, they are buying the improvements as well as the land. Fee simple, it's the most complete form of ownership.

If the purchase is for a leasehold-type property, the investor is purchasing a temporary right to hold land or property and is only leasing the land. The lessor (the landowner) does not give the lessee (tenant) any actual ownership rights in the property, only possessive rights. With a leasehold-type property, the terms are customarily long-term leases, which are measured in decades or even centuries. For example, a 99-year lease term is quite common. Prior to the end of the lease agreement, the investor may or may not have the opportunity to purchase or re-lease the land. An example of this type of leasehold agreement is the 99-year lease signed by Britain and China for Hong Kong on June 9, 1898.

The advantage of a leasehold-type arrangement is that the purchase price is much lower—sometimes as low as 50% of the fee simple-type ownership arrangement. Conversely, the disadvantage of leasehold ownership is that the investment ends at the end of the lease. Moreover, lease payments could increase during the term of the lease, and the property value will decrease towards the end of the lease.

A title search, known as an *"abstract"* or *"abstract of title,"* will also identify any outstanding easements, judgments, liens, mortgages, past-due taxes, or any other outstanding claims against the property. Additionally, other items that can appear in the abstract or report are soil survey and water conservation, as well as covenants from homeowner's associations (HOA).

An abstract of title traces back to the original owner of the property, usually starting with the country of origin and follows a detailed lineage to the present. It will disclose ownership in succession, conveyances, details of mortgages, surveys of the boundaries of the property and legal description, any code violations, and compliances. A title search is an essential due diligence step because it will disclose all outstanding claims and attachments to the property. It is crucial for private mortgage investors to know that the property title is clean before committing to the loan opportunity.

Verify the Lien Position

The term first lien position means that the lender or investor has primary priority in the event of a loan default, which subsequently could end up in a foreclosure action proceeding if the defaulted situation does not get remedied. In essence, being in the first lien position on the title will diminish collection risks should there be a borrower's default. Therefore, having a first lien position loan will provide the investor the security that, in the event of a borrower's default, the lender will receive the collateral following the foreclosure process, thus mitigating a complete loss of investment funds as usually occurs with other types of investments.

Require Hazard Insurance to Protect the Collateral

The mortgage lender, whether private or traditional, will require the borrower to carry hazard insurance coverage because the property is the collateral for the loan; therefore, it needs to be protected. Hazards, such as weather events, fires, and vandalism, are considered property risks, which can be mitigated by requiring adequate insurance coverage. In contrast to mortgage insurance, hazard insurance benefits both the borrower as well as the lender.

Make Sure an Attorney Reviews all the Closing Documents

While it is important that private money lenders be knowledgeable in every facet of the lending business, it is also of paramount importance to work with a competent real estate attorney. An attorney that is well versed in all of the intricacies of the private or hard mortgage lending industry is a crucial component to mitigate investment risk.

Having an experienced attorney as part of the investor's team to review all of the loan closing documents and agreements will prevent exposure to otherwise avoidable risks. Engaging a competent attorney in the lending process is an essential risk-mitigating strategy. This is money well spent, and in the opinion of the author, mandatory.

All the vetting and due diligence steps that have been described are imperative to mitigate and minimize the risks of entering into a bad investment loan by the private mortgage lender. Furthermore, to assist with the risk-mitigating process, it is also crucial to have a proper understanding of what constitutes mortgage fraud in order to avoid these potential risks. The next section will address this most important topic.

Understanding and Avoiding the Risks for Mortgage Fraud

Every industry encounters ethical violations and criminal activities, and the mortgage lending industry is no exception. Mortgage fraud is not just limited to predatory lending practices, which essentially are the unfair, deceptive, or fraudulent practices of some lenders during the loan origination process. In other words, mortgage fraud is the imposition of unjust and abusive loan terms on borrowers (Office of Inspector General, 2006, June).

Mortgage fraud, as defined by the Federal Bureau of Investigation (FBI), is described as the material misstatement, misrepresentation, or omission relating to the property or potential mortgage relied upon by an underwriter or lender to fund, purchase, or insure a loan. Consequently, based on the description of this definition by the FBI, it is apparent that mortgage fraud can be committed by the individual borrowers, the mortgage lenders, or both.

It is important to understand that mortgage fraud involves at least two parties: the party providing false information and the party that relies on that information to complete a transaction. In mortgage fraud analysis, law enforcement officials have recognized the existence of two major categories of mortgage fraud, which are as follows:

❖ Fraud for property or housing

❖ Fraud for profit

Fraud for Property or Housing

"Fraud for property or housing" is the type of fraud where a borrower intentionally provides or submits false, incomplete, or inaccurate information in order to qualify for a loan or to obtain more favorable terms than they could achieve without the misrepresented information. Therefore, fraud for housing is what

is classified as borrower-initiated fraud. Essentially the perpetrator inflates their income, assets, or both, as well as misrepresenting their employment status in an attempt to qualify for a loan they would normally not qualify for.

This type of fraud may or may not require a certain degree of collusion from the loan originator, real estate professional, or the appraiser. Fraud for housing is considered to be the least expensive type of fraud to lenders or investors because the objective of the borrower is to acquire and retain the property. Thus, the borrower's intention is to make the mortgage payments. However, problems do arise when borrowers fail to make their payment, which is attributed to the fact that they did not have the financial wherewithal to make those payments. That is why borrower-initiated fraud-type loans are described as being self-underwritten loans. The misrepresentation of the loan information is initiated by the borrowers, which subsequently influences the underwriting process. This type of loan carries a higher failure rate than lender-underwritten loans.

If these loans end up defaulting, according to Dungey (2007), their only redeeming quality or saving grace is that the lender usually will recover more of their funds in a foreclosure than in a fraud-for-profit type case. The penalties imposed on these borrowers will infrequently come in the form of prosecution. The borrower's usual punishment is limited to losing the home and becoming a subprime borrower for the next four to seven years because of the damage to their credit rating.

Fraud for Profit

"Fraud for profit" is a situation where an individual or group of individuals intentionally commits fraud in an attempt to extract money from a property or a transaction. This type of fraud is classified as *"industry insider fraud"* because it requires collusion among several participants, such as real estate brokers and realtors, mortgage broker/lenders, closing agents, or appraisers. Therefore,

fraud for profit is considered a more complex type of scheme that involves multiple parties—that can include mortgage lending professionals—in a financially motivated secret plot in an attempt to defraud the lender of large sums of money.

Such collusion or participation does not always necessitate action on the part of the cooperating or participating professionals. It can merely be an implicit act where the professional fails to disclose or correct a misrepresentation made by an applicant whom the professional knows to be false or fraudulent. While there is an infinite number of variations on fraud for profit, according to results uncovered from FBI investigations, the following fraud-for-profit schemes appear to be the most prevalent:

- ❖ Misrepresented and fraudulent loan documentation
- ❖ Property flipping
- ❖ Straw buyers
- ❖ Silent second
- ❖ Foreclosure rescue schemes
- ❖ Identity fraud
- ❖ Appraisal fraud

Misrepresented and Fraudulent Loan Documentation

The falsification or misrepresentation of documents is considered a type of white-collar crime. There are a variety of white-collar crimes that are deemed non-violent crimes, typically committed in commercial or business situations for financial gain. The term *"white-collar"* refers to the fact that people who commit these crimes are usually high-powered professionals, in contrast to *"blue-collar"* laborers. These crimes involve altering, changing, or modifying a document with the intent to deceive another person. It can also involve the passing along of copies of documents that are known to be false (Clarke, n. d; La Mance, n. d.). In many states like Florida, falsifying or misrepresenting documents to qualify and obtain a mortgage loan is considered mortgage fraud and is a crime punishable as a second-degree felony under Florida Statute No. 817.545.

Property Flipping

Property flipping is a practice whereby a recently acquired property is quickly resold, customarily for a substantial profit. Most property flipping occurs within days or weeks of acquisition, and usually with minimal or no cosmetic improvements. In this type of fraudulent scheme, a real estate property is purchased, promptly appraised at a falsely inflated value, and is then quickly resold. The falsified appraisal is what facilitates this type of fraud, and it is what makes it illegal.

It is important to understand that there is nothing inherently illegal with selling properties within days of their acquisition. However, what makes these transactions fraudulent or unlawful is that the condition of the property is misrepresented, or the property value is artificially inflated.

Straw Buyers

By definition, a straw buyer is an individual who consents to the use of their name and personal credit information by another individual for the purpose of obtaining a mortgage loan with the goal of never inhabiting or residing in the purchased property. In return for the favor, the straw buyer will be offered thousands of dollars to facilitate the transaction, or they may not know that their name and information were used to apply for a loan, as in the case of identity theft.

The straw buyers are customarily willing participants in the mortgage fraud plot or network. Since the initiator of the fraud scheme usually leaves the country after successfully obtaining a large loan amount for the overvalued property, it is not an infrequent occurrence that the straw buyers might end up being sued by the lenders for extending the loan funds. The straw buyers will be legally responsible for participating in the criminal offense, whether or not they were aware of their involvement in the perpetrator's fraudulent mortgage scheme.

However, it is possible straw buyers were deceived into believing they were investing in real estate properties that would subsequently be rented out, with the rental payments used to pay the mortgage loan. If any remaining monies were left, it would be used for profit distribution. Despite the possibility of this deception, ignorance is not a defense, and straw buyers will be responsible legally and financially for the misdeeds of others. Therefore, every individual engaged in any type of commerce or business dealings should understand the concept of caveat emptor, which means *"buyers beware."*

Generally, caveat emptor is the contract law principle that controls the sale of real property once the closing has taken place. However, it may also apply to the sales of other goods or services. The term arises from the fact that buyers customarily have an asymmetrical information disadvantage as it relates to the good or service being purchased, while the seller is more abundantly informed.

Thus, caveat emptor is an implicit warning to buyers that sellers are not bound to volunteer negative information about the items they are selling. It is assumed that unless the seller gives an express warranty, the buyer assumes all risk for any loss due to the defects in the goods or property being purchased. That is why it is of paramount importance to learn how to perform a thorough vetting and due diligence process when engaged in the private mortgage lending business. It is crucial that private money lenders be able to discern all the possible tactics that borrowers and other real estate professionals use to misrepresent information to qualify for a loan or receive a commission.

Silent Second

A silent second is a type of second mortgage loan that is part of a home sale transaction without the knowledge of the first lender. The silent component refers to the seller and buyer not divulging to the primary lender the existence of a second mortgage loan that will be used as the down payment for the purchase of the property. In other words, in a silent second type of mortgage fraud, there is a lack of full disclosure to the first mortgage lender. Typically, the down payment money is used by the lender issuing the first mortgage as security to mitigate their investment risk. However, in a silent second scheme, the borrower lies to the lender regarding the source of the down payment funds.

This type of mortgage fraud is akin to 100% financing because the majority of the down payment is in the form of financing. The danger of this scheme to the primary lender is that the homebuyer only has a minimal amount of capital invested in the property— skin in the game. Should property values decrease, the buyer's equity will be non-existent, which will reduce the incentive of the borrower to keep up with the mortgage payments.

Foreclosure Rescue Schemes

All foreclosure rescue schemes essentially target those individuals whose houses are in danger of imminent foreclosure because of mortgage defaults and are thus desperate to try to prevent losing their homes. Therefore, a foreclosure rescue scheme is a type of fraud that takes advantage of homeowners who have fallen behind on their mortgage payments. While there are many types of foreclosure rescue schemes, the author will describe just a few so that the reading audience can get a sense of the many possibilities that can occur.

Three common foreclosure rescue schemes that are prevalent in the marketplace are as follows:

❖ Equity skimming schemes

- ❖ Lease-buyback schemes

- ❖ Consulting service schemes

All of these schemes will cause different types of harm to the homeowners. However, invariably, all these schemes will result in the owners being forced out of their homes. Thus, losing even more money as a result of all the potential complications and consequences that can arise from such fraudulent schemes.

Equity Skimming Schemes

In equity-skimming or stripping, the perpetrator assumes ownership of the house while allowing the former owner to continue living in their home, provided that rent is paid to the perpetrator, who is now the new owner. To appease the homeowners, the perpetrator will often reassure the property owners that the ownership is temporary in nature and that the victim will later reassume ownership of the home once the terms of the loan are renegotiated.

Ultimately, the result of this scheme is an eviction from the home and complete loss of equity with additional financial losses to the victim. The perpetrator, once ownership is obtained, will either sell the property or allow it to go into foreclosure.

Lease-Buyback Scheme

In this scheme, the foreclosure rescue perpetrator promises the homeowner that their home will be saved from foreclosure, that their damaged credit will be repaired, and that their past-due credit cards and other personal debts could potentially be paid off. In order to accomplish that objective, the homeowner must temporarily sign their property deed over to someone with a better credit score. Moreover, the homeowner is allowed to stay in the home while making lease payments to the perpetrator. Furthermore, the homeowner is promised that they will be able to buy back the house after a certain period of time has passed. However, once the homeowner has signed over the property deed to the perpetrator, they essentially have lost their home.

Consulting Service Schemes

In this foreclosure scheme, a company promotes itself as a foreclosure rescue service offering to act as an agent for the property owner to renegotiate the terms of the loan with the lender, in return for a fee. These companies, after collecting their fee, never actually contact the lender. If they do attempt to negotiate with the lender on behalf of the homeowners, these firms are unlikely to have any negotiating skills that will resolve the property owner's problem. Therefore, the value of the fee may be disproportionate to the service the homeowners will receive. Additionally, these consulting service companies may also encourage the original borrower to avoid any communication with the lender under the premise that such contact would interfere with their efforts to secure a loan modification. In fact, they discourage any contact with the lender because doing so will reveal that the consulting firm has not contacted the lender at all.

Identity Fraud

In this type of mortgage fraud, the mortgage loan applicant uses the name, personal information, and credit history of the stolen identity to apply for a loan.

Appraisal Fraud

Appraisal fraud is a part of most mortgage fraud schemes. The fraud occurs when the home's fair market value is deliberately and fraudulently overstated or understated, depending on the objective of the fraud. When the value is inflated, more money can be obtained. Conversely, when the value is deflated, it can be used to get a lower price on a foreclosed home.

Generally, in this type of fraud, the seller receives the check at closing for the inflated amount, and the seller then pays off the appraiser and any other participant involved in the scheme.

Subsequently, the borrower does not make any mortgage payments, and the house goes to foreclosure. Appraisers have been complaining for decades about the pressure they are subjected to from real estate agents and lenders to submit a property value that supports the purchase price against the money to be loaned. However, despite the conflict of making a living and the pressure imposed on appraisers by other real estate professionals to commit fraud, appraisers have a fiduciary duty to protect the public.

To help fight the prevalence of mortgage fraud and other crimes, on May 20, 2009, Congress passed the Fraud Enforcement and Recovery Act (FERA), which became Public Law 111-21. FERA is an act designed to improve enforcement of mortgage fraud, securities, and commodities fraud, financial institution fraud, and other frauds related to federal assistance and relief programs, for the recovery of funds lost to these frauds and for other purposes. This act essentially amends the federal criminal code to include within it the definition of financial institution: a mortgage lending business or any person or entity that makes, in whole or in part, a federally related mortgage loan. Furthermore, it also defines *"mortgage lending business"* as an organization that finances or refinances any debt secured by an interest in real estate, including private mortgage companies and their subsidiaries, and whose activities affect interstate or foreign commerce.

Therefore, FERA of 2009 essentially expanded the reach of federal law enforcement officials in enforcing mortgage fraud laws. Sentences under FERA can include $1 million fines and up to 30-year prison sentences, which means that mortgage fraud is a serious crime, punishable by significant penalties. Such crimes are commonly prosecuted as wire fraud, bank fraud, and conspiracy. It is also important to know that some states have their own laws that address crimes related to mortgage fraud.

For example, in the state of Florida, Chapter 817 is the law that addresses fraudulent practices. As a result of the mortgage crisis of 2007 to enhance and strengthen Chapter 817, House Bill 743 was crafted by the Florida legislative committee in collaboration with Glenn Theobald, past Miami-Dade County Mortgage Fraud Task Force chairman. House Bill 743 was sponsored by former State Representative Carlos-Lopez Cantera, the current Florida Lieutenant Governor. Moreover, similar Senate Bill 1116 was sponsored by prior Florida Senator Gwen Margolis.

These two bills passed the Florida House and Senate unanimously, which subsequently were signed into law by former Florida Governor Charlie Crist on July 1, 2008. The objective of these two bills was to enhance Chapter 817 by adding section 817.545, which addressed mortgage fraud specifically. As of 2019, Florida Statute 817.545—Mortgage Fraud—reads as follows:

817.545—Mortgage Fraud

(1) For the purposes of the section, the term "mortgage lending process" means the process through which a person seeks or obtains a residential mortgage loan, including, but not limited to, the solicitation, application or origination, negotiation of terms, third-party provider services, underwriting, signing and closing, and funding of the loan. Documents involved in the mortgage lending process include, but are not limited to, mortgages, deeds, surveys, inspection reports, uniform residential loan applications, or other loan applications; appraisal reports; HUD-1 settlement statements; supporting personal documentation for loan applications such as W-2 forms, verifications of income and employment, credit reports, bank statements, tax returns, and payroll stubs; and any required disclosures.

(2) A person commits the offense of mortgage fraud if, with the intent to defraud, the person knowingly:

(a) Makes any material misstatement, misrepresentation, or omission during the mortgage lending process with the intention that the misstatement, misrepresentation, or omission will be relied on by a mortgage lender, borrower, or any other person or entity involved in the mortgage lending process; however, omissions on a loan application regarding employment, income, or assets for a loan which does not require this information are not considered a material omission for purposes of this subsection.

(b) Uses or facilitates the use of any material misstatement, misrepresentation, or omission during the mortgage lending process with the intention that the material misstatement, misrepresentation, or omission will be relied on by a mortgage lender, borrower, or any other person or entity involved in the mortgage lending process; however, omissions on a loan application regarding employment, income, or assets for a loan which does not require this information are not considered a material omission for purposes of this subsection.

(c) Receives any proceeds or any other funds in connection with the mortgage lending process that the person knew resulted from a violation of paragraph (a) or paragraph (b).

(d) Files or causes to be filed with the clerk of the circuit court for any county of this state, a document involved in the mortgage lending process, which contains a material misstatement, misrepresentation, or omission.

(3) An offense of mortgage fraud may not be predicated solely upon information lawfully disclosed under federal disclosure laws, regulations, or interpretations related to the mortgage lending process.

(4) For the purpose of venue under this section, any violation of this section is considered to have been committed:

(a) In the county in which the real property is located; or

(b) In any county in which a material act was performed in furtherance of the violation.

(5)(a) Any person who violates subsection (2) commits *a felony of the third degree*, punishable as provided in s. 775.082, s. 775.083, or s. 775.084.

(b) Any person who violates subsection (2), and the loan value stated on documents used in the mortgage lending process exceeds $100,000, commits *a felony of the second degree,* punishable as provided in s. 775.082, s. 775.083, or s. 775.084.

Since private mortgage investing mostly deals with the lending aspect of the industry, the mortgage investor has to be vigilant of the potential misconduct and misrepresentations of the borrowers seeking to obtain private funds. *Moreover, if the private mortgage investor is also a source of lending for the hard money brokers/ lenders, they should also be vigilant of these lenders as well.* Although this industry offers the income investors tremendous opportunities to generate a safe, consistent, and abundant passive income stream, the private lender must be aware that the industry is also riddled with corruption. That is why it is vital to adequately vet and thoroughly perform due diligence of the borrowers and lenders.

The private mortgage lending business requires a substantial learning curve if the investor wants to be directly involved in the lending process. Therefore, the primary reason investors do not pursue this type of alternative investment is the lack of experience. Underwriting or assessing the risk associated with a hard mortgage loan is a different process than evaluating other types of investments. That is why it is recommended that a novice investor who would like to pursue this type of investing they should seek an honest and knowledgeable private mortgage broker/lender to be used as a mentor. Not possessing the proper level of knowledge of how to vet and underwrite this type of alternative investment will result in unnecessary errors being made, leading to substantial risks and possible losses. Consequently, this lack of expertise will lead to undesirable results and disappointment for the investor who is learning by trial and error.

At the risk of being overly redundant, it should be emphasized again that one of the most prudent and safest things an investor can do to mitigate the risks associated with private mortgage investing is to choose an experienced and ethical hard mortgage lender to assist in evaluating these loan opportunities. Proven and trusted professionals with an established network of resources are the best and most important individuals to help guide the novice mortgage investor through the necessary steps towards a successful investment.

The research undertaken to write this book has demonstrated that private mortgage lending is a safe and suitable investment vehicle that can generate an excellent return on investment (ROI) without taking on too much risk. In the private money lending industry, currently, the interest rate that can be achieved is determined by the lender who is willing to make the loan. Private money lenders (PMLs) are able to charge these high-interest rates, ranging from 7.5% to 12%, in consideration for issuing the loan because the borrowers who seek these types of loans do not qualify for conventional bank loans.

Additionally, these borrowers are not willing to subject themselves to the paperwork scrutiny demands of conventional bank loans or the long waiting time to qualify for these types of loans. The kind of return attainable with private mortgage lending is comparable, and at times better, than those garnered from traditional investments like stocks and bonds. Moreover, these returns can be achieved with more control and safety than traditional market investments.

10

Legal Ways of Holding Title to the Investment Loans

T here are several ways that individuals engaged in the private money lending business can hold title to the assets or loans that are being made. Typically, the legal way to hold title will be determined by the number of loans the lender plans to originate. The lender can hold title personally as sole ownership or through any of the concurrent forms of tenancy ownerships, which generally take the following three forms as shown below:

- ❖ Personally as sole ownership
- ❖ Tenancy in common
- ❖ Joint tenancy with right of survivorship
- ❖ Tenancy by the entirety

Personally as Sole Ownership

The simplest way to hold title to a property or a loan is as sole ownership. As the name implies in sole ownership, the lender alone holds all rights to the loan. This form of ownership is often used by the private money lenders who are beginning their lending activity practice, or simply because they prefer to do it that way. However, holding the title as a sole owner will have a tax implication for the lender because the interest that is earned is treated as ordinary income. For lenders who are married but who want to engage in the lending business by themselves, in order to claim sole ownership of the loan, the spouse should be willing to sign a document, called a quitclaim deed (QCD), which effectively denies the spouse any rights to the loan.

Tenancy in Common (TIC)

Tenancy in common and tenants in common (TIC) refer to arrangements under which two or more individuals are co-owners of a parcel of real estate or a right without the right of survivorship. Therefore, tenancy in common is a specific type of concurrent or simultaneous ownership of real property or a right, such as a loan in the case of private mortgage lending by two or more parties.

This form of co-ownership allows each co-owner to choose who will inherit the ownership interest to be alienated or transferred upon the death of any of the owners of record. In TIC, all tenants hold an individual, undivided ownership interest in the property. This means that each party has the right to alienate—which in legal jargon means to convey or transfer—their ownership interest in a property or a right. This is usually executed by a specific action rather than by the due course of law. This transfer can be done by deed, will, or other conveyances.

In a tenancy by the entirety, which is a concurrent estate between married individuals, neither tenant has the right of alienation (transfer) without the consent of the other party. When a tenant by the entirety dies, the surviving spouse receives the deceased spouse's interest, therefore, acquiring full ownership over the property or right. This process is called a right of survivorship, which is also part of joint tenancy.

In a joint tenancy, a tenant may transfer the property or right; however, once that transfer occurs, the tenancy is changed to a TIC. In essence, when this transfer takes place, no tenant will have the right of survivorship any longer. Another difference between the three concurrent forms of tenancies—tenants in common, joint tenants, and tenants by the entirety—is that tenants in common may hold unequal ownership interests. In contrast, joint tenants and tenants by the entirety own equal shares of the property. Moreover, tenants in common may acquire their interests from different conveyance instruments. Conversely, joint tenants and tenants by the entirety must obtain their interests at the same time and in the same document.

Therefore, tenancy in common is a broader way for a few individuals, who sometimes are not related, to hold title together for a property or a right. In this way, multiple people can hold either equal or unequal portions of one property or right. For example, two individuals can each own 50%, or one may own 60%, with the remaining 40% split between other individuals or any combination thereof. All of these ownership combinations are legally acceptable. Moreover, in a TIC, any owner can independently sell, give, or will their share of the property or right at any time. Because any future transfer could potentially create some friction between the co-owners, a written agreement between the owners specifying how owners can transfer their interest in the property is a customary practice and highly recommended.

As it is with any legal arrangement, there are always advantages and disadvantages with the lawful structure, as has been briefly explained above. Some of the advantages and disadvantages of tenancy in common (TIC) are as follows:

Advantages of Tenancy in Common (TIC)

The advantages of tenancy in common include the following:

- ❖ Provides for unlimited ownership
- ❖ Provides for the unequal ownership
- ❖ Transfer of ownership

Provides for Unlimited Ownership

One of the primary advantages of tenancy in common is that it allows for an unlimited number of individuals to hold title to a property or a right, such as a sole mortgage loan or fractionalized, pooled private mortgage investment. This form of concurrent tenancy can also be advantageous when investing in expensive real estate properties or a jumbo mortgage loan. It is beneficial because a group of individuals can pool their financial resources to purchase a highly-priced property or grant a mortgage loan that individually would have been unaffordable to one investor.

Provides for Unequal Ownership

In contrast to a joint tenancy, which requires the titleholders to have equal ownership of the property or right, a TIC allows the various owners or investors to divide their ownership interest in any proportion that is agreeable to everyone. The typical distribution is for the owners or investors to assign the percentage of ownership based on the contributions of each owner to the property or the right.

Transfer of Ownership

Each owner in a tenancy in common has the right to designate an heir in their testamentary will. If an owner expires, their share of the property or right passes to the person listed in the will. If the property that is transferred to the heir is income-producing, the heir will receive the deceased investor's portion of the income generated by that property. The testamentary will is the legal instrument that permits the investor to provide real property or personal financial inheritance when the grantor passes away.

Occasionally, there has been some confusion regarding the limitations of a *"will."* Historically, it was believed that a *"will"* was limited to conveying real property only, while a *"testament"* applied to dispositions of personal property—hence the reason for the use of the term *"Last Will and Testament."*

However, historical records have indicated that these terms have been used interchangeably; therefore, the word "will" validly applies to both personal and real property. Additionally, a will may also create a testamentary trust that is effective only after the death of the testator (Dukeminier, Johanson, Lindgren, and Sitkoff, 2005).

Disadvantages of Tenancy in Common (TIC)

The disadvantages of tenancy in common include the following:

- ❖ Nonpayment
- ❖ Dissolving a tenancy in common

Nonpayment

Since tenancy in common (TIC) permits an unlimited number of investors to hold title to the property in proportion to the amount of money invested by each investor, this feature of TIC can become a disadvantage. For example, if one of the tenants or owners is unable to meet his or her financial obligation, such as nonpayment of the mortgage obligation or nonpayment of the property maintenance or repair expenses, this situation will financially affect the other owners.

In the case of a private mortgage loan, if that is the investment, then the nonpayment problem can result when there is a property default that will require pursuing a foreclosure action. In this scenario, if one of the owners does not have sufficient funds to cover the proportion of his or her financial obligation to cover the attorney's expenses in the foreclosure process, subsequently, the other tenants will be financially affected.

In these types of situations, if one owner fails to make a payment, the other owners must cover the expenses. Typically, this problem is usually resolved by the other owners facilitating a loan to the nonpaying owner or merely buying off the rights of the owner who is having financial difficulty.

Dissolving a Tenancy in Common

Dissolving a tenancy in common can be a complex legal matter. In a situation where all owners are in agreement to sell the property, the process would be to divide the proceeds according to their existing ownership proportions. However, if all the owners are not in agreement with the sale of the property, one owner can usually obtain a partition action that essentially is a court order that forces the sale of the property. This situation can pose a legal problem as well as being a disadvantage to the owner(s) who wanted to keep the property.

Joint Tenancy with Right of Survivorship (JTWROS)

Joint tenancy is a form of ownership whereby two or more persons share equally in the value of the property or asset involved. The individuals are called joint tenants, and each person has equal rights to keep or dispose of the property. The concept of joint tenancy is to create an equitable form of property transference, whether it is for a married couple, parents and children, or even business partners.

If one of the participants dies, the remainder of the property is transferred to the survivors. This is referred to as the joint tenants with the right of survivorship (JTWROS). Joint tenants can share real estate, brokerage accounts, bank accounts, and other rights. In any case, certain provisions must accompany a joint tenancy arrangement. For example:

- ❖ The joint tenants must own an undivided interest in the property, which means that each tenant will own an equal share in the property or right.
- ❖ The estates of both tenants are fixed and unalterable for life.
- ❖ The joint tenants hold the property under the same title.
- ❖ The joint tenants enjoy the same privileges until one of them passes away.

Advantages of Joint Tenancy

The advantages of joint tenancy include the following:

- ❖ Simplicity

❖ Avoidance of probate court

Simplicity

The primary advantages of a joint tenancy agreement for small estates are its ease and low cost. A fairly simple application is filled out by an attorney or qualified counsel and signed by all the parties concerned. It is quick and inexpensive.

Avoidance of Probate Court

Under normal conditions, when a person passes away, their testamentary will is reviewed by a probate court. It is up to the court to decide whether the willed document is valid and legally binding. The court will also determine if there are any assets and liabilities still outstanding. After determining the debts that must be settled, the remaining assets are distributed among the heirs.

Should the individual die intestate, which means without leaving a testamentary will. Then the distribution process becomes extremely complicated because the court must determine who is entitled to inherit the assets. This complicated probate process will be very costly, as well as time-consuming, taking months and sometimes years to unravel the deceased's bequeathed assets.

With a joint tenancy with right of survivorship (JTWROS), the ownership transfer is automatically executed to the other surviving spouse or business partner. Therefore, avoiding the lengthy and stressful probate process. The only person legally permitted to inherit any assets from the deceased party is the joint tenant. A JTWROS supersedes all provisions of a will or any trust previously established.

Disadvantages of a Joint Tenancy

Holding assets in a joint tenancy will have some disadvantages that could result in some undesirable consequences. The list below will demonstrate some of the disadvantages of holding title in joint tenancy:

- Unnecessary estate taxes
- Change ownership interest into a tenancy in common
- Possibility of creating a gift tax liability
- Unintended consequences of disinheritance
- The property could be subjected to a probate proceeding
- Assets are subjected to creditors
- No fiduciary duty exists

Unnecessary Estate taxes

Placing property in joint tenancy can result in unnecessary estate taxes. By holding title as a joint tenant, it can adversely affect the income tax basis of the assets because the surviving spouse only receives a 50% step-up in basis following the death of the first spouse. This situation could result in the living spouse having to pay unnecessary income taxes if any assets were sold following the death of the deceased spouse (Mahony, 2014).

Change Ownership Interest into Tenancy in Common

In a joint tenancy, any tenant or owner can change the nature of their interest into a tenancy in common (TIC). Subsequently, they can sell or give away their interest at any time during life or at death.

Possibility of Creating a Gift Tax Liability

Placing property in joint tenancy or making major improvements to property already in joint tenancy may cause a gift tax liability unless the joint tenants are U.S. citizens who are married to each other.

Unintended Consequences of Disinheritance

Placing property in joint tenancy may have the unintended consequence of disinheriting children or others. The reason being that property held in joint tenancy passes to the survivor, in spite

248

of what the deceased joint tenant's testamentary will directs and no matter who the decedent's heirs are under state law.

Property Could be Subjected to Probate Proceeding

If the joint owners die in a common disaster, the asset will be subject to a probate proceeding with the additional issue of determining which owner died first.

Assets are Subjected to Creditors

The assets are exposed to the creditors of all the joint owners. If a joint owner has credit issues, files for bankruptcy, is entangled in a lawsuit, or is subject to a divorce proceeding, then the property could be subject to seizure, sale, or collection.

No Fiduciary Duty Exists

In contrast to a trustee in a revocable trust, who in the document states that there is a fiduciary duty to the trust beneficiaries in the management of the assets and care of the same; in a joint tenancy, no such fiduciary duty exists to the other joint owner. For example, in a joint tenancy, if one of the owners gets into financial trouble that leads to loss of the property, there is limited legal recourse for the other joint tenants.

Perusing the list of advantages and disadvantages of joint tenancy should demonstrate to the reader that while a joint tenancy with right of survivorship (JTWROS) is a legal instrument that is useful between married individuals, it should not be employed as the foundation of their estate plan. The reason joint tenancy can undermine an estate plan is that joint tenancy property passes to the surviving joint tenant instantly upon death. This means that such property does not pass according to the deceased's testamentary will or trust if there is one. In other words, joint tenancy has priority over a will or trust (Ridgway, n. d.).

Tenancy by the Entirety (TBE)

Tenancy by the entirety (TBE) is another form of concurrent or joint property ownership. TBE it's offered by some states such as Alaska, Arkansas, Delaware, District of Columbia (DC), Florida,

Hawaii, Indiana, Illinois, Maryland, Massachusetts, Michigan, New Jersey, North Carolina, Ohio, Pennsylvania, Tennessee, Vermont, Virginia, and Wyoming. Tenancy by the entirety is an ownership form that is available only for a husband and wife and must be created by will or deed. The husband and wife hold title together and must make all decisions on the property jointly.

This form of ownership is beneficial because it offers protection from creditors. For example, if one of the spouses has a large debt, the creditor cannot go after the property with this type of joint ownership. For instance, if either the husband or wife is sued, a creditor may place a lien against their interest. However, unlike joint tenancy or tenancy in common, the creditor is not permitted by law to file a petition to partition proceeding.

The creation of a tenancy by the entirety is similar to the creation of a joint tenancy, with the provision that the parties must be married to be able to use a tenancy by the entirety. There are five criteria that must be met in order to form a tenancy by the entirety. They are as follows

- ❖ To use it the parties must be married.
- ❖ The couple must acquire the property or right at the same time.
- ❖ The two parties must acquire title by the same will or deed.
- ❖ The husband and wife must have identical or equal interests in the property or right.
- ❖ The couple must have an equal right to possession.

To maintain the integrity of tenancy by the entirety, all of these five criteria or conditions must be met. Should any of these five conditions be missing, the presumption of most courts will be to assume that the more favored tenancy in common was formed.

At the moment, some attorneys may be reluctant to utilize tenancy by the entirety as a method of holding title because case law has not clearly clarified the advantages and disadvantages of this form of concurrent asset ownership. The current trend among states is to abolish tenancy by the entirety. Many states no longer favor it because often creditors of one spouse cannot levy against property held in tenancy by the entirety (LaMance, n. d.).

Ways to Terminate a Tenancy by the Entirety

Should there be a need to terminate a tenancy by the entirety, there are four ways to accomplish this task. Termination can be done by divorce, joint conveyance, by express or implied agreement, or death.

❖ Termination by Divorce

Upon divorce, a tenancy by the entirety is terminated because the condition of marriage no longer exists. Subsequently, the terms of the divorce will determine the disposition of the property.

❖ Termination by Joint Conveyance

Husband and wife can agree to convey title to the property to a third party. This can be done through gift or deed.

❖ Termination by Express or Implied Agreement

Through mutual agreement, the husband and wife can terminate the tenancy by the entirety. Subsequently, in the majority of cases, a tenancy in common will be formed.

❖ Termination by Death

Upon the death of one of the spouses, the surviving spouse will inherit the title to the entire property.

Advantages of Tenancy by the Entirety

The advantages of a tenancy by the entirety include the following:

- ❖ Creditor protection.
- ❖ Consent is required to transfer property.
- ❖ Right of survivorship.

Creditor Protection

The main advantage of tenancy by the entirety is that judgment creditors of one party cannot enforce their liens against the property. Therefore, this type of ownership will provide creditor protection in a more effective manner than the other two forms of concurrent or joint ownership.

Consent Required to Transfer Property

Neither party can dispose of, divide, or alienate (transfer) their share of the asset without the consent or approval of the other spouse.

Right of Survivorship

There is an automatic right of survivorship with tenancy by the entirety, which means that when one spouse dies, the other gets full title to the property.

Disadvantages of Tenancy by the Entirety

The disadvantages of a tenancy by the entirety include the following:

❖ Property cannot be severed.

❖ One party cannot convey the title.

Property Cannot Be Severed

Property held in tenancy by the entirety cannot be severed by a partition action filed by one of the parties. This provision of a tenancy by the entirety can pose a problem if one spouse disappears or becomes incompetent; there can be subsequent difficulties in transferring or encumbering the property.

One Party Cannot Convey Title

With a tenancy by the entirety, one party cannot convey title to an adult child as is possible under joint tenancy. This situation could create a problem in the eventuality that one of the owners should suddenly die in a car accident that results in the death or injury of other motorists. Since the property is automatically transferred to the surviving spouse in a tenancy by the entirety, this situation can leave the estate of the living spouse vulnerable to future lawsuits.

A Domestic Partner as a Sole and Separate Loan Investor

A domestic partnership is a legal interpersonal relationship between two individuals who live together and share a common domestic life but are neither joined by marriage nor a civil union. This partnership is not identical to a marriage; however, it provides some of the same benefits. Depending on the state where the domestic partners reside, the relationship may also be referred to as a civil union. Still, the definitions may vary from one city or state to the next.

The origin of the term "domestic partnership" was first proposed by gay rights activist Tom Brougham in August of 1979 as a new category of relationship. Initially, the requirements to be classified as domestic partners were based on the fact that two people had to be living together and were also qualified to marry, except that the partners were of the same gender. In the last decade of the twentieth century and continuing into the twenty-first, a number of city and county governments have enacted domestic partnership laws, which include Seattle, New York City, and Broward County, Florida. Moreover, requirements were subsequently added for the partners to maintain mutual financial responsibility and for both to be at least eighteen years of age and able to enter into a legal contract (Domestic Partnership, n. d.).

The terminology for such unions is still an evolving process, and the exact level of rights and responsibilities conferred by a domestic partnership varies widely from one place to another. Some legislatures have voluntarily established domestic partnership relations by statute instead of being ordered to do so by a court. Although some jurisdictions have instituted domestic partnerships as a way to recognize same-sex unions, domestic partnerships may involve either different-sex or same-sex couples (Bishop, 1989).

In a situation where a domestic partner who wishes to hold title solely under his or her name, the title company insuring the title will require that the domestic partner of the person acquiring the title disclaims or relinquishes title and interest to the property or the particular right. This process establishes that both domestic partners want the title to the property to be granted to one partner as that person's separate and sole property or right.

Community Property

Community property is a marital property system or matrimonial regime that has its origins in civil law jurisdictions. However, it can also be currently found in civil law jurisdictions. Community property is a system of property ownership between spouses who provide for the creation or absence of a marital estate. When a matrimonial state is created, it provides the guidelines for what properties are included in that estate, how and by whom it is managed, how it will be divided, and inherited at the end of the marriage.

Therefore, community property is a form of joint ownership of property between married couples. The title on the property is deemed to be jointly owned by both spouses regardless of which spouse purchased the asset until they are divided through divorce, annulment, or death. The major characteristics of holding title by community property are governed by the states in which the spouses reside during their marriage. Consequently, most property acquired by either spouse during the marriage and while domiciled within the community property state is considered to be community property or *communion bonorum*, and is owned jointly by each spouse. The only exceptions to community property ownership are property acquired through gift or inheritance (Stuntz, 2005).

Currently, property acquired during a marriage is recognized in nine U.S. states as community property. In these states, community property is analogous to tenancy by the entirety. *The states that recognize this form of joint ownership are Arizona, California,*

Idaho, Louisiana, Nevada, New Mexico, Texas, Washington, and Wisconsin. In Alaska, married couples can elect to have some or all of their property treated as community property by stating so in a written contract.

In a community property state, the husband and wife each own half the property, and each can *"will"* their half to someone else. They also incur any debts in equal proportions. If the community property is owned with right of survivorship, the surviving spouse will receive the entire property (Stuntz, 2005).

Other Ways of Vesting Title

The term *"vest"* is an important term in the law because it means that a person has an absolute right to some present or future interest in something of value. When a right has vested, the person is legally entitled to what has been promised and may seek relief in court if the benefit is not forthcoming.

For hard money lenders who are engaged in the business of making private mortgage investments for their personal portfolio, there are other ways to hold title to the property or right other than personally or through any of the three types of concurrent tenancies previously described.

There are some other forms of holding title to property or a legal right. All of these forms of holding title have their particular advantages and disadvantages. However, if the private money lender (PML) is planning to engage more intensely in the mortgage lending activity, it might be more tax-efficient for investors to hold title to the loans through one of the various types of corporate entities. These other entities might have more favorable tax consequences. These other entities are as follows:

- ❖ C corporation
- ❖ S corporation or subtitle S
- ❖ Limited liability company (LLC)

❖ Single-purpose entity (SPE)

❖ Series limited liability company (SLLC)

❖ Partnership

❖ Self-directed IRAs

Corporations exist in part to shield the personal assets of shareholders from personal liability for the debts or actions of a corporation. In contrast, in a general partnership or sole proprietorship in which the owner could be held responsible for all of the debts of the company, a corporation traditionally limits the personal liability of the shareholders.

In the business world, there are three types of corporations: a C corporation, an S corporation, and a limited liability company (LLC). They all initially begin as a C corporation before electing or choosing to become an S corporation or an LLC.

C Corporations

A traditional corporation, or a C corporation, is a business structure that is created as a separate, distinct legal entity from its owners or shareholders. Once a corporation is formed, the corporation can have its individual bank accounts, own property and investments, conduct business, and even establish a line of credit, irrespective of the personal accounts or credit of the shareholders.

As previously mentioned, the primary advantage of having a business structured as a corporation is because shareholders are not personally liable for the debts and legal liabilities incurred by the corporation. For example, if a corporation is sued for any kind of business reason, the shareholders will not be required to satisfy the debts of the corporation from their own personal assets. This corporate feature safeguards the assets and properties of the individual shareholders. Therefore, it is more appealing and safer to conduct business for potential investors. The limits of this protection have narrowed somewhat in recent years, and shareholders are increasingly being held personally liable for the wrongdoings of their corporations.

Once a corporation is established, the shareholders must name—by way of an election—a board of directors that is responsible for the operation of the business, making business decisions, and managing all business-related affairs. After the board of directors is elected by the shareholders, they, in turn, will appoint the corporate officers to specific roles, which customarily include a secretary, a treasurer, and directors. However, to ensure that the benefits of the limited liability protection afforded by the corporation continue to protect the shareholders, it is essential to perform and behave like a corporation.

Performing and behaving like a corporation means that the corporation must observe certain corporate formalities. These formalities are processes, such as a required annual meeting of the board of directors, the necessity to maintain the corporate minutes up-to-date, and the separation of corporate and personal funds. Moreover, it is also necessary to maintain all written agreements for all corporate transactions, which include internal transactions such as internal loans, executive compensation agreements, etc.

The preservation of limited liability protection is the primary reason for the existence of a corporation. However, as stated above, if certain corporate formalities are not diligently followed, this corporate protection of limited liability can be lost. The limited liability protection can be lost through the following:

❖ The piercing of the corporate veil.

❖ Defective incorporation.

❖ The improper signing of documents.

The Piercing of the Corporate Veil

Once a business has been incorporated, it essentially has created a separate and distinct legal entity. This incorporation grants the stockholders and the business certain rights and benefits by state law, which can subsequently be enjoyed by the owners of the company. However, these benefits come with some administrative formalities, as previously mentioned, in order to make sure the incorporation is going to protect the stockholders when it's needed the most.

For example, a court may pierce through the corporate veil of liability protection if the corporation does not follow proper corporate formalities, if it is undercapitalized, or if it can be demonstrated that it is a fraudulent incorporation. If the corporate formalities are not followed, the corporation may be deemed not to be functioning as a true corporation, but rather, operating as co-equal owners. To prevent the piercing of the corporate veil, it is imperative that the corporation keeps corporate minutes from the board of directors meetings and not to commingle personal assets with corporate assets.

Following these simple procedures will ensure that the corporation will be viewed as a separate entity in the unfortunate event that it is sued. Liability protection is only as strong as the proper management of the corporate entity. Keeping this concept in mind will serve the business owners well in minimizing business risk (Larson, 2010, December; Piercing the Corporate Veil, 2010, September 14).

Defective Incorporation

Defective incorporation involves mistakes or errors in the creation of the corporation itself. This means that some of the legal requirements of creating a corporation have not been met. Individuals (shareholders) may be held personally liable if the corporation is not set up properly but still proceeds to do business. In such cases of defective incorporation, one can escape personal liability under certain conditions. For example, if a good-faith effort was made to incorporate and a substantial portion of the laws of incorporation was followed, limited liability protection may be granted.

The Improper Signing of Documents

Corporate officers should always sign documents and transact business under the name of the corporation. By signing documents under the corporate name, it will help avoid a claim that the officer is personally liable for a corporation's default or that the officer was transacting business on his or her own behalf and not on behalf of the corporation.

The officer's title should be clearly written next to his or her name and signature. When signing documents on behalf of a corporation, both the name of the corporation and the signer's representative position within the corporation must be stated.

Advantages of a C Corporation

- ❖ Limited liability for shareholders
- ❖ Certain tax benefits
- ❖ Prestige for the business and corporate officers
- ❖ Credibility
- ❖ Ability to raise capital and attract investors

Disadvantages of a C Corporation

- ❖ Double taxation pitfall
- ❖ Increased paperwork
- ❖ Necessity of exercising and maintaining corporate formalities

S Corporation or Subtitle S

With the Tax Reform Act (TRA) of 1986, the S corporation became a highly desirable entity for corporate tax purposes. An S corporation is not a different type of corporation. It is a special tax designation applied for and granted by the IRS to corporations that have already been formed. An S corporation, for federal income tax purposes, is a closely-held corporation that makes a valid election to be taxed under Subchapter S of Chapter 1, sections 1361 through 1379 of the Internal Revenue Code. Generally, S corporations do not pay any federal income taxes. This type of corporation is what is called a *pass-through type of entity* where income or losses are divided among shareholders, which subsequently must be reported on the shareholder's own individual income tax return. Therefore, according to the IRS, S corporations are corporations that elect to pass corporate income, losses, deductions, and credits through to their shareholders for federal tax purposes.

To qualify for S corporation status, the corporation must meet the following requirements:

- ❖ Be a domestic corporation
- ❖ Have only allowable shareholders
  - May be individuals, certain trusts, and estates
  - May not be partnerships, corporations, or non-resident alien shareholders
- ❖ Have no more than 100 shareholders
- ❖ Have only one class of stock
- ❖ Not be an ineligible corporation (i.e., certain financial institutions, insurance companies, and domestic international sales corporations)

Many entrepreneurs and small-business owners are partial to the S corporation because it combines many of the advantages of a sole proprietorship, partnership, and corporate forms of business structure. The S corporations essentially have the same basic advantages and disadvantages of a general or close corporation with the added benefit of the S corporation special tax provisions.

When a standard corporation, whether general, close, or professional, makes a profit, it pays a federal corporate income tax on the profit. If the company declares a dividend, the shareholders must report the dividend as personal income and pay more taxes. However, S corporations avoid this double taxation because all the income or losses are reported only once on the personal tax returns of the shareholders. Thus, income is taxed at the shareholder level and not at the corporate level. Moreover, like standard corporations and unlike some partnerships, the S corporation shareholders are exempt from personal liability for business debt.

Restrictions of S Corporations

To elect S corporation status, the corporation must follow certain specific guidelines. As the result of the 1996 Tax Law, also known as the *William S. Lee Quality Jobs and Business Expansion Act,* which became effective January 1, 1997, many of these qualifying guidelines have been changed. A few of these changes are noted below:

❖ Prior to the 1996 Tax Law, the maximum number of shareholders was 35. The maximum number of shareholders for an S corporation was increased to 75 and is currently 100.

❖ Previously, S corporation ownership was limited to individuals, estates, and certain trusts. Under the new law, the stock of an S corporation may be held by a new, electing small business trust. All beneficiaries of the trust must be individuals or estates, except that charitable organizations may also hold limited interests. Interests in the trust must be acquired by gift or bequest and not by purchase. Each potential current beneficiary of the trust is counted towards the 100 shareholder limit on S corporation shareholders.

❖ S corporations are now allowed to own 80% or more of the stock of a regular C corporation, which may elect to file a consolidated return with other affiliated, regular C corporations. The S corporation itself may not join in that election. In addition, an S corporation is now allowed to own a qualified subchapter S subsidiary. The parent S corporation must own 100% of the stock of the subsidiary.

- ❖ Qualified retirement plans or Section 501(c) (3) charitable organizations may now be shareholders in S corporations.

- ❖ All S corporations must have shareholders who are citizens or residents of the United States. Nonresident aliens cannot be shareholders.

- ❖ S corporations may only issue one class of stock.

- ❖ No more than 25% of the gross corporate income may be derived from passive income.

- ❖ An S corporation can generally provide employee benefits and deferred compensation plans.

- ❖ S corporations eliminate the problems faced by standard corporations whose shareholder-employees might be subject to IRS claims of excessive compensation.

- ❖ Not all domestic general business corporations are eligible for S corporation status.

These exclusions include the following:

- A financial institution that is a bank
- An insurance company taxed under Subchapter L
- A domestic international sales corporation (DISC)
- Certain affiliated groups of corporations

How to File as an S Corporation

To become an S corporation, the applicant must know the mechanics of filing for this special tax status. The first step is to form a C corporation, or close Professional Corporation, in the state of the applicant's choice. Second, the applicant must obtain the formal consent of the corporation's shareholders.

This consent should be noted in the corporation's minutes. Once the filing is approved, the company must complete Form 2553, Election by a Small Business Corporation. This form must be filed with the appropriate IRS office in the region where the application is located. The applicant should review the IRS's instructions for Form 2553 to determine the proper deadline for completing and submitting this form.

The company or attorney that creates the corporation for the business owner can assist the applicant in preparing and submitting the IRS Form 2553 as part of the incorporating process. This is a simple enough process that the applicant's accountant or the applicant himself can perform.

Advantages of S Corporations

Some of the advantages of an S corporation include the following;

- ❖ Eliminating double taxation
- ❖ Limited liability protection to shareholders
- ❖ Potential for a greater number of investors
- ❖ Easier accounting rules

Eliminating Double Taxation

In an S corporation, profits and losses are passed through to the company shareholders, and taxes are only paid once. Everyone should check with their state to determine how it handles S corporations. For example, some states do not recognize S corporations and will tax such businesses as regular C corporations. Some states charge S corporations a state tax, although the corporation will not have to pay federal tax.

Limited Liability Protection for Shareholders

As the owner of an S corporation, the shareholder's personal assets are separate from those of the business. Therefore, these assets are protected in case any judgments occur against the business.

Potential for a Greater Number of Investors

Originally, the maximum number of shareholders an S corporation could have was 35. Subsequently, it was increased to a maximum of 75, and currently, an S corporation can have as many as 100 shareholders.

Easier Accounting Rules

S corporations without any inventory can use the cash method of accounting, which is a much simpler method than the accrual method. The business owner should verify with their accountant which option makes more sense for their business.

Disadvantages of S Corporations

The disadvantages of S corporations include the following:

- ❖ Rules and fees
- ❖ Shareholder restrictions
- ❖ Salary requirements

Rules and Fees

Like a C corporation, S corporations are required to file several official state and federal documents, such as the Articles of Incorporation. Additionally, corporations are required by law to document many aspects of their existence. This documentation includes the corporate minutes, which are notes taken during meetings of shareholders and the board of directors. This meeting must be held regularly during the year, as well as paying the annual corporate filing fee. All of these requirements are important to prevent piercing the corporate veil and losing the limited liability protection.

Shareholder Restrictions

Realize that if an S corporation has shareholders, the shareholders will be taxed for any income the company has, even if no income distributions are made. Conversely, in a C corporation, the shareholders are taxed only if they receive dividend distributions. Additionally, S corporations are only allowed to issue one class of stock, which may discourage some investors.

Salary Requirements

The Internal Revenue Service (IRS) requires all officers and owners of S corporations to take a salary, even if the company is not yet making a profit. Even though this could be problematic for new businesses struggling to make payroll. A reasonable salary is what a person with the appropriate skills needed for the position would be paid on the free market.

Taking a salary from the corporation, although there is no profit, is a confusing area of S corporation taxation. Because when a company is starting out, the business typically goes through a two or three-year cycle where sometimes it is losing money, and other times it is breaking even. After those few years of struggle, the business will either fail or start making a profit. However, in the start-up years, the funds being used customarily are considered the paid-in capital from the shareholders to start the venture. Therefore, if the salary the owner is receiving—if any—is the owner's own money, how can a shareholder be receiving a salary and paying taxes when there are no profits.

Although this is the language used by the IRS regarding this topic, it is a wise practice to consult with a tax professional who has expertise of handling small business taxation issues. The accountant could perform an examination of the cash-flow projections for the business to find a solution that will be defensible before the IRS in the event that the corporation is not distributing any salary and gets audited.

Limited Liability Company (LLC)

Limited liability companies (LLCs) have long been a traditional form of business structure that has been used in Europe and Latin America. An LLC is a hybrid entity that combines the limited liability protection of a corporation with the flexibility and simplicity of a partnership. The main feature an LLC has in common with a corporation is the limited liability aspect, and the primary characteristic it shares with a partnership structure is the availability of pass-through income taxation.

The LLC business structure was introduced in the United States by the state of Wyoming in 1977 with the passage of its *Limited Liability Act*. Subsequently, in 1988, the IRS authorized that LLCs be taxed in a way similar to partnerships as pass-through entities. Even though an LLC is considered a business entity, essentially, it is a type of unincorporated association, and thus it is not a corporation (Stafford, 2010, June 17). However, it is often more flexible than a corporation, and it is well-suited for companies with a single owner. Many business professionals believe LLCs present a superior alternative to corporations and partnerships because they combine many of the advantages of both.

A vital component of limited liability companies is the need for having an LLC operating agreement. An LLC operating agreement is a formal document that allows the members to create a structure for the LLC that is customized to the needs of the business. Therefore, the operating agreement allows the owner(s) to structure financial and working relationships with other co-owners in a way that is beneficial to the business. Additionally, the operating agreement is used to establish the members' ownership percentage, their share of profits and losses, their rights and responsibilities, as well as determining what will happen to the business if a member leaves or dies.

Many states do not legally require an LLC to have an operating agreement. Moreover, each state has laws called *"default rules"* that dictate basic operating rules for LLCs. Therefore, if an LLC does not have an operating agreement, then the company will be governed by the state's default rules, which might not be in the LLC's best interest. By having this essential operating agreement, the owner(s) can choose the rules that will govern the LLC's inner workings, rather than having to follow default rules that may or may not be right for the LLC.

The main reason for creating an operating agreement is to ensure that courts will respect the limited liability protection feature of the LLC. Having this agreement is especially vital in a one-member LLC where, without the formality of the agreement, the LLC will appear to be more like a sole proprietorship. Therefore, having a formal written operating agreement will lend credibility to the LLC's separate existence. Experts contend that it is foolish to operate an LLC without this document, even for a one-owner company (Laurence, n. d.).

Advantages of LLCs

A limited liability company (LLC) has many advantages as a form of business entity. The list below demonstrates some of the advantages of an LLC business structure:

- ❖ It is a pass-through taxation entity
- ❖ Limited liability protection
- ❖ Entity classification election
- ❖ Only one owner is required
- ❖ Harder to pierce the LLC's veil
- ❖ Enduring legal business entities
- ❖ Assignment of member interest

It is a Pass-Through Taxation Entity

Just like sole proprietorships, partnerships, and S corporations, LLCs are classified as pass-through entities for federal income tax purposes. These types of entities are not subject to income tax. Instead, the owners are directly taxed individually on the income, taking into account their share of the profits and losses. This means that there is no double taxation unless the LLC elects to be taxed like a C corporation.

Limited Liability Protection

Like shareholders of a corporation, all LLC owners are protected from personal liability for business debts and claims. This protection means that if the business itself cannot pay a creditor, such as a supplier, a lender, or a landlord. The creditor cannot legally come after the LLC member's house, car, or other private possessions. Only the LLC assets are used to pay off business debts; thus, LLC owners stand to lose just the money that they invested in the LLC. In essence, this is the limited liability feature of this type of entity. Therefore, LLC members are protected from some or all the liability acts and debts of the LLC, which are dependent on state shield laws.

Entity Classification Election

An LLC can elect to be taxed as a sole proprietorship, partnership, S corporation, or C corporation, which provides for a greater degree of flexibility. This entity classification election is made by filing IRS Form 8832.

Only One Owner is Required

A limited liability company (LLC) is a corporation and partnership hybrid that allows the members or owners the decision-making freedom of a partnership along with the liability protection of a corporation. However, each state interprets this hybrid status differently, which may determine the type of ownership required. Typically, most states require that an LLC have at least one member or owner.

Harder to Pierce the LLC's Veil

It is harder to pierce the LLC's corporate veil because this business structure does not have as many formalities to maintain, as is the case for corporations. As long as the LLC and the members do not commingle funds, it would be difficult to pierce this veil. Moreover, there are no annual shareholder meeting requirements, as well as less administrative paperwork and recordkeeping requirements. Currently, only Tennessee and Minnesota are exempt from these requirements. However, laws and regulations are invariably evolving; therefore, the reader should follow the recommended premise of always seeking the counsel of a professional well-versed on the subject to avoid any legal problems.

Enduring Legal Business Entities

LLCs can be enduring legal business entities with lives that extend beyond the illness or even the death of their members or owners. This feature can help avoid potential business termination problems, as with the death of a sole proprietor. However, to have this enduring live feature, the LLC must include the appropriate provisions in the operating agreement.

Assignment of Member Interest

The membership interests of LLCs can be assigned, and the economic benefits of those interests can be separated and assigned, which provides the assignee with the economic benefits of distributions of profits and losses—similar to a partnership—without transferring the title to the membership interest. However, the assigning of a membership interest is subject to the LLC act of each state.

Disadvantages of LLCs

While a limited liability company (LLC) offers many advantages over other forms of business entities, there are also some disadvantages. Some of the drawbacks to selecting an LLC over another type of business structure are as follows:

- ❖ Legal uncertainty
- ❖ Raising capital
- ❖ Earnings are subject to self-employment taxes
- ❖ Potential to lose pass-through tax status
- ❖ Loss of accounting cash method
- ❖ Loss of stock option incentives
- ❖ Lack of uniformity
- ❖ The requirement of LLCs to elect partnership treatment

- ❖ Unequal tax treatment
- ❖ Minority discounts
- ❖ Possible recognition of appreciated assets

Legal Uncertainty

As previously mentioned, in 1977, Wyoming became the first state to enact rules and regulations for the formation and operation of an LLC. Therefore, the newness or originality of the LLC is one of the disadvantages of the structure. LLC laws are still evolving, and case history is limited in terms of interpreting LLC business laws.

Raising Capital

Raising capital can be a challenging endeavor for an LLC because the company does not have the ability to issue stocks and bonds like a corporation. This means the company has to rely on the contributions of its members to finance its business activities.

Earnings are Subject to Self-Employment Taxes

The earnings of most members of an LLC are generally subject to self-employment taxes. This varies from the earnings of an S corporation, in which after paying a reasonable salary to a shareholder who also works for the business, the remaining earnings can be passed through as distributions of profits and thus are not subjected to self-employment taxes.

Potential to Lose Tax Pass-Through Status

LLCs are considered partnerships for federal income tax purposes. Therefore, if 50% or more of the capital and profit interests of the LLC are sold or exchanged within a twelve-month period, the LLC will lose its federal pass-through tax provision.

Loss of Accounting Cash Method

If more than 35% of the LLC losses can be allocated to non-managing members, the limited liability company may lose its ability to use the accounting cash method.

Loss of Stock Option Incentives

A limited liability company that is treated as a partnership cannot take advantage of stock option incentives when engaged in tax-free reorganizations or issuance of Section 1244 stock. This type of equity or stock is named after the section of the Internal Revenue Code (IRC) that describes its treatment under tax law. Section 1244 of the tax code allows losses from the sale of shares of small, domestic corporations to be deducted as ordinary losses instead of as capital losses—up to a maximum of $50,000 for individual tax returns or $100,000 for joint returns (Investopedia, n. d.).

Lack of Uniformity

There is a lack of uniformity among limited liability company statutes. Businesses that operate in more than one state may not receive consistent treatment.

Requirements of LLCs to Elect Partnership Treatment

In order to be treated as a partnership, an LLC must have at least two members. Conversely, S corporations can operate with only one shareholder. Although all states allow single-member LLCs, the entity is not permitted to elect partnership classification for federal tax purposes with just one member. The business files Schedule C as a sole proprietor unless it elects to file as a corporation.;

Unequal Tax Treatment

It is essential to understand the tax treatment of LLCs to address the structure selection appropriately. For example, some states do not tax partnerships; however, they do tax LLCs. An LLC is an entity created by state statute, and depending on the elections made by the LLC and the number of members; the IRS will treat an LLC either as a corporation, partnership, or as part of the owner's tax return, which is classified as a *"disregarded entity."* A disregarded entity is a business entity that is separate from its owner but, elects to be *disregarded as separate* from the business owner for federal tax purposes. Specifically, a domestic LLC with at *least two members* is classified as a partnership for federal income tax purposes unless it files Form 8832 and affirmatively elects to be treated as a corporation.

Conversely, a single-member LLC (SMLLC) is treated as a disregarded entity unless it files Form 8832 and affirmatively makes the election to be treated as a corporation. In other words, if a single-member LLC does not elect to be treated as a corporation, the LLC is a disregarded entity, and the LLC's activities should be reflected on its owner's federal tax return (IRS.gov, n.d.).

An individual owner of a single-member LLC that operates a trade or business is subject to the tax on net earnings from self-employment in the same manner as a sole proprietorship. If the single-member LLC is owned by a corporation or partnership, the LLC should be reflected on its owner's federal tax return as a division of the corporation or partnership (Single Member LLCs, n. d.).

Minority Discounts

Minority discounts for estate planning purposes may be lower in a limited liability company than in a corporation. Since LLCs are easier to dissolve, there is greater access to the business assets. Some experts believe that limited liability company discounts may only be 15% compared to between 25% and 40% for a closely-held corporation.

Possible Recognition of Appreciated Assets

Conversion of the status of an existing business to a limited liability company could result in tax recognition on appreciated assets, which can have a negative tax consequence.

Federal Taxation Treatment of LLCs

Before January 1, 1997, the Internal Revenue Service (IRS) determined whether an LLC would be taxed like a partnership or a corporation by analyzing its legal structure or by requiring the members to elect the tax status on a special form. Effective January 1, 1997, the IRS simplified the interpretation of this process.

The IRS stated that pursuant to these new IRS regulations, if a limited liability company has satisfied IRS requirements, it can be treated as a partnership for federal tax purposes. As such, LLCs are required to file the same federal tax forms as partnerships and take advantage of the equivalent benefits. However, this is still a highly evolving technical area that requires further clarification. Should additional information on this subject be required, it is recommended that the Internal Revenue Service or a competent professional such as a qualified tax accountant or attorney be consulted.

Single Purpose Entity (SPE)

Single-purpose entities (SPEs) are sometimes required by mortgage lenders to facilitate some real estate financing transactions. A single-purpose entity is an entity that exists for only one single purpose, which is the ownership and operation of a parcel of property. An SPE essentially is an LLC or corporation that holds title to real estate and owes a mortgage to a lender. As the name implies, an SPE owns only one asset and the mortgage to that asset; thus, it does not have any other assets or liabilities.

The SPE will usually lease its only property to another company, comprised of the same owners. The second company, in contrast, can execute leases to tenants, hire a management company or provide for necessary services, and generally incur all liabilities associated with the management of the property. The SPE business structure is usually required by a lender as a condition of extending a mortgage loan.

The purpose of this type of entity is to insulate the collateral from the claims of other creditors. For example, if the second company must file for bankruptcy because it is not able to pay creditors, that does not stop the lender from foreclosing unless the SPE also files for bankruptcy. If the SPE files for bankruptcy, it is much easier for the lender to lift the automatic stay and proceed with the foreclosure because it has the only vote for issues such as approving a plan of reorganization under Chapter 11.

If there were many creditors, consisting of the janitorial service, utilities, tenants, and others, then those other creditors could force the mortgage lender to consent or comply with a plan of reorganization that is not in the lender's best interests. This process is called a *"cram-down,"* which is the involuntary imposition by a court of a reorganization plan over the objection of some classes of creditors. However, with only one creditor, which is the mortgage lender, there is no possibility that a cram-down can occur. For the lenders, requesting an SPE structure can prove beneficial in protecting their loans in the event of a bankruptcy. Although the SPE structure cannot provide absolute protection to the lender, case law in this area has evolved to a point where lenders have a substantial degree of comfort that some significant protections are created. Furthermore, since the cost and burden of record-keeping of the SPE requirements do not fall on the lender's shoulders, it is an additional protection that is cost-effective for lenders (Single-Purpose Entity. n. d.).

Series Limited Liability Company (SLLC)

A series limited liability company, commonly known as a series LLC and sometimes abbreviated as SLLC, is a form of a limited liability company that provides liability protection across multiple series or cells. Consequently, each series theoretically is protected from liabilities arising from the other series. The series LLC is a relatively new concept in business ownership structure; however, the concept of multiple LLCs has been around for some time. In its overall structure, the series LLC has been described as a master LLC that has separate divisions.

This corporate structure has been compared to an S corporation with qualified subsidiaries (Qsub). A qualified subchapter S subsidiary (Qsss), also known as a Qsub or Qsss, is simply an S corporation that is owned by another S corporation. Therefore, a Qsub is treated as a subsidiary of the parent S corporation. The benefit of this structure is that only the parent S corporation needs to file a tax return to the federal and state governments because the income and deductions of the Qsub are combined with the parent S corporation income and deductions. To be treated as a Qsub, the parent S corporation needs to make the election by filing IRS Form 8869 by March 15th of the first year that the parent S corporation wants to treat the subsidiary S corporation as a Qsub (Nelson, n. d.).

An SLLC is the latest—and is considered by far—the most sophisticated form of business entity ever created, as some experts contend. The concept behind this business structure is that a single entity may be formed in a state, but separate series or cells may be internally created within the LLC. The series LLC is an innovative concept that was created by the state of Delaware in 1996 under Delaware's Code Annotated Title 6, Section 18-215 of the Delaware statute. This type of LLC structure has been receiving more and more attention lately.

The series LLC is essentially a single umbrella entity that has the ability to partition its assets and liabilities among the various sub-LLCs or series. Consequently, each sub-LLC may have different assets, economic structures, members, and managers. The profits, losses, and liabilities of each series are legally separate from the other series, thereby creating a sort of firewall between each series. The benefit of this corporate structure is that it eliminates the administrative burden and expense of forming multiple LLCs. The structure is very similar to a parent corporation with subsidiaries only without the expense, formalities, and taxation implications (Staub, n. d.).

The assets of a particular series are protected from enforcement against the assets of the parent LLC or any other series or cells if the following requirements are maintained:

- The LLC agreement provides for the establishment of one or more series.

- Separate and distinct records are maintained for each series; the assets are accounted for separately from the assets of the parent LLC or any other series as described in the LLC operating agreement.

- Notice of such limitation of liability is set forth in the LLC's certificate of formation (see Del. Code Ann. Tit. 6; Section 18-215(b)). However, a member or manager may agree to be obligated personally for any or all of the debts, obligations, and liabilities of one or more series (see Delaware Code Annotated Title 6, Section 18-215(c).

Series LLCs are considered to be the most advanced business structure and planning tool of the future. It is a business structure that offers advantages in planning for various types of business. For example, it can be used in such businesses as hedge funds, venture capital funds, oil and gas arrangements, as well as fractional ownership or sharing arrangements. Moreover, complex business arrangements can sometimes be better managed using a series LLC (Rutledge, 2009).

As previously mentioned, the first state to enact the concept of series LLCs (SLLCs) was Delaware. Within the Delaware series LLC statute, there was a provision that provided for the protection of the assets of one series from the liabilities of another series. Because of this feature of series asset protection, the concept of the SLLC was originally introduced to help the mutual fund industry avoid having to file numerous Securities and Exchange Commission (SEC) reports for their various classes of funds. Moreover, because a series LLC business structure permits multiple series or cells to operate independently from the parent LLC, the motivation for the mutual fund industry to use this type of entity was because it allowed them to operate many funds under one business entity. Therefore, it provided the benefit of filing one SEC report under one umbrella—the parent LLC—and still permitted the individual fund activities to conduct business separately (Rutledge, 2009).

Other states that have enacted their own version of the series LLC structure have stopped short of these internal walls that the Delaware SLLC provides. However, they still give each series or cells what amounts to a different business entity—having separate rights, powers, and duties from the other series, as well as distinct rights or obligations to participate in profits or losses.

The states that have adopted series LLCs, other than Delaware, are Illinois, Iowa, Nevada, Oklahoma, Tennessee, Texas, Utah, Wisconsin, and the Commonwealth of Puerto Rico. There are several other states considering series LLC legislation. The fact that a state has not adopted a series LLC statute does not prohibit one from forming a Delaware series LLC and having it registered to do business within the state, though there may be complications in doing so.

Like LLCs in general, the Delaware series LLCs are not without certain risks. There are numerous unresolved issues regarding the series LLC, including, without limitation, tax and creditor/debtor issues, such as the interaction between the Federal Bankruptcy Code and state series LLC law. Furthermore, some practitioners have expressed some concerns that the Internal Revenue Service will not permit the series LLC to file just one tax return for all the series combined, which is the primary benefit of an SLLC. For example, the California Franchise Tax Board's position is that each series in a Delaware series LLC is considered a different LLC. Therefore, it must file its own Form 568 Liability Company Return of Income and pay its own separate LLC annual tax and fee if it is registered or doing business in California (Limitedliabilitycompanycenter. com, n. d.).

To address some of these concerns, the IRS, on November 8, 2010, issued a Notice of Proposed Rulemaking (NPRM) by proposing regulation 119921-09 on domestic series limited liability companies. This reg. 119921-09 should help give taxpayers and their advisors more confidence in using series LLCs as a method of dividing a business venture into a variety of units or cells to accomplish a variety of business objectives (Staub, n. d.).

The commitments from the IRS under the proposed regulation 119921-09 to treat an LLC and its series units together as separate entities under federal tax law should make taxpayers who have avoided implementation of a series LLC structure, out of caution, reconsider the benefits from this business arrangement. Advocates of series LLCs perceive the new regulations as an attempt by the IRS to give series LLCs equal footing with a master LLC type of structure, within which an upper-tier LLC owns one or more lower-tier LLCs. Many practitioners are hopeful that the use of series LLCs will expand as a result of this added attention by the IRS.

Despite optimism over the expansion of series LLCs into different business operations, the primary limit to the progress of this business structure may not be the IRS as much as the state laws themselves. It is not clear whether the IRS action will incite the remaining states without series LLC statutes to adopt them. However, what is apparent is the continuing importance of looking to individual state series LLC laws to determine rights and obligations.

Advantages of a Series LLC

The advantages of a series LLC include the following:

- ❖ Reduced startup costs
- ❖ Protection of assets
- ❖ Flexibility of administration
- ❖ A less complex entity structure than a corporation or subsidiary structure
- ❖ Less sales tax
- ❖ Only one state registration
- ❖ Only one tax return

Reduced Startup Costs

Only one filing fee is required, and an attorney can set up the parent and series or cells at less cost than setting up multiple LLCs. This feature makes this entity structure cost-efficient.

Protection of Assets

The use of a series limited liability company (SLLC) has shown a certain degree of popularity and growing sophistication that is being employed in asset protection strategies. The use of the various series or cells to partition the SLLC assets, debts, obligations, liabilities, and rights among separate series facilitates segregating the company's assets and liabilities. The act of segregating the SLLC's assets and liabilities can provide a greater degree of asset protection that could help businesses avoid bankruptcy and protect their assets. The formation of this business structure essentially can protect the assets within each series or cell from judgments against assets in other series.

Flexibility of Administration

Anyone can set up as many LLCs as they want; however, each LLC would be separate and would have to be administered individually, which would increase the cost of operation. Therefore, a series LLC allows the owners or members to save on administrative time and expenses.

A Less Complex Entity Structure than a Corporation or Subsidiary Structure

A series LLC does not possess the same complexities of taxes, structure, and formalities as a corporation with various subsidiaries.

Less Sales Tax

Depending on the regulations in the state of domicile, the rent paid by one cell to another cell in the series might not be subject to sales tax. However, each state has its own regulations; therefore, this information should always be verified to determine what applies to the SLLC in question.

Only One State Registration

Only the parent LLC must be registered with the state, which means fewer legal costs and registration fees. It also means just one annual or biennial fee is needed for the series.

Only One Tax Return

Only the parent LLC is required to file a tax return, which includes all the series or cells of the LLCs. However, the complexity of the tax return will be greater than a return for a single company, which will require an accountant well-versed in such tax returns.

Disadvantages of a Series LLC

The disadvantages of a series LLC include the following:

- ❖ No separate registered agent
- ❖ Separate bank accounts and accounting
- ❖ Cost of formation
- ❖ Bankruptcy treatment uncertainty

No Separate Registered Agent

It is likely that the state will require a separate registered agent for each LLC in the series, which means an additional expense for all of these registered agents.

Separate Bank Accounts and Accounting

Each LLC series will need its own bank account, and because each series is producing separate financial statements, each must have distinct accounting records. If there are numerous series, then the administrative burden is greater.

Cost of Formation

The cost of forming a series LLC may be higher than the cost of forming a regular LLC. For example, the state of Illinois charges \$600 to form a typical LLC and \$850 for a series LLC. It is important to note that these costs can be quite fluid and can change rather quickly. However, the benefit is that should more series be required in the future; there are no additional fees for increasing the number of series.

Bankruptcy Treatment Uncertainty

Although the SLLC can offer a substantial reduction in cost and effort for business owners, as a business structure, it has not garnered much use in the business world, due mainly to the uncertainties surrounding the entity (Dawson, 2010). Because the series LLC concept is relatively new, there are many legal issues still to be clarified. For example, there is no authority on how series LLCs will be treated in jurisdictions where there are no series statutes, or whether the SLLC's limited liability protection provision will be upheld in federal court.

A related but more limited question is whether a separate series is considered a *"person"* who may file for bankruptcy, or whether the parent LLC is required to file on behalf of the series, which can potentially expose all the other series to the claims of the creditors in bankruptcy. Moreover, it will be important to see whether a single series or cell will have the ability to stand on its own as a different entity from its parent LLC in a bankruptcy proceeding. However, because of the lack of legislation, case law, and practice, these questions are still uncertain (Dawson, 2010).

It is crucial at this juncture to stress the importance of seeking competent legal and financial counsel for anyone who is contemplating the adoption of this type of business structure. The purpose of this section of the book is to provide general information about a new and changing type of business entity for the benefit of the reading audience. Moreover, while every effort has been made to research and validate the legal veracity of the information contained in this chapter, it is prudent to consult with a competent and well-versed professional on the subject before embracing any of the concepts herein described.

Partnerships

According to the Internal Revenue Service (IRS), a partnership is a relationship between two or more persons that join together to carry on a trade or business. With each person contributing money, property, labor, or skill, and each expecting to share in the profits and losses of the company whether or not a formal partnership agreement is made. Therefore, a partnership arises whenever two or more people co-own a business and share in the profits and losses of the company.

The legal system of common law addresses three types or forms of partnerships, which differ based on the level of involvement of the partners as it relates to management rights and personal liability. The three forms of partnerships are as follows:

- ❖ General partnership
- ❖ Limited partnership (LP)
- ❖ Limited liability partnership (LLP)

General Partnerships

A general partnership involves two or more partners who perform the full range of business functions for the management of the company. Consequently, general partners share equal rights and responsibilities in connection with the management of the enterprise, as well as meeting all the financial obligations of the partnership. In other words, any individual partner can bind the entire group to a legal obligation in addition to each partner assuming full responsibility for all business debts and obligations.

Although partnerships possess very restrictive personal liability responsibility, it does have a tax treatment advantage. The partnership profits are not taxed directly to the business, but instead, they are passed through to the partners, who subsequently must include their gains on their individual tax returns, which could be at a lower tax rate.

Limited Partnership (LP)

In a limited partnership, the law restricts the personal liability of each limited partner to the amount of money they invested in the business. The reason for this protection is that a limited partner is considered a passive owner that merely injects or contributes capital to the business. Hence, they are not held personally liable should anything go wrong with the business. However, this form of partnership requires that there should be at least one general partner that must accept general partnership status, exposing this partner to full personal liability for the business's debts and obligations. Therefore, the general partner retains the right to control the business, while the limited partners do not participate in any management decisions. Conversely, the two classes of partners, general and limited, will benefit from the business profits.

Limited Liability Partnership (LLP)

In a limited liability partnership (LLP), there are no general partners. Every partner is considered a limited partner in theory and has limited personal liability. However, in this form of partnership, the limited liability partners can participate in the micro-management of the business and still be afforded partial, if not complete, protection against personal liability for the mistakes of other partners. This feature of an LLP is an incentive for investors to help finance companies because their risk of personal liability is diminished.

Moreover, limited liability partnerships (LLPs) retain the tax advantages of the general partnership structure, in addition to offering some personal liability protection to the participants. The individual partners in a limited liability partnership are not personally responsible for the wrongful acts of other partners, or for the debts or obligations of the business. Because the LLP form changes some of the fundamental aspects of the traditional partnership, some state taxing authorities may subject a limited liability partnership to non-partnership tax rules. However, as far as the IRS is concerned, these businesses are viewed as partnerships, and thus it is allowed for partners to use the pass-through tax treatment.

Definitions of Partnership and Partner

The Internal Revenue Code (IRC) 26 U.S. CODE § 7701, states that a *"partnership"* may include any of the following arrangements. A limited partnership, a syndicate, a group, a pool, a joint venture, or any other unincorporated type of organization through which any business, financial operation, or venture is carried on, as long as it is not within the meaning of regulation, a trust, an estate, or a corporation. The term *"partner"* includes a member in such a syndicate, group, pool, joint venture, or organization. Therefore, a joint undertaking merely to share expenses is not a partnership. Mere co-ownership of property that is maintained and leased or rented is not a partnership. However, if the co-owners provide services to the tenants, then a partnership does exist.

Business Owned and Operated by Spouses

Generally, if a husband and wife jointly own and operate an unincorporated business and share in the profits and losses, they are partners in a partnership, and they must file Form 1065. The purpose of IRS Form 1065 is to file an information return, which is used to report the income, gains, losses, deductions, credits, etc. from the operation of a partnership. A partnership does not pay tax on its income but passes through any profits or losses to its partners.

Partners must include partnership items on their tax or information returns. Therefore, a partnership is an arrangement in which parties agree to cooperate to advance their mutual interests to carry on business for profit as co-owners, as governed by the Uniform Partnership Act. A partnership may hold title to real property or private mortgage loan investments in the name of the partnership.

There are distinct partnership advantages and disadvantages, as with any other type of business structure.

Advantages of Partnerships

Some of the advantages of partnerships include the following:

- ❖ Are easy to establish
- ❖ Ability to raise more capital
- ❖ Incentive to attract potential employees
- ❖ Possibility of creating synergy
- ❖ Can be cost-effective
- ❖ Possibility of team enhancement

Are Easy to Establish

Partnerships are relatively easy to establish. In most U.S. states, the investor merely files the required paperwork with the state's division of commerce and pays the applicable fee(s), which is usually $100 or less. There could be additional requirements, such as a business license, occupational license, permits, surety bond, and insurance. Setting up the partnership is the easy part of the process.

Ability to Raise More Capital

With more than one owner, the ability to raise funds may be increased, both because two or more partners may be able to contribute more funds and because their borrowing capacity may be greater.

Incentive to Attract Potential Employees

Prospective employees may be attracted to the business if given the incentive and opportunity to become a partner.

Possibility of Creating Synergy

A partnership may benefit from the combination of complementary skills of two or more people. Essentially, there is a wider pool of knowledge, skills, and contacts.

Can be Cost-Effective

Partnerships can be cost-effective, as each partner specializes in certain aspects of their business.

Possibility of Team Enhancement

Partnerships create a team approach that can provide moral support, which may facilitate a more creative brainstorming and synergistic working environment.

Disadvantages of Partnerships

Some of the disadvantages of partnerships include the following;

- ❖ Liable for the actions of other partners
- ❖ Work and time contribution conflicts
- ❖ Potential for disagreements to arise
- ❖ Partnerships may have a limited life span
- ❖ Growth limitations
- ❖ Requires flexibility in decision-making
- ❖ General partners have unlimited liability

Liable for the Actions of Other Partners

Business partners are jointly and individually liable for the actions of the other partners, which depends on the form of partnership.

Work and Time Contribution Conflicts

Profits must be shared with others. The partners will have to decide how they value each other's time and skills. Problems could arise when a partner is contributing less time due to personal circumstances.

Potential for Disagreements to Arise

Since decisions are shared, disagreements can occur. A partnership is for the long term, and expectations and situations can change, which can lead to dramatic and traumatic split-ups.

Partnerships May Have Limited Life Span

The partnership may have a limited life; it may end upon the withdrawal or death of a partner.

Growth Limitations

A partnership usually has limitations that keep it from becoming a large business.

Requires Flexibility in Decision-Making

The partners will have to consult with each other and be open to more negotiating because decisions need to be made jointly. Therefore, partners will be required to be more flexible and patient.

General Partners Have Unlimited Liability

A significant disadvantage of a partnership is unlimited liability. General partners are liable without limit for all debts contracted, and errors made by the partnership. For example, if one partner owns 1% of the partnership and the business fails, that partner will be called upon to pay 1% of the partnership's debt, and the other partners will be responsible for covering their 99 % obligation. However, if the partners owning the remaining 99% cannot meet their obligations, then the partner who owns the 1% may be obligated to pay all the debts, even if that partner must sell off all of his or her possessions to do so. This feature makes partnerships too risky for most situations.

Business Partnerships Need a Prenuptial Agreement

If the decision is made to set up a partnership business structure, then a safe business practice to follow is to create a business prenuptial agreement to protect the business in the event a partner leaves. This prenuptial agreement serves the same function as a premarital agreement, but for a business. In America, the divorce rate is 41% for first marriages, and 60% and 73% for second and third marriages, respectively (Baker, n. d.).

Based on those statistics, it would be a wise decision to have a prenuptial agreement. However, the biggest impediment in asking for one is because such a request suggests a lack of trust. The success rate for business ventures is even worse than for marriages. For example, the failure rate for a first-year business is 85%, and for second and third-year businesses, the failure rates are 70% and 62%, respectively. Therefore, having a pre-business agreement is of paramount importance. In the business world, there are individuals who still believe that a handshake is an honorable, noble, and romantic way of doing business. However, while such chivalrous behavior and business arrangements make great theater, in real life, they are short-sighted, ignorant, and risky (Ritholtz, 2012, January 4).

In business dealings, just as in marriage, misunderstandings are common. It is also not a well-known fact that success may create more problems than does failure. Money affects our behavior, and no one is cognizant of how they will react to the process of making or losing money until they have experienced the actual event (Adams, n. d.). Therefore, it is good practice when going into business with a partner to get a pre-business prenuptial agreement. If the investor is already in business, it is never too late to sit down with the partner and draft an agreement that will be mutually beneficial to all parties.

The pre-business prenuptial agreement should describe what will happen to the company in the event that any of the following should occur:

- ❖ Terminating the business relationship.
- ❖ Contemplating retirement.
- ❖ Going through a personal bankruptcy.
- ❖ Wishing to sell their company shares to another investor.
- ❖ Going through a divorce.
- ❖ Partner passes away.

Moreover, the agreement should also delineate the job description of the partners, define the limits of their authority, establish the remuneration guidelines, and create a buy-out agreement. Establishing these pre-business guidelines will reduce or remove most of the uncertainties that can develop in any business venture.

Investing through a Self-Directed IRA

An Individual Retirement Account (IRA) is a form of retirement account that provides investors with certain tax benefits for retirement savings. Some common examples of IRAs used by investors include the following:

❖ Traditional IRA

❖ Roth IRA

❖ Simplified Employee Pension (SEP) IRA

❖ Savings Incentive Match Plan for Employees (SIMPLE) IRA.

All IRA accounts are held for investors by custodians or trustees. These may include banks, trust companies, or any other entity approved by the IRS to act as a trustee or custodian. A self-directed IRA arrangement is an IRA that permits the owner of the account to make a wider range of investments than can typically be made with a traditional type of IRA. The flexibility offered by a truly self-directed IRA is probably one of the best benefits that the government has provided to the investor in the history of tax-advantaged government retirement plans. The range of permissible investments that can be used in a self-directed IRA is greater than for the traditional IRA.

In fact, the Internal Revenue Code (IRC) does not describe what a self-directed IRA can invest in; however, it does state what is not allowed as an investment. These types of unallowable investments are classified as prohibited transactions, which, in essence, are investments that are in violation of IRS tax rules and laws as they relate to self-directed IRAs (Investor alert, 2011). Defined in IRC

4975(c) (1) and IRS Publication 590, these rules were established to ensure that everything the IRA engages in is for the exclusive benefit of the retirement plan.

The term *"self-directed IRA"* is actually a descriptive name devised by the marketplace. In reality, the IRS does not care what people call an IRA because their only concern is that investors do not violate the rules that have to be followed by all IRA account holders. The objective of the prohibited transaction rules is twofold: 1) to encourage the use of IRAs for the purpose of accumulating retirement savings, and 2) to prohibit those in control of IRAs from taking advantage of the tax benefits for their personal account. In essence, the goal of these prohibited transactions is meant to protect the security and the retirement integrity of the IRA account.

Essentially, the only two types of investments that the IRS disallows or prohibits from being purchased by a self-directed IRA are life insurance contracts and collectibles. Collectible investments can encompass the following items:

- Any work of art
- Rugs
- Antiques
- Metals
- Gems
- Stamps
- Sports or entertainment cards and related memorabilia.
- Alcoholic beverages, such as wines or scotch collections.
- Coins—the exceptions allowed are certain U.S. gold, silver, and platinum coins minted by the Treasury Department. The investor may also invest in certain gold, silver, platinum, and palladium bullion that is allowed to be used to settle a Commodities Exchange-regulated futures contract.

Furthermore, the account holder cannot be engaged in any self-dealing activity, which, in essence, constitutes prohibited transactions. The IRC Section 4975 defines a prohibited transaction as a transaction between a plan (the IRA) and a disqualified person. According to the IRS prohibited transaction rules, disqualified persons are defined to be the IRA account holder, other fiduciaries, certain family members such as lineal descendants and spouses of lineal descendants, businesses, corporations, LLCs, trusts, and partnerships where the account holder controls more than 50% of the ownership, or anyone who is considered to be a disqualified person.

Custodians and trustees of self-directed IRAs will allow investors to invest retirement funds in other types of assets. For example, investors are permitted to invest in such things as real estate, promissory notes, tax lien certificates, tax deed sales, private placement securities, and private mortgage investing, which is the focus of the research undertaken to write this book. While self-directed IRAs may offer investors access to these arrays of private investment opportunities, it is important to note that investments in these kinds of assets may possess unique risks that investors should understand and consider. Those risks can include a lack of disclosure and liquidity, as well as the risk of fraud.

To mitigate investment fraud as it relates to self-directed IRAs, the Securities and Exchange Commission (SEC) recommends that investors avoid unsolicited investment offers of any kind. However, investors should be especially cautious of unsolicited investment offers that promote the use of self-directed IRAs. That is why becoming an educated consumer regarding all forms of investment vehicles is crucial to prevent being exposed to investment fraud.

The reason why fraud is such a temptation in this industry is that according to a 2011 report by the Investment Company Institute, U.S. investors held approximately $4.7 trillion in IRAs. The estimates from various sources approximate that investors hold 2%, or $94 billion, of IRA retirement funds in self-directed IRAs. This large amount of money held in self-directed IRAs makes them attractive targets for fraud promoters. Fraud promoters also may target other types of retirement accounts by attempting to lure investors into transferring money from those accounts to new, self-directed IRAs in order to participate in the fraud promoter's scheme (Investor alert, 2011).

Despite these potential risks, self-directed IRA accounts give investors much more control over their investments than traditional IRA accounts. This control stems from the account owner's ability to choose the type of investments they wish to own. For example, private mortgage investing is a permissible investment within a self-directed IRA. In essence, with a self-directed IRA, almost any investment vehicle is permissible to the investor for their consideration, except for prohibited transactions such as collectible items. However, as previously explained, gold and silver investments are permissible by the IRS. Therefore, a self-directed IRA account allows the investor a greater degree of diversification in their investment portfolio than from the customary stocks, bonds, mutual funds, and CDs. Participation in these other types of investments can help reduce the overall volatility of the investor's portfolio by way of diversification.

This chapter has provided numerous examples of the many ways that investors can hold title to the private mortgage investments they make. Some of the ways of holding ownership title can be better than others, which can provide tax benefits as well as providing limited liability protection. However, there is not a single best way to invest; the ultimate decision of how to hold title to mortgage investments lies with the personal preference of the investors and the number of loans that are made.

11

Managing the Private Mortgage Investments

C urrently, the private mortgage lending industry has billions of dollars in private mortgage notes and deed of trust, which are being held by individual private lenders/investors. It is expected that more private mortgages are being made every day as the result of the housing financial crisis of 2008 and the tightness in lending rules being implemented by traditional banks, which makes it harder for borrowers to qualify for a loan.

Moreover, because the Federal Reserve has artificially opted to create a low-interest-rate environment in an attempt to stimulate the economy, this situation has incentivized individual investors to search for alternative ways to increase their return on investment (ROI). One investment option that has been discovered by investors seeking higher yields is investing in private mortgage loans. This trend of maintaining a low-interest-rate environment is expected to continue under the Trump administration. Therefore, as more private money lenders/investors discover that they can generate a safer and more consistent income stream from private mortgage investing, this industry will continue to grow substantially.

Consequently, as the result of a lack of mortgage servicing and managing expertise by most of these new private mortgage lenders/ investors, this situation poses both a dilemma for the mortgage investor and an opportunity for the servicing industry. The majority of these novice private mortgage lenders are either unfamiliar with the process of managing or servicing the loans they are making, or they merely do not have the time or the inclination to undertake their own mortgage servicing duties. This lack of knowledge, time, or desire to manage these assets is what presents the opportunity for mortgage servicing companies to grow and fill this need.

Besides these individual private lenders, even the smaller to medium-size private money lending firms simply do not have the time, the up-to-the-minute servicing compliance knowledge, nor the systems and tools required to handle in-house the loan servicing functions. This servicing function entails the tracking of interest payments, late-payment fees, payment collection, disbursement of investors' interest payments, and the handling of the occasional foreclosures and legal issues that occur from time to time. For these private lending broker firms, the best way to continue their lending activity is to outsource the loan managing and servicing functions. These mortgage servicing firms for a fee will provide all the services necessary to manage these assets for the mortgage lenders/investors or broker/lender firms.

Therefore, because of the growth in the private money loan industry, the servicing side of the industry has also evolved and grown from the need to service these private mortgage loans that are increasingly being made by individuals and private lending companies. Thus, the mortgage management process encompasses all the necessary functions required to maintain the mortgage loan from its inception upon approval through its eventual payoff or foreclosure (in the event of a default). However, whether the mortgage managing and servicing functions are outsourced or done in-house by the private lenders themselves, they are an essential component in mitigating the risk of these types of investments.

Mortgage Management Process

Loan servicing is the process by which a company such as a mortgage bank or mortgage servicing firm collects interest, principal, and escrow payments from a loan borrower. The payments that are collected by the servicer are then remitted to the various pertinent parties. For example, payment distributions typically include paying property taxes and insurance from escrowed funds, remitting principal and interest payments to investors holding private mortgage promissory notes, and remitting fees to mortgage guarantors, trustees, and other third parties providing services.

The level of service varies depending on the type of loan and terms negotiated between the servicer and investor procuring their services. Some of the services provided by servicers may include activities such as monitoring delinquencies, preparing and mailing borrower reminder letters and account statements, submitting late-payment notices, making collection calls, and executing foreclosures if required— just to name a few. In exchange for performing these functions, the servicer typically receives specified servicing fees in addition to other ancillary sources of income, such as participating in early prepayments and late fee charges.

The following list describes most of the functions that take place to maintain the mortgage management process properly. However, just like in any other business, as investors and servicing companies are exposed to different types of scenarios that might come up during the course of conducting business, they will gain more experience that could potentially increase the size of the list below.

❖ Preparing borrowers statements

❖ Mailing out borrowers' payment reminder letters

❖ Collecting and disbursing mortgage interest payments

❖ Sending late payment notices and collection of late payment fees

- ❖ Monitoring and ensuring that property taxes are paid
- ❖ Monitoring and ensuring hazard Insurance coverage is in place
- ❖ Monitoring property values to assess the market
- ❖ Monitor for property liens
- ❖ Maintaining proper recordkeeping of all pertinent documentation
- ❖ Initiate foreclosure and collective action in the event of a default
- ❖ Preparing payoff statements
- ❖ Issuing end of the year IRS forms 1098 and 1096
- ❖ Compliance notice

Preparing Borrowers Statements

Customarily, management servicing companies will prepare and submit a mortgage payment letter to all customers on a monthly basis to remind them of the upcoming mortgage payment.

Mailing out Borrowers' Payment Reminder Letters

Occasionally, some borrowers will be late in submitting their mortgage payments. Therefore, the mortgage servicing company will send reminder letters to their mortgagors, letting them know that mortgage payments have not been received.

Collecting and Disbursing Mortgage Interest Payments

If a mortgage servicing company has been contracted to perform the loan management process, they will be the ones being paid the monthly mortgage payments by the borrower. Subsequently, the servicing company will pay or disburse to the lender their interest payments minus the management fees as per agreement.

Sending Late Payment Notices and Collection of Late Payment Fees

In the event that the borrower pays the mortgage payment late (after the customary ten or 15-day grace period), the mortgage servicing company will send a letter to the borrower reminding them that a late fee has been incurred as the result of exceeding the grace period. Most mortgage payments are due on the first of each month, and payments received after the 10th or the 16th are subject to a late fee. This late fee is typically 5% of the monthly mortgage payment.

Borrowers who develop a tendency to pay past their grace period and do not include the late charge with their payment may start a cycle of repeated late charges. In this type of situation, the mortgage lender or company may deduct the late fee from the payment; thus, the payment is posted short.

Monitoring and Ensuring that Property Taxes are Paid

If an escrow account was not set up during the initial documents at closing, the lender has the added responsibility of monitoring the borrower's tax payments every year. If the borrower falls behind on his property taxes, the lender could end up in the middle of a property tax lien sale, which, in essence, it is a foreclosure brought forth by the county where the property is located.

The lender who is confronted by this type of situation would most likely intervene by paying the property taxes in order to stop the county foreclosure sale. All of these potential problems can be avoided if the lender requires that an escrow account is made a condition of receiving the loan. This way, the lender is the one responsible for paying the taxes. The escrow account can also be set up to pay for hazard insurance.

Although the lender has the right to make the escrow account a condition for receiving the loan, this is usually a negotiable option.

If the borrower is allowed to pay the taxes and insurance coverage, typically the mortgage agreement will have the language to the effect that if the borrower fails to pay these obligations on time, then the lender has the right to set up the escrow account. Thus, the escrow account becomes the responsibility of the lender to collect and pay the taxes and insurance.

Monitoring and Ensuring Hazard Insurance Coverage is in Place

In the same way that the lender or servicing company monitors payments of property taxes, hazard insurance coverage is also monitored to ensure the loan is protected. If the borrower (mortgagor) has not paid their hazard or homeowner's insurance, and it has lapsed, the lender should purchase a policy and add the cost to the monthly installment payments.

If the hazard insurance has been escrowed and paid by the lender, their name should appear as a loss payee in the policy. This way, in the event of a lapse in coverage, the lender will be informed of the non-payment of insurance. Thus, in the event of damage to the property, the lender will receive the funds for the repairs and not the borrower. If the borrower receives the money for the damages directly, there is no guarantee the repairs will be completed according to code specifications, if at all. In fact, the lender should always be named as a loss payee in the insurance policy, even if an escrow account is not set up to collect for this expense.

At a minimum, once a year, the borrower's hazard or homeowner's insurance coverage should be monitored and reviewed to ensure that there is sufficient coverage for the mortgage and that the lender as the noteholder is the mortgagee on the policy. Reviewing appropriate insurance coverage is particularly essential in areas of growing house values.

Monitoring Property Values to Assess the Market

At least twice per annum, one should cultivate the habit of inspecting the homes in which loans have been made. The lender or representative should drive by the property to assess if any serious signs of disrepair or lack of property maintenance can be seen. Surprisingly enough, during this type of drive-by inspection, mortgage lenders have often discovered that the borrower is not maintaining the property as stipulated in the mortgage agreement. Occasionally, the lender uncovers that the borrower is not living in the property and has rented it out to a tenant.

Monitor for Property Liens

Research the county tax records once or twice a year for new liens on the property. These new liens could be in the way of a second mortgage, which may not be allowed per the mortgage note agreement. If there is no escrow account set up for the property, there could be tax lien certificates, tax deed liens, and state or federal tax liens. It is vital for the private lender to monitor the properties they have funded so they can mitigate any adverse legal issues that can occur from time to time.

Maintaining Proper Recordkeeping of all Pertinent Documentation

The lender or servicing company should ensure detailed records are kept of all payments made on the loans. These should include the date of payment, check number, returned check information, amortization schedule, late payments, and copy of postdated envelopes that will assist in proving late-payment fees, should it become necessary to confirm late-payment arrival. Moreover, all correspondence and all transactions associated with the asset should be kept. All of this documentation will be required if there is a dispute, a default, or litigation of any kind.

Initiate Foreclosure and Collection Action in the Event of a Default

If the borrower defaults on the mortgage payments, the lender should contact a qualified real estate attorney to initiate any legal remedies provided by the law. The lender should not attempt to negotiate a solution to the problem with the borrower without the advice and guidance of a competent attorney well-versed in the foreclosure field.

Preparing Payoff Statements

A payoff letter is requested by the borrower from the lender in order to pay off a loan. Once the payoff letter is requested, the lender or servicing company will prepare a payoff statement. The payoff statement is a document signed by a lender indicating the amount required to pay a loan balance in full and satisfy the debt. This document is used in the settlement process to protect both the lender's and borrower's interests.

Typically, payoff statements can apply to any sort of loan; however, they are most commonly prepared for mortgages. The payoff statement will provide for the borrower or mortgagor what is called the payoff amount, which differs from the current loan balance. The payoff amount is the total amount the borrower will actually have to pay to satisfy the terms of the mortgage loan and pay off the entire debt.

The payoff amount is different from the current loan balance, which is the amount the borrower or mortgagor owes as of the date of the payoff statement. The payoff also includes the payment of any interest the lender is owed up through the day the borrower intends to pay off the loan. Additionally, it may include other fees the borrower has incurred that have not been paid. For example, this could include late payment fees, prepayment penalties, and attorney's fees, just to name a few (see Appendices F & G).

Once the mortgage has been paid off, the borrower will receive a satisfaction of mortgage, which is essentially a legal document generated by a mortgage lender or the lender's attorney. The satisfaction of mortgage document confirms that the lender no longer has any control over, or ownership of, the property because the loan has been fully paid. This document is customarily submitted directly by the lender to the county clerk so the clerk can update the property deed.

This document is the borrower's proof that the property is owned free and clear. It is always a good idea to search the county records to make sure the satisfaction of mortgage has, in fact, been filed. If it has not, the mortgagor can submit the satisfaction of mortgage directly to the clerk to update the deed.

Issuing End of the Year IRS Forms 1098 and 1096

IRS Form 1098 must be submitted for reporting earned mortgage interest of $600 dollars or more that has been received by the private money lender from any individual, including a sole proprietor, during the year while engaged in the lending business. The $600 dollar threshold applies separately to each mortgage. Therefore, a separate Form 1098 must be filed for each mortgage. IRS Form 1096 is used to summarize all the information that is physically mailed to the IRS. If the lender paper-files Form 1098 with the IRS, then he or she must send Form 1096 as the transmittal document for all the 1098 forms the lender has issued.

Compliance Notice

Every mortgage servicing and loss mitigation company must comply with federal and state regulations by being licensed and registered in the name of the company associated with their specific business address. Consumers—for their protection before contracting with any of these companies—should verify their compliance by checking with www.nmlsconsumeraccess.org by entering the company name or any information requested by the site. Once this is done, the consumer should follow the instructions being requested by the website. They will be able to access the company's federal and state ID numbers.

The National Mortgage Licensing System & Registry (NMLS) Consumer Access website is a free service for consumers to confirm that the financial services company or professional with whom they wish to conduct business is authorized to conduct business in their state. Users of NMLS Consumer Access are subject to the Terms of Use Agreement.

The mortgage management and servicing function can be performed by either a standalone mortgage servicing company or by a mortgage broker business that is also engaged in the mortgage lending side of the business. Mortgage brokerage firms that also provide the mortgage servicing component for their investors/lenders as an extension of the primary business, typically do it because it allows for another source of revenue for the firm. Additionally, it helps them to optimize the customer services function and to instill further management controls over their investors.

Performing the mortgage servicing and management function is a tedious process that requires a great deal of knowledge to execute this function effectively. For the novice private lender, the learning curve is steep. That is why most new—and at times experienced— lenders outsource these functions for their private mortgage lending business. They just want to participate in the private lending business without the time-consuming hassle of the day-to-day activities. However, a word of caution to the investor/lender is appropriate at this point: like in any other business industry, not all mortgage servicing and managing companies provide excellent service, although most of them do an adequate job.

It is always a good idea for the investor to learn to perform all of the functions involved in the mortgage managing and servicing process. Once the investor/lender has acquired a certain degree of competency in the process regarding all of the activities of mortgage servicing, then it would be safe to outsource the service. The implementation of this strategy is crucial because not only will the investor learn, but it will also let them know if the mortgage managing and servicing company is performing competently. In this way, if the servicing company is not rendering an adequate service, the investor can take over the managing function until another service provider can be found or simply keep doing it themselves and save the servicing fees.

Customarily, mortgage servicing companies charge between 1% and 2% of the monthly mortgage payments. Some companies have a schedule of various fees that they charge for the different functions or services they provide. These fees can add up to a hefty sum, especially if a substantial amount of funds has been invested in private loans. Therefore, it is essential that if these fees are being paid, the investor should feel safe that the job has been performed efficiently and competently.

It is important to point out—again—that a conflict of interest situation could arise when the broker/lender business is both the referral source for the loan opportunity and the mortgage servicing company. The conflict could be even greater with broker lenders who, besides referring and servicing loans, also invest in the private mortgage opportunities they offer to their investors. Although this practice is common with some brokers, a further conflict of interest might arise if the private lender/investor must use the mortgage servicing of the referring broker as a condition to participating in the loan referral opportunity. While not all broker lenders are unethical, having a business structure as just described poses substantial risks for the private money lending investors. Be careful with business structures where the broker lender wants to retain too much control over his loan referrals. For an explanation of conflict of interest, the reader can peruse Chapter 3.

12

Private Mortgage Investing

Versus

Income Producing Property Ownership

T his chapter will examine the advantages and disadvantages of whether it is better to invest in private mortgages, or it is best to own the income-producing real estate property. Firstly, the advantages and disadvantages of direct ownership will be addressed, followed by the same analysis for private mortgage investing. Secondly, the mathematical calculations for both types of investments will be demonstrated so the reader can obtain a visual appreciation of the difference between both types of investment.

Investing in income-producing properties with the objective of renting them to generate an extra income stream or cash flow has proven to be a wise strategy for many real estate investors. However, investing in real estate with the goal of multiplying the investor's returns is not always as simple as it is claimed to be. Real estate investments can also prove to be very risky for investors who are not familiar with the advantages and disadvantages of purchasing income-producing investment properties.

Notwithstanding these risks, possessing a thorough understanding of the benefits or advantages of real estate investing will show that the advantages have proven to prevail over the disadvantages.

Therefore, to survive in the real estate rental market, it is essential for the investor to understand the advantages and disadvantages of purchasing these types of properties.

Advantages of Income Producing Real Estate

Some of the advantages of purchasing income-producing real estate are as follows:

- ❖ Generating an extra income stream.
- ❖ Real estate values are less volatile than stock market investment.
- ❖ Tax benefits of real estate investing.

Generating an Extra Income Stream

Purchasing a property for the purpose of renting can be a wise decision to generate an extra income stream. However, this type of investment is only considered advantageous when the landlord is able to rent the property at a rate higher than the total costs of the investment, thereby hopefully generating a positive cash flow or income stream. The costs of the investment include the mortgage payment, property taxes, insurances, maintenance costs, and miscellaneous expenses.

Real Estate Values are Less Volatile than Stock Market Investment

Real estate is considered a long-term investment, and over time, most properties will tend to appreciate in value. What makes real estate a less volatile investment as compared to stock market investments is that real estate properties always have a residual or base level value in contrast to stocks or a business, where everything can be lost overnight.

Tax Benefits of Real Estate Investing

If the rental property is generating a loss, the tax laws can help the investor financially by reducing the owner's tax liability. The investor is allowed to depreciate the value of the real estate to create a reduced current cash flow against a non-cash expense. However, if the property is operating at a loss, it could be that the investment is not being effectively managed or that the purchase was executed without the proper financial due diligence.

Disadvantages of Income Producing Real Estate

An income-producing or rental real estate investment, as with any type of investment, also has its disadvantages. Some of these disadvantages include the following:

- ❖ Finding qualified tenants can be a difficult task
- ❖ Minimizing vacancy rates
- ❖ Unforeseen extra expenses
- ❖ Legal risks
- ❖ Maintenance of the real estate property

Finding Eligible Tenants can be a Difficult Task

When an investor purchases a property for the purpose of generating rental income, the most significant challenge they may face is finding a responsible tenant who will take proper care of the property and pay the rent on time. Finding good tenants can be a challenging task, especially in bad rental locations or in a bad economy.

In fact, bad tenants can prove to be the biggest risk in getting involved in the business of owning income-producing property. The reason bad tenants pose the most significant risks is that these types of tenants could damage the property intentionally or unintentionally and never pay the rent on time, or simply plan to be evicted while living on the property for free. They could even involve the landlord/investor in legal proceedings, which could make things worse. On many occasions, the landlords might have to resort to an eviction process to remove the tenants who violate the rental agreements, which could be a very expensive *"Pandora's box."*

Minimizing Vacancy Rates

Depending on the location of the rental property, it could take time to fill vacancies. For the income-producing property investor, the worst-case scenario is to have too many vacancies because the expenses continue in the way of mortgage payments, property taxes, insurance, maintenance cost, and management company fees if the landlord is using this type of service. Even if the property is fully paid, there still can be a substantial amount of expenses.

Unforeseen Extra Expenses

Unforeseen expenses is another major disadvantage of owning rental property. There can be many hidden expenses that result from property ownership. For example, there are costs associated with home repairs, advertising to find the tenants, screening prospective tenants, rental registration with the local city or county, and property management, and legal fees, just to name a few.

Legal Risks

Landlords are exposed to litigation risks from their properties. Thus, they face the need to protect their assets with appropriate steps like obtaining insurance or titling the property ownership under a legal entity like an S corporation or a limited liability company (LLC) to reduce personal liability exposure (see Chapter 10). However, all extra steps that are implemented to mitigate the risks of legal exposure will increase the costs of maintaining the property.

Maintenance of the Real Estate Property

Property ownership includes many types of responsibilities. The investor must ensure the proper maintenance and care of the property, which can involve an enormous amount of time, and frequently it will require more financial resources than was first envisioned. Moreover, depending on the municipality of the real estate, there can be legal requirements such as installing appropriate security devices, smoke detectors, and any other device that is called for by the building code. Therefore, rental property is not always a guaranteed type of investment.

Investing in Private Mortgages

A careful review of the previous information will reveal the fact that investing in direct ownership of the income-producing property can entail a great deal of work for the owner because the investor will need to be involved in the day-to-day management of the property. If the investor decides to delegate or outsource these managerial functions to a property management company, the investor will forgo or relinquish a large portion of the investment return.

Even if the property's daily managerial functions are outsourced, this does not remove the investor from the responsibility of participating in numerous management decisions. For example, the investor will still need to be involved in supervising the effectiveness of the management company, making all the decisions regarding property repairs, capital improvements, and establishing rental rates, just to name a few. Therefore, a real estate property owner—depending on their degree of involvement in the management of the property—can be more of a business owner or operator than an investor.

Conversely, if the investor is only interested in capturing the high-yield potential of investing in real estate without the time-consuming inconvenience associated with the management of direct property ownership, then private mortgage investing could be a better alternative investment.

Private mortgage lending is an indirect way of investing in real estate that it is considered a safer way to invest, as long as some guidelines are strictly followed. However, just as with any other investment, private mortgage investing also poses some advantages and disadvantages.

Advantages of Mortgage Investing as Compared to Direct Property Ownership

❖ Private mortgage investors can typically earn between a 7.5% to 12% annualized return on their investment.

❖ Private lending is a secure investment as long as certain investing guidelines are strictly adhered to, such as not lending more than a 65% to 70% LTV and only lending on first lien position mortgages on a physical asset such as a real estate property.

❖ If the loan defaults, the lender can seize the property through a foreclosure action, which could be a positive event, allowing the investor to participate in the property's appreciation.

❖ Private lending allows an investor to invest funds in real estate without the risks and headaches associated with rental or income-producing property.

❖ Private lending is a short-term type of investment, customarily six months to two or three years. Therefore, investors have the ability to move their money in and out if desired.

❖ Engaging in private mortgage lending, the investor is, in essence, the bank. Hence, the mortgage investor receives the monthly interest payments, and the direct real estate investor receives all the work.

❖ Transaction costs are higher for the direct real estate purchase investor in comparison to the private mortgage investor because the borrower pays for the real estate transactional costs, including the attorney's fees.

Disadvantages of Mortgage Investing as Compared to Direct Property Ownership

❖ Private mortgage lending does not have the same favorable tax advantages that direct property ownership does, like mortgage interest deduction, and 1031 tax-free exchanges.

❖ While private mortgage lending does generate exceptional yields, which can be better than what most income-producing rental properties create, it does not have the appreciation potential of direct property ownership. However, this situation can and does occur in the event of a foreclosure. For example, because private lenders originate mortgage loans where the loan-to-value (LTV) ratio fluctuates from 65% to 70%, in the event of a foreclosed property, the lender could end up with a 30% to 35% appreciation on their loan, less the attorney's foreclosure and court costs.

❖ If hard mortgage lending is done with a longer-term time horizon and not the typical short-term maximum of three years, then private lending can be exposed to the risk of inflationary loss in the same way that long-term bonds are exposed to inflationary risk.

ROI Comparisons between Property Ownership and Mortgage Lending

Purchasing income-producing real estate is often thought of as an excellent investment because it can be rented to generate an extra income stream. However, if the investor is not careful, they could end up buying a property that is a poor investment.

As previously described, there are advantages and disadvantages associated with these two types of investments. To determine if a property qualifies as a good investment, whether as a property purchase or as a private mortgage investment, the investor needs to calculate the real estate return on investment (ROI).

Return on investment (ROI) for income-producing properties is a calculation used by investors to measure the potential profitability of a real estate investment. The ROI calculation measures the annual percentage yield on the initial amount invested in the property. When evaluating income properties or a private mortgage investment, knowledgeable investors will analyze the past, present, and future returns to determine whether they should initiate the investment.

The determination of whether a property or an investment is healthy, appropriate, or safe can be done by applying certain useful formulas that are specifically designed for that purpose. There are many formulas that are used to assess investments. This chapter will only address the ones that are applicable to the example being presented.

Formulas Use to Determine the Health and Appropriateness of the Investment

Formula 1:

Yield is represented as a percentage and is calculated by applying the following formula:

ROI or Yield = Annual Gross Revenue / Value

The yield of an investment is the gross revenue, which in the world of real estate is simply the sum of all the unit rents plus any additional sources of income attributable to a building. In the case of private mortgage investments, it is the sum of all mortgage payments and any other fees generated by the loan. For example, in a 10-unit building, if each apartment rents for $800 per month, the monthly yield will be $8,000, and the annual yield or return would be $96,000. However, if the building can generate $500 of additional revenue from a vending machine concession area or an on-site Laundromat, then the monthly yield would be $8,500 or $102,000 per annum.

Therefore, if the purchase price for the 10-unit apartment building is $700,000, and assuming the apartment complex is fully rented, the investment will generate an annual revenue stream of $102,000. Applying *"formula 1"* in this scenario will produce a ROI of 14.57%, as shown by the calculation below:

ROI = $ 102,000/$ 700,000 = 14.57 %

However, calculating the ROI or yield alone to determine the health of a real estate investment has its limitations because the calculation focuses exclusively on the income side of the operation's structure and does not take into account the expenses incurred by the building. Thus, this metric is only useful in determining that the cash flow been represented by the seller of the building appears to correlate with other buildings of similar nature and location. Of course, to be able to make that determination, the investor would need to possess sufficient knowledge of the marketplace comparables.

To mitigate the investment risk of the building, the investor needs to make a more precise determination of the health of the investment by taking into account the expense structure of the asset. To accomplish this task, the net operating income (NOI) needs to be calculated.

Net operating income is the measurement of the income potential that can be generated by an income-producing real estate investment, which takes into account the expense structure of the asset. The NOI provides a very detailed look at the health of the investment, and it is used as the grounding basis for estimating the value of the investment property through the capitalization rate analysis.

The formula to calculate the NOI is as follows:

Formula 2:

NOI = Gross Income – Operating Costs
(Financing costs not included)

The NOI formula does not take into account the cost of money or the debt service, which is the mortgage payment—in essence, the financing costs. The reason the mortgage payment is not included in the calculation is that the mortgage payment depends on the amount and terms of the leverage or loan, or lack thereof, if the property is paid in full.

Consequently, the mortgage expense is left out in an attempt to perform an orange to oranges analysis of the income potential of the building. Thus, the most reasonable way to accomplish this analysis is by excluding the cost of money or financing costs. This is why the NOI is used to ground or underpin the valuation process in commercial real estate.

Continuing with the example of the 10-unit apartment building that generates $102,000 of gross income, and assuming that the total expenses to operate the building efficiently is $3,800 per month or $45,600 per year, the NOI would be calculated as follows:

NOI = Gross Income – Operating Costs

NOI = $ 102,000 - $ 45,600 = $ 56,400 per year, or $ 4,700.00 per month

Therefore, calculating the NOI provides a more realistic picture of the income potential of the 10-unit apartment building, keeping in mind that if the building was purchased with leverage, then there is a mortgage payment that needs to be debited from the NOI calculation. However, to simplify the calculation, let's assume that the building was purchased for cash, so there are no debt services or financing costs.

Conversely, let's invest the same $700,000 in a private mortgage loan at a 12% rate of return, assuming there are no additional income streams generated from the investment, such as loan origination points and possibly late fees. Furthermore, it is also assumed that the investor is managing his or her own loan; therefore, there is no mortgage servicing fee expense.

Then the calculations for the ROI and the NOI for the private mortgage loan investment would be as follows:

ROI = Loan Amount x Interest Rate

ROI = $ 700,000 x 12% = $ 84,000 per year, or $ 7,000 per month

NOI = Gross Income – Operating Costs

NOI = $ 84,000 – $ 0.00 = $ 84,000

It should be evident to the reader that calculating or determining the property's NOI provides a better perspective for the investor of the income-generating potential of the building, which cannot be achieved by merely calculating the gross income or yield by itself.

However, if the investor wants to know what the purchase value of the building should be, then the NOI is not a sufficient calculation for that purpose. To accomplish that task, another calculation has to be performed for which knowing the NOI of the building is essential in determining its value. To be able to assess the value of the property, the capitalization rate or *"cap rate"* must be determined. The cap rate formula uses the NOI results as the basis for the calculation. The *cap rate* is the rate of return an investor would be willing to receive on the investment that has been considered for purchase. Therefore, the investor is the one who ultimately decides what kind of ROI would be required to incentivize him or her to make the purchase decision.

To generate the additional information that would be necessary for determining which of these two investments—purchasing an income-producing property or originating a private mortgage loan—would be a better alternative, two other formulas need to be introduced. They are the *"cap rate"* and the *"value"* formulas.

Formula 3:

CAP Rate = NOI / Price (Value)

Formula 4:

Value = NOI / CAP Rate

The calculation for the 10-unit income-producing apartment property, assuming the $700,000 purchasing price and a desired 12% cap rate or ROI is as follows:

Formula 3:

Cap Rate = NOI / Price or Value

Cap Rate = $45,600 / $700,000 = .0651 or 6.51%

Formula 4:

Value = NOI / Cap Rate

Value = $45,600/ 0.12 = $380,000

In this example, it is clear that to pay $700,000 for the income-producing property would be overpaying for the building if the investor's goal is to receive a 12% cap rate. With an NOI of only $45,600 in order to generate the desired cap rate of 12%, then the investor should only pay $380,000 for the property.

The calculation for an investment in a private mortgage loan of $700,000 and a rate of return of 12% is as follows:

Formula 3:

Cap Rate = NOI / Price or Value

Cap Rate = $84,000/$ 700,000 = 0.12 or 12%

Formula 4:

Value = NOI / Cap Rate

Value = $ 84,000 / 0.12 = $ 700,000

These simple calculations demonstrate the superiority of private mortgage investing over income-producing property ownership with substantially less work involved. Of course, there could be many other variables that could be introduced into these calculations, but the results would be quite similar. Moreover, there are other formulas that can be used in determining the health and appropriateness of an investment, but what has been presented in this chapter is sufficient to accomplish the objective of comparing these two types of investment vehicles.

The important point to remember is that this example clearly conveys to the reader the advantages of engaging in private mortgage investing as compared to income-producing property ownership. The study results vividly demonstrate that it is better to be the bank than the owner of the property. Moreover, the research undertaken to write this book whose objective was to determine the suitability and safety of private mortgage lending has demonstrated that this form of investment does have unique characteristics worthy of consideration by investors. It is especially suitable for investors in search of a consistent passive income stream, either for retirement or as a cash flow generating business.

13

Private Mortgage Investing

Study Conclusions

T he goal of this research project was to explore the suitability of private mortgage lending as an alternative investment vehicle to generate a safe and meaningful passive income stream. Additionally, the study further examined the usefulness of the investment as both a stand-alone cash-flow generating business model and a more consistent way to provide retirement income with a higher degree of safety. Passive income refers to income earned from sources other than direct employment earnings. In essence, it means earnings that are generated without having active participation in its creation.

It is essential to understand that learning to create a passive income stream should be the ultimate goal of everyone who wants to retire early and in comfort. In fact, learning to generate sufficient passive income to cover all monthly expenses will lead to financial independence. According to investor Sam Dogen (2015, March 2), creating a consistent passive income stream is considered the holy grail of personal finance. Although there are many investments that can generate passive income, not all are created equal. However, the contention of all the study participants was that the passive income generated from private mortgage investing is the safest and less labor-intensive of all passive income sources.

This book is organized in a way that will provide the reader with the necessary information to build the educational foundation to understand the intricacies that demonstrate private mortgage lending is an investment vehicle worthy of consideration. It is a significant investment strategy for every investor seeking to generate an abundant high-income stream with less market risk than stock market investments.

Therefore, to achieve the study's objective of determining whether private mortgage lending/investing is an alternative investment worthy of consideration, the author designed a qualitative research study to explore the suitability of this type of investment. To address the suitability of this investment vehicle, the researcher design the study by selecting a group of private money brokers/lenders, as well as individual private mortgage investors were selected. This sample of participants was purposefully selected for inclusion in the study because of their unique richness of information and expertise with this investment class.

Moreover, the sample size used in this study followed the guiding principle of saturation as proposed by Glaser and Strauss (1967), which states that any additional participant interviewed after a saturation point is no longer contributing any further insights on the issue under investigation. In other words, saturation is reached at the point where no new information or themes are observed in the data being collected (Guest, Bunce & Johnson, 2006).

The results of the data collected from the questionnaires and interviews with the study participants conclusively demonstrated that private mortgage investing is, in fact, an investment-worthy of learning. The research study showed that the reason mortgage investing is considered a safe investment is because of the numerous risk-mitigating strategies available for the investor to reduce the level of investment risk.

The feature that is most attractive about this type of investment is the use of hedging with the protective equity of the real estate asset being used as collateral that ensures the mortgage is secured. In essence, the hedging with the protective equity of the property is what makes it safer than other investments. Unlike stocks and bonds investing where investors can lose their entire investment, with private mortgages, the investor will consistently retain some value in the investment because it is a tangible asset. Real estate under the worst possible conditions will always maintain a certain degree of value in comparison to stock market investments that can merely evaporate overnight as the result of bad company news.

An interesting finding from the study that was serendipitously discovered was the reason why private mortgage investing was not such a well-known investment vehicle. The study identified that the reason why the investment is not well-known was that investors who have been fortunate enough to have been exposed to this knowledge are not inclined to broadcast or share this information with other potential investors. They guard the information as a sort of secret that, if disseminated to others, would reduce the available investment opportunities for themselves.

Perhaps this lack of information sharing could be attributed to some form of jealousy or greed on the part of investors that makes them reluctant to divulge valuable information that might have taken them a long time to learn, and possibly at considerable risk. This observation might likely be the source of the resistance to share and make it easy for other investors who they feel are always seeking to circumvent the learning process and piggyback on someone else's efforts and risks.

Every investor knows that there are no risk-free investments. There are risks associated with any investment, and investing in private mortgages is no exception. The most that can be achieved is to mitigate the risk of the investment vehicle. This investment risk mitigation can be accomplished through the acquisition of knowledge and experience, which is one of the objectives of this book. However, the qualitative research study results demonstrated that private mortgage investing could, in fact, be used to generate a safe passive income stream, both as a cash flow business model and produce retirement income.

Throughout the book, the author has stated numerous times that the learning curve for safe real estate and private mortgage investing is quite steep. While initially, it is advisable to seek the mentorship of an ethical and experienced broker/lender to learn the underwriting guidelines and the due diligence process to evaluate the loan opportunities safely, the ultimate responsibility for the safety of the investments lies with the investor.

Most of the learning that takes place in the private mortgage lending industry occurs by happenstance. There are no formal or structured educational programs to learn this type of information. However, there are a few helpful books available on the subject listed on the *"Further Reading Recommendation"* page at the end of the book. Consequently, the author hopes that this research project will provide an additional source of information that will serve to develop the necessary educational foundation to begin the process of learning the intricacies of this unique and valuable investment vehicle.

Retirement should be a time for enjoyment and relaxation, not for worrying and suffering, as is the case for many investors. This type of retirement distress has been particularly pronounced in the artificially created low-interest-rate environment we find ourselves in that began under the Obama administration and continues under the Trump administration. That is why it is crucial to learn how to find and invest in alternative investments that can help investors thrived in all market conditions.

The research for this book is both relevant and important because it is an attempt to identify and determine if private mortgage lending/investing, as an alternative investment vehicle, can generate the return on investment (ROI), the safety, and the tranquility that retirees and soon-to-be retirees want and need. Moreover, the study did not limit its exploration just to retirement goals; it also examined whether private mortgage investing was additionally suitable as a stand-alone cash flow generating business. Thus, this study explored the suitability of private mortgage investing as a less risky, more consistent, and predictable way to invest for a safer road to a sound financial life and tranquil retirement.

The risks associated with private mortgage lending can be avoided or minimized by effectively performing the due diligence on the investment by following the vetting and underwriting guidelines, such as the following risk-mitigating steps. The following list should be adhered to by the investor to minimize investment risk as it relates to private mortgage investing:

❖ Consider the property market.

❖ Request an appraisal report on the property to determine value.

❖ Do not lend more than 65% to 70% of the loan-to-value (LTV) ratio on residential loans and no more than 50% on raw, undeveloped land.

❖ Perform a property title search.

❖ Do only first-lien position loans.

❖ Limit the lending activity to non-homesteaded properties (non-owner occupied).

❖ Require hazard insurance, including flood insurance, to protect the collateral. If insurance payments are not escrowed, verify annually with the borrower that the insurance premiums have been paid.

❖ Make sure the insurance company has named lender as loss payee.

❖ Make sure to use an attorney to review all the closing documents.

❖ Make sure the borrower has a realistic exit strategy.

- ❖ Preferably request that taxes are escrowed; if not, verify every year that taxes are being paid.

- ❖ If the loan is on a property with a homeowner's association (HOA), regularly verify that fees are being paid.

- ❖ Although the amount of protective equity is the most important aspect of private mortgage lending, make sure to assess the borrower's credit history and ability-to-repay. Adhere to the Dodd-Frank Act guidelines even if not required, merely as a safety measure.

- ❖ Be prepared to foreclose and always let the attorney deal with the borrower's issues.

- ❖ Keep informed about property values and property market conditions annually, at a minimum.

- ❖ Embrace the philosophy of being a perpetual student. Always ask yourself, *"How can I do better, and how can I further mitigate risk?"*

- ❖ Always have a plan in the event the borrower dies or walks away from the property.

- ❖ Keep in mind that mortgage fraud is prevalent, and it can be initiated by the borrower, the lender, or both. In fact, approach this business with the mindset that everyone is lying.

- ❖ Never take any shortcuts in the vetting and due diligence process. What this means is that even if your mother is the referring source for the loan opportunity, perform the vetting and due diligence process thoroughly.

This risk mitigating and due diligence process list is not an exhaustive list of all the possible steps that can be taken to minimize investment risks while engaged in the private mortgage lending business. However, all of these steps are essential in reducing the risks associated with this type of investment. Because every loan opportunity is a different deal that needs to be evaluated, the investor—as a perpetual student—will undoubtedly add to this list as problems arise and are resolved.

All the investors who participated in the research study unanimously concurred that the advantages of private mortgage investing far outweigh paper investments, such as stocks, bonds, and derivatives. Additionally, all the study participants further stated that they all had lost money in the stock market; however, none had lost any money in private mortgage investing.

The study participants cited numerous reasons why they considered private mortgage lending to be a superior investment vehicle compared to other types of investments. The reasons cited were remarkably consistent among all participants, brokers/lenders, and individual investors.

The reasons cited by the participants' were as follows:

❖ Less volatility than stock market investment. Hence, greater consistency and safety of the return on investments (ROI).

❖ Because private mortgages are short-term bridge loans with durations of six months to 24 months on average, they have the potential for compounding a couple of times a year, especially with the six-month maturities.

❖ Greater control over when and how much to invest.

❖ It is a simple investment to understand in comparison to other investment vehicles, although the learning curve is steep to invest with safety.

❖ More predictable returns than the stock market investments because the rate of return is fixed from the onset (at closing).

❖ Potential to generate double-digit returns with a higher degree of safety, even in low-interest-rates economic environments like the one we have been experiencing for the past twelve years.

❖ Real estate is a tangible asset. Thus, under a worst-case scenario, there will always be a certain degree of value, unlike paper investing such as stocks where an investor can lose 100% of their investment in the event of a company's failure leading to bankruptcy.

❖ In the private mortgage lending business, a worst-case scenario is a foreclosure and bankruptcy. However, since the investor is only lending at a 65% to 70% loan-to-value ratio, if a foreclosure and bankruptcy occur, then this situation could be a positive event for the lender. If the investor doesn't get paid and is able to keep the property, then they would be acquiring property at wholesale values. Moreover, the protective equity of 30% to 35% should be sufficient to recover the legal costs of the foreclosure process.

The objective of this qualitative research study was to explore and analyze the suitability and safety of private mortgage lending/ investing. The study findings demonstrated that this investment class does, in fact, have unique characteristics worthy of consideration by investors in search of a consistent passive income stream, either for retirement or as a cash flow generating business.

Therefore, this research study effectively confirmed and validated the research questions it set out to answer, which were:

1). Can private mortgage investing, as an alternative investment vehicle, generate a competitive rate of return comparable to stock market returns?

This investment vehicle can consistently generate a return on investment (ROI) of 7.5% to12% year after year in the current economic environment. These ROIs are quite comparable to historical stock market returns. In contrast, when the market generates these returns, it has to be under bull market conditions, unlike mortgage investing, which can produce these types of high single-digit and double-digit returns year after year, regardless of market conditions. This predictability of return on investment is what makes private mortgage investing an excellent investment vehicle for creating passive income for retirement.

2). Is private mortgage investing a better and safer income-generating investment choice for individual investors who are already retired or at near-retirement age?

The answer to this research question is also affirmative because, under a worst-case scenario, a real estate asset will always retain some value, unlike stocks and bonds, where the investor can lose their entire investment merely on bad or negative market news. Additionally, mortgage investing is a non-correlated type of investment that does not follow the market; thus, it is not subjected to the uncertainty and volatility of the market. Because of this feature, the return on investment generated from private mortgage investing is more consistent, predictable, and high enough to produce a passive income stream that is quite suitable for retirement, or as a cash flow generating business. Therefore, it is an excellent investment choice to sustain a comfortable retirement lifestyle, depending on the amount of funds available for investing.

Furthermore, private mortgage lending/investing can be hedged with various hedging strategies—such as maintaining lower loan to value (LTV) loans and applying cross-collateralization—that helps mitigate investment risk. These hedging strategies make this investment vehicle safer and more secure for the lender/investor.

3). Is private mortgage investing an investment strategy that is suitable for any type of investment portfolio?

Again, the answer to this question was also affirmative because private mortgage investing is a strategy that is suitable for anyone seeking to generate a safe passive income stream. Private mortgage lending/investing can also be a good business model to generate cash flow with substantially less work than direct property ownership or managing a regular type of business. Therefore, it is a strategy that can be employed by any individual with sufficient funds who merely wants to generate cash flow (see Chapter 12). In essence, mortgage lending is a form of private banking. Instead of renting real estate properties, the investor rents their money, and consequently, the rents collected are the interest payments.

In concluding this project, it is the sincere hope of the author that the reading audience finds this book helpful in understanding the field of private mortgage investing. The private mortgage lending/ investing market is an industry that is worthy of notice for income investors because the potential rewards that can be attained from learning how to use this type of investment class can be quite profitable, as well as life-changing.

Author's Note

Dear Reader,

Thank you for taking the time to read my book and helping me present the information behind the research that went into the creation of *Private Money Lending: Learn How to Consistently Generate a Passive Income Stream.* I hope learning about this investment class was as valuable to you as it was for me.

I hope you enjoyed reading the book and founded valuable. If you did, I would appreciate it very much if you could leave a short review on the site where you purchased the book. Your help in spreading the word is much appreciated.

Thank you!

Gustavo J. Gomez

Official author's website: www.gustavojgomez.com

Amazon author's page: amazon.com/author/gustavojgomez

FLORIDA CHRISTIAN
UNIVERSITY

This book represents an extensive scientific research study completed as a result of doctoral studies undertaken at Florida Christian University (FCU) in Orlando, Florida. Founded in 1985, Florida Christian University is a not-for-profit, Global Reach Institution of higher education for students seeking to integrate professional studies and Christian ethics foundations.

The research study contained herein represents the efforts and dedication of a student who attended, and was approved under the requirements of the program of Doctor of Philosophy in Business Administration at Florida Christian University, hereby willing to share his knowledge and findings.

Florida Christian University expects that this initiative can offer students, professionals, and managers, tools that can contribute to their continuing education. This knowledge, added to personal and professional practice, is intended to contribute even more to the specialization, updating, and improvement of this field.

Florida Christian University (FCU),

Professor Bruno Portigliatti, BA, MBA, JD

President and Chancellor

Appendices

Appendix A

US Business Cycle Expansions and Contractions

Contractions (recessions) start at the peak of a business cycle and end at the trough

BUSINESS CYCLE REFERENCE DATES		DURATION IN MONTHS			
Peak	Trough	Contraction	Expansion	Cycle	
Quarterly dates are in parentheses		Peak to Trough	Previous Trough to this Peak	Previous Trough to this Peak	Peak from Previous Peak
	December 1854 (IV)	--	--	--	--
June 1857(II)	December 1858 (IV)	18	30	48	--
October 1860(III)	June 1861 (III)	8	22	30	40
April 1865(I)	December 1867 (I)	32	46	78	54
June 1869(II)	December 1870 (IV)	18	18	36	50
October 1873(III)	March 1879 (I)	65	34	99	52
March 1882(I)	May 1885 (II)	38	36	74	101
March 1887(II)	April 1888 (I)	13	22	35	60
July 1890(III)	May 1891 (II)	10	27	37	40
January 1893(I)	June 1894 (II)	17	20	37	30
December 1895(IV)	June 1897 (II)	18	18	36	35
June 1899(III)	December 1900 (IV)	18	24	42	42
September 1902(IV)	August 1904 (III)	23	21	44	39
May 1907(II)	June 1908 (II)	13	33	46	56
January 1910(I)	January 1912 (IV)	24	19	43	32
January 1913(I)	December 1914 (IV)	23	12	35	36
August 1918(III)	March 1919 (I)	7	44	51	67
January 1920(I)	July 1921 (III)	18	10	28	17
May 1923(II)	July 1924 (III)	14	22	36	40

BUSINESS CYCLE REFERENCE DATES		DURATION IN MONTHS			
Peak	Trough	Contraction	Expansion	Cycle	
Quarterly dates are in parentheses		Peak to Trough	Previous Trough to this Peak	Previous Trough to this Peak	Peak from Previous Peak
	November 1927 (IV)				
October 1926(III)	March 1933 (I)	13	27	40	41
August 1929(III)	June 1938 (II)	43	21	64	34
May 1937(II)	October 1945 (IV)	13	50	63	93
February 1945(I)	October 1949 (IV)	8	80	88	93
November 1948(IV)	May 1954 (II)	11	37	48	45
July 1953(II)	April 1958 (II)	10	45	55	56
August 1957(III)	February 1961 (I)	8	39	47	49
April 1960(II)	November 1970 (IV)	10	24	34	32
December 1969(IV)		11	106	117	116
November 1973(IV)	March 1975 (I)	16	36	52	47
January 1980(I)	July 1980 (III)	6	58	64	74
July 1981(III)	November 1982 (IV)	16	12	28	18
July 1990(III)		8	92	100	108
March 2001(I)	March 1991(I)	8	120	128	128
December 2007 (IV)	November 2001 (IV)	18	73	91	81
	June 2009 (II)				
Average, all cycles:					
1854-2009 (33 cycles)		17.5	38.7	56.2	56.4*
1854-1919 (16 cycles)		21.6	26.6	48.2	48.9**
1919-1945 (6 cycles)		18.2	35.0	53.2	53.0
1945-2009 (12 cycles)		11.1	58.4	69.5	68.5
* 33 cycles					
** 15 cycles					

The National Bureau of Economic Research (NBER) does not define a recession in terms of two consecutive quarters of decline in real GDP as it is the custom. Rather, it defines a recession as a significant decline in the economic activity spread across the economy, lasting more than a few months, normally visible in real GDP, real income, employment, industrial production, and wholesale retail sales.

Latest announcement from the NBER's Business Cycle Dating Committee was on September 20th, 2010.

Business Cycles Turning Points, Peak or Trough, and Announcement Date

Turning Point Date	Peak or Trough	Announcement Date
June 2009	Trough	September 20, 2010
December 2007	Peak	December 1, 2008
November 2001	Trough	July 17, 2003
March 2001	Peak	November 26, 2001
March 1991	Trough	December 22, 1992
July 1990	Peak	April 25, 1991
November 1982	Trough	July 8, 1983
July 1981	Peak	January 6, 1982
July 1980	Trough	July 8, 1981
January 1980	Peak	June 3, 1980

Prior to 1979, there were no formal announcements of business cycle turning points. The determination that the last expansion began in June 2009 is the most-recent decision of the Business Cycle Dating Committee of the National Bureau of Economic Research.

Source: The National Bureau of Economic Research, Inc. (NBER)

Appendix B

Foreclosure Process and Foreclosure Laws

The foreclosure process is the legal remedy available to lenders in order to reclaim the collateral that was used as the basis for a mortgage loan when a borrower defaults on their legal obligations. Each state has specific laws regarding the mortgage foreclosure process. The foreclosure process differs from state to state, which depends on whether a state is a *"Mortgage"* or a *"Deed of Trust"* state, as shown below:

- ❖ **Non-Judicial Foreclosure:** Used in *"Deed of Trust"* states. They are foreclosures that are processed without court intervention.

- ❖ **Judicial Foreclosure:** Used in *"Mortgage"* states and require court filings and court appearances.

- ❖ **Strict Foreclosure**: The least common type of foreclosure in which the lender simply takes the property without an auction sale. It is only allowed by law in a few states (see table below), and it is only utilized in certain cases.

Foreclosure Laws Comparison
Table of the 50 States

STATE	Security Instrument Use	Type of Foreclosure Use	Initial Step	Timeline in Months	Right of Redemption (Months)	Deficiency Judgment	Timeline + Redemption (Months)
ALABAMA	Trust Deed	Non-judicial	Publica-tion	1	12	Allowed	13

STATE	Security Instrument Use	Type of Foreclosure Use	Initial Step	Timeline in Months	Right of Redemption (Months)	Deficiency Judgment	Timeline + Redemption (Months)
ALASKA	Trust Deed and Mortgage	Non-judicial and Judicial	Notice of Default	3	0	Allowed	3
ARIZONA	Trust Deed and Mortgage	Non-judicial and Judicial	Notice of Sale	3	0	Allowed	3
ARKANSAS	Trust Deed and Mortgage	Non-judicial and Judicial	Com-plaint	4	0	Allowed	4
CALIFORNIA	Trust Deed	Non-judicial	Notice of Default	4	0	Prohib-ited	4
COLORADO	Trust Deed and Mortgage	Non-judicial and Judicial	Notice of Default	2	2.5	Allowed	4.5
CONNECTI-CUT	Mortgage	Judicial and Strict	Com-plaint	5	0	Allowed	5
DELAWARE	Mortgage	Judicial	Com-plaint	3	0	Allowed	3
DISTRICT of COLUMBIA (D.C.)	Trust Deed	Non-judicial	Notice of Default	2	0	Allowed	2

STATE	Security Instrument Use	Type of Foreclosure Use	Initial Step	Timeline in Months	Right of Redemption (Months)	Deficiency Judgment	Timeline + Redemption (Months)
FLORIDA	Mortgage	Judicial	Complaint	5	0	Allowed	5
GEORGIA	Security Deed	Non-judicial	Publication	2	0	Allowed	2
HAWAII	Trust Deed	Non-judicial	Publication	3	0	Allowed	3
IDAHO	Trust Deed	Non-judicial	Notice of Default	5	0	Allowed	5
ILLINOIS	Mortgage	Judicial and Strict	Complaint	7	0	Allowed	7
INDIANA	Mortgage	Judicial and Strict	Complaint	5	3	Allowed	8
IOWA	Trust Deed and Mortgage	Non-judicial and Judicial	Petition	5	6	Allowed	11
KANSAS	Mortgage	Judicial	Complaint	4	12	Allowed	16
KENTUCKY	Mortgage	Judicial	Complaint	6	0	Allowed	6
LOUISIANA	Mortgage	Judicial	Petition	2	0	Allowed	2
MAINE	Mortgage	Judicial and Strict	Complaint	6	0	Allowed	6

STATE	Security Instrument Use	Type of Foreclosure Use	Initial Step	Timeline in Months	Right of Redemption (Months)	Deficiency Judgment	Timeline + Redemption (Months)
MARYLAND	Mortgage	Judicial	Notice	2	0	Allowed	2
MASSACHU-SETTS	Trust Deed	Non-judicial	Complaint	3	0	Allowed	3
MICHIGAN	Trust Deed and Mortgage	Non-judicial and Judicial	Publication	2	6	Allowed	8
MINNESOTA	Trust Deed and Mortgage	Non-judicial and Judicial	Publication	2	6	Prohibited	8
MISSISSIPPI	Trust Deed	Non-judicial	Publication	2	0	Prohibited	2
MISSOURI	Trust Deed	Non-judicial	Publication	2	0	Allowed	2
MONTANA	Trust Deed and Mortgage	Non-judicial and Judicial	Notice	5	0	Prohibited	5
NEBRASKA	Mortgage	Judicial	Petition	5	0	Allowed	5
NEVADA	Trust Deed	Non-judicial	Notice of Default	4	0	Allowed	4
NEW HAMPSHIRE	Trust Deed	Non-judicial and Strict	Notice of Sale	2	0	Allowed	2

STATE	Security Instrument Use	Type of Foreclosure Use	Initial Step	Timeline in Months	Right of Redemption (Months)	Deficiency Judgment	Timeline + Redemption (Months)
NEW JERSEY	Mortgage	Judicial	Com-plaint	3	0.25	Allowed	3.25
NEW MEXICO	Mortgage	Judicial	Com-plaint	4	0	Allowed	4
NEW YORK	Mortgage	Judicial	Com-plaint	4	0	Allowed	4
NORTH CAROLINA	Trust Deed	Non-judicial	Notice Hearing	2	0	Allowed	2
NORTH DAKOTA	Mortgage	Judicial	Com-plaint	3	1	Prohib-ited	4
OHIO	Mortgage	Judicial	Com-plaint	5	0	Allowed	5
OKLAHOMA	Trust Deed and Mortgage	Non-judicial and Judicial	Com-plaint	4	0	Allowed	4
OREGON	Trust Deed	Non-judicial	Notice of Default	5	0	Allowed	5
PENNSYLVA-NIA	Mortgage	Judicial	Com-plaint	3	0	Allowed	3
RHODE ISLAND	Trust Deed and Mortgage	Non-judicial and Judicial	Publica-tion	2	0	Allowed	2

STATE	Security Instrument Use	Type of Foreclosure Use	Initial Step	Timeline in Months	Right of Redemption (Months)	Deficiency Judgment	Timeline + Redemption (Months)
SOUTH CAROLINA	Mortgage	Judicial	Com-plaint	6	0	Allowed	6
SOUTH DAKOTA	Trust Deed	Non-Judicial	Com-plaint	3	6	Allowed	9
TENNESSEE	Trust Deed	Non-judicial	Publica-tion	2	0	Allowed	2
TEXAS	Trust Deed	Non-judicial	Publica-tion	2	0	Allowed	2
UTAH	Trust Deed and Mortgage	Non-judicial and Judicial	Notice of Default	4	0	Allowed	4
VERMONT	Trust Deed and Mortgage	Non-judicial, Strict, and Judicial	Com-plaint	7	0	Allowed	7
VIRGINIA	Trust Deed	Non-judicial	Publica-tion	2	0	Allowed	2
WASHINGTON	Trust Deed	Non-judicial	Notice of Default	4	0	Allowed	4
WEST VIRGINIA	Trust Deed	Non-judicial	Publica-tion	2	0	Prohib-ited	2

STATE	Security Instrument Use	Type of Foreclosure Use	Initial Step	Timeline in Months	Right of Redemption (Months)	Deficiency Judgment	Timeline + Redemption (Months)
WISCONSIN	Trust Deed and Mortgage	Non-judicial and Judicial	Com-plaint	Varies	0	Allowed	12
WYOMING	Trust Deed	Non-judicial	Publica-tion	2	3	Allowed	5

❖ **16** States use Trust Deed only and allow Non-Judicial Foreclosure.

❖ **17** States use Mortgage only and allow Judicial Foreclosure.

❖ **12** States use both Trust Deed and Mortgage and allow both Non-Judicial and Judicial Foreclosures.

❖ **4** States use Mortgage only and allow both Judicial and Strict foreclosures.

❖ **1** State use Trust Deed only and allow both Non-Judicial and Strict foreclosures.

❖ **1** State use both Trust Deed and Mortgage and allow all three types of foreclosures: Non-Judicial, Judicial, and Strict.

Source: www.rogerbutcher.com/index.php?option=com_content&view=article&id=40Foreclosure-timeline-all-states & catid=27: articles & Itemid=32

Appendix C

Comparison Table between

Deed of Trust and Mortgage

	Deed of Trust	Mortgage
Law Definition	A document that embodies the agreement between a lender and a borrower to transfer an interest in the borrower's land to a neutral third party—a trustee—to secure the payment of a debt by the borrower.	A legal document by which the owner (buyer) transfers to the lender an interest in real estate to secure the repayment of a debt, as evidenced by a mortgage note.
Description	A document that allows a loan to be secured for a property with the involvement of a third party called a trustee, like escrow or a title insurance company.	A mortgage is a method of using property (real or personal) as security for the payment of a debt.
Types	The Trustee's Deed, The Re-Conveyance Deed, and the Deed of Trust.	Mortgage by Demise, Mortgage by legal charge, and Equitable Mortgage.
Use	To secure loan(s) to buy a property, either commercial or residential.	Mortgage is seen as the standard method by which individuals and businesses can purchase residential and commercial real estate without the need to pay the full value immediately.
Parties Involved	Borrower (trustor), Lender (beneficiary), and a third party like escrow or an insurance title company (trustee).	Borrower (trustor) and Lender (beneficiary)

Source: www.diffen.com/difference/Deed_Of_Trust_vs_Mortgage

Appendix D

Dodd–Frank Wall Street Reform

and Consumer Protection Act

The purpose of this act is to promote the financial stability of the United States markets by improving accountability and transparency in the financial system. It is intended to end the concept of *"too big to fail"* in order to protect the American taxpayer by ending bailouts, and to protect consumers from the abusive practices of financial service and other situations where abuses exist.

The Dodd-Frank Act of 2010
is composed of sixteen titles

Table of Contents			
1	Origins and proposal		
2	Legislative response and passage		
3	Overview		
4	Provisions		
	4.1	Title I – Financial Stability	
		4.1.1	Duties
		4.1.2	Membership
		4.1.3	Resources
		4.1.4	Authority
		4.1.5	Financial reporting to the Council
		4.1.6	Office of Financial Research
		4.1.7	Financial Research Director's independent reports to Congress
		4.1.8	Resources

Table of Contents

Table of Contents

Table of Contents

Source: http://www.ask.com/wiki/Dodd_Frank

Appendix E

The Loss and Gain Asymmetry

Gains and losses of equal percentage magnitude have asymmetrical effects on wealth, with losses having the greater effect.

Loss (%)	Gain (%) Needed to Break Even
10%	11%
15%	18%
20%	25%
25%	33%
30%	43%
40%	67%
50%	100%
60%	150%
70%	233%
80%	400%
90%	900%

The lesson to be learned about investment losses is this:

A cursory look across the table above will demonstrate that limiting investment losses to the smallest amount possible is an excellent and crucial practice because it will take a small gain to recuperate the investment and break even. Conversely, a large loss like 50% will require a 100% gain to recuperate the investment and break even (Chevreau, 2010). Considering the psychological pain that type of loss can create, it is almost impossible to recuperate from those types of losses because the investor will either sell the position, taking the loss to avoid further pain, or retain the position in the hopes of recuperating the losses and surely inflicting substantially more pain. This is the reason for the saying by Daniel Drew in the late 1800s: *"Cut your losses short and let your profits run"* (Slagle, 2008).

Appendix F

Sample Payoff Request Letter

Date:

Mortgagor:

Social Security:

Address:

Mortgage No:

Premise:

Dear Sir or Madam:

Please be advised that our client(s) wishes to satisfy the above referenced mortgage. If you would be so kind, please forward to us a payoff statement letter setting forth the amount necessary to fully satisfy our client mortgage obligation.

If applicable, please include the real estate tax escrow balance and the last taxes paid by the bank.

Sincerely,

_____

Appendix G

Sample Payoff Statement Letter

December 10, 20xx

XYZ Mortgage Services, LLC
C/o G. M. Doe
18090 SW 156th Street
Roaddale, Fl 35677

> Re: Mortgagor: Maximilian R. Magnus
>
> Mortgagee: TTT Investments, LLC
>
> Property: 17456 SW 65th Lane
>
> Roaddale, Fl 35689

Dear Mr. Magnus,

Please be advised that I represent TTT Investments, LLC.

As requested, the estoppels letter for the payoff of the above-captioned mortgage is as follows:

The unpaid principal balance as of 12/10/xxxx	$166,266.00
Interest from 11/01/xxxx through 12/15/xxxx at $ 55.04/diem	$2,696.96
Late payment fee	$none
Re-conveyance Fee	$298.00
Current balance due on December 15th, xxxx	$169,260.96
Less: xxxx Property taxes (Escrow account)	$2,665.30
Total Due December 15th, xxxx	$166,595.66
Per Diem interest rate after December 15th, xxxx	$55.04

This payoff letter is good through December 15th, xxxx. After that, include the per diem interest rate.

Please wire the payoff funds as per the following instructions:

Bank: USA Bank 7788 NW 56th Avenue Roaddale, Fl 35788

ABA: XXXXXX   ACC #: XXXXXX   Beneficiary: XYZ Mortgage Services, LLC IOTA ESTATE ACCOUNT

Please call if you need further assistance.

Sincerely,

Appendix H

Inverse Relationship between Interest Rates and Bond Prices

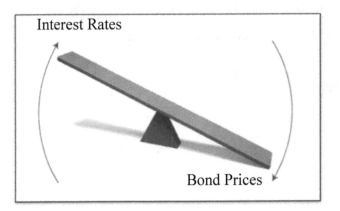

The above seesaw demonstrates the inverse relationship that exists between interest rates and bond prices:

- ❖ Higher market interest rates result in lower bond prices.
- ❖ Lower market interest rates result in higher bond prices.

Source: www.investor.gov

Appendix I

Effect of a 1% Decrease in Interest Rate on Bond Prices and Yield to Maturity

Financial Term	Today	One Year Later ↓
Market Interest Rate	3%	2%
Coupon Rate (semi-annual payments)	3%	3%
Face Value	$1,000	$1,000
Maturity	10 years	9 years remaining
Price	$1,000	$1,082
Yield to Maturity	3%	2%

*Lower market interest rates result in higher bond prices and lower bond yields.

Effect of a 1% Increase in Interest Rate on Bond Prices and Yield to Maturity

Financial Term	Today	One Year Later ↑
Market Interest Rate	3%	2%
Coupon Rate (semi-annual payments)	3%	3%
Face Value	$1,000	$1,000
Maturity	10 years	9 years remaining
Price	$1,000	$925
Yield to Maturity	3%	4%

*Higher market interest rates result in lower bond prices and higher bond yields.

Source: www.investor.gov

Appendix J

Hard Money State Rankings Report

The Hard Money State Rankings List for 2012 is compiled through the use of accurate, real-time, Internet-based data collected from housing funding sales trends and lender behaviors, such as recorded deeds and final closing statements. *Alternative Lending Magazine* is an expert on the field of hard money funding programs and alternative lending scenario modeling. It is the primary guide to the unconventional mortgage market.

The list below represents the hard money state rankings according to *Alternative Lending Magazine* for 2012, with the top three states highlighted in bold letters.

1. California	15. Virginia
2. Texas	16. Tennessee
3. Florida	17. Louisiana
4. Illinois	18. Indiana
5. Arizona	19. South Carolina
6. Georgia	20. Washington
7. Ohio	21. Utah
8. Michigan	22. Oregon
9. Nevada	23. Alabama
10. New Jersey	24. (Tie) Missouri - Kansas
11. Maryland	25. (Tie) Missouri - Kansas
12. New York	26. Colorado
13. Pennsylvania	27. New Mexico
14. North Carolina	28. Oklahoma

29. West Virginia

30. Arkansas

31. Iowa

32. Wisconsin

33. South Dakota

34. Rhode Island

35. Massachusetts

36. Minnesota

37. North Dakota

38. Wyoming

39. (Tie) Connecticut - Idaho

40. (Tie) Connecticut - Idaho

41. Kentucky

42. Nebraska

43. Vermont

44. Mississippi

45. New Hampshire

46. Montana

47. Hawaii

48. Delaware

49. Maine

50. Alaska

http://www.prweb.com/releases/2013/2/prweb10396981.htm

General Inquiries and Operations
Palo Alto, CA 94301
info@alternativelendingmagazine.com

Glossary

A

Acceleration clause: A clause in your mortgage that allows the lender to demand payment of the outstanding loan balance for various reasons. The most common reasons for accelerating a loan are if the borrower defaults on the loan or transfers title to another individual without informing the lender.

Adjustable-rate mortgage (ARM): A mortgage in which the interest changes periodically, according to corresponding fluctuations in an index. All ARMs are tied to indexes.

Adjustment date: The date the interest rate changes on an adjustable-rate mortgage.

Amortization: The gradual elimination of a liability, such as a mortgage, in regular payments over a specified period of time.

Annual percentage rate (APR): The actual cost to the borrower of a mortgage, including interest, mortgage insurance, and loan origination fees (points) calculated over the life of the loan. This will be higher than the note rate. Certain fees to third parties (e.g., appraisal, title insurance, etc.) are not included in this calculation.

Application: The form used to apply for a mortgage loan that contains information about a borrower's income, savings, assets, debts, and more.

Appraisal: A written opinion of value of the property based on an appraiser's analysis of the property.

Appraised value: Is an opinion of a property's fair market value based on an appraiser's knowledge, experience, and analysis of the property. Since an appraisal is based primarily on comparable sales, and the most recent sale is the one on the property in question, the appraisal usually comes out at the purchase price.

Appraiser: An individual qualified by education, training, and experience to estimate the value of real property and personal property. Although some appraisers work directly for mortgage lenders, most are independent.

Appreciation: The increase in the value of a property due to changes in market conditions, inflation, or other causes.

Assessed value: The valuation placed on property by a public tax assessor for purposes of taxation.

Assessor: A public official who establishes the value of a property for taxation purposes.

Asset: Items of value owned by an individual. Assets that can be quickly converted into cash are considered "liquid assets." These include bank accounts, stocks, bonds, mutual funds, and so on. Other assets include real estate, personal property, and debts owed to an individual by others.

Assignment: When ownership of your mortgage is transferred from one company or individual to another, it is called an assignment.

Assumable mortgage: A mortgage that can be assumed by the buyer when a home is sold. Usually, the borrower must "qualify" in order to assume the loan.

B

Balloon mortgage: A mortgage whose payments will not be sufficient to pay off the entire balance of the loan by the end of the term of the loan. The payment required at the end of the loan term is called a balloon payment.

Balloon payment: Within the mortgage loan arena, this term is used to identify a payment made that is significantly larger in size than any of the previous payments. Typically, this is a lump sum payment used to pay off any remaining balance that exists.

Bankruptcy: By filing in federal bankruptcy court, an individual or individuals can restructure or relieve themselves of debts and liabilities. Bankruptcies are of various types, but the most common for an individual seems to be a "Chapter 7 No Asset" bankruptcy, which relieves the borrower of most types of unsecured debts. A borrower cannot usually qualify for an "A" paper loan for a period of two years after the bankruptcy has been discharged and requires the re-establishment of an ability to repay debt.

Boom and bust cycle: Is a process of economic expansion and contraction that occurs repeatedly.

Bridge loan: Short-term loan used to bridge the gap. For example a loan used to buy a property until a permanent loan can be secured.

C

Cap: Adjustable rate mortgages have fluctuating interest rates, but those fluctuations are usually limited to a certain amount. Those limitations may apply to how much the loan may adjust over a six-month period, an annual period, and over the life of the loan, and are referred to as "caps." Some ARMs, although they may have a life cap, allow the interest rate to fluctuate freely, but require a certain minimum payment that can change once a year. There is a limit on how much that payment can change each year, and that limit is also referred to as a cap.

Cash-out refinance: This is the refinancing of an existing mortgage in which the borrower receives cash in excess of what is used to pay off the existing mortgage, closing costs, points, and other fees associated with the transaction.

Chain of title: An analysis of the transfers of title to a piece of property over the years.

Clear title: A title that is free of liens or legal questions as to ownership of the property.

Closing: This has different meanings in different states. In some states a real estate transaction is not consider "closed" until the documents record at the local recorder's office. In others, the "closing" is a meeting where all of the documents are signed and money changes hands.

Closing costs: These are expenses—in addition to the purchase price of the property—that are incurred by buyers and sellers in transferring ownership of a property, including but not limited to: origination fees, title insurance, and recording fees.

Cloud on title: Any conditions revealed by a title search that adversely affect the title to real estate. Usually, clouds on title cannot be removed except by deed, release, or court action.

Co-borrower: An additional individual who is both obligated on the loan and is on the title to the property.

Collateral: In a home loan, the property is the collateral. In the event of a payment default the borrower risks losing the property if the loan is not repaid according to the terms of the mortgage or deed of trust.

Combined loan-to-value: The total of all liens on the property divided by the appraised value, expressed as a percentage.

Community property: In some states, especially in the southwest, property acquired by a married couple during their marriage is considered to be owned jointly, except under special circumstances. This is an outgrowth of the Spanish and Mexican heritage of the area.

Comparable sales: Recent sales of similar properties in nearby areas that are used to help determine the market value of a property. This is also referred to as "comps."

Condominium: A type of ownership in real property where all of the owners own the property, common areas, and buildings together, with the exception of the interior of the unit to which they have title. Often mistakenly referred to as a type of construction or development, it actually refers to the type of ownership.

Conflict of Interest: A conflict of interest is a set of circumstances, which creates a risk that professional judgment or actions regarding a primary interest will be unduly influenced by a secondary interest (Lo & Field, 2009). There are two classifications of conflict of interest: *"Primary interest"* refers to the principal goals of the profession or activity, such as the protection of clients, the health of patients, the integrity of research, and the duties of public office. *"Secondary interest"* includes not only financial gains, but also such motives as the desire for professional advancement and the wish to do favors for family and friends.

Conforming loan: A mortgage that is equal to or less than the dollar amount established by the conforming loan limit set by Fannie Mae and Freddie Mac's federal regulator, the Office of Federal Housing Enterprise Oversight (OFHEO) and meets the funding criteria of Freddie Mac and Fannie Mae.

Construction loan: A short-term, interim loan for financing the cost of construction. The lender makes payments to the builder at periodic intervals as the work progresses.

Contingency: A condition that must be met before a contract is legally binding. For example, home purchasers often include a contingency that specifies that the contract is not binding until the purchaser obtains a satisfactory home inspection report from a qualified home inspector.

Conventional mortgage: Refers to home loans other than government loans (VA and FHA).

Conventional mortgage loan: Conventional loans cover a vast array of loan programs offered by banks. They can have either fixed or variable rates or payments. These loans are not government insured or guaranteed, so they do not include FHA loans or VA loans. They also do not include private money or hard money loans.

Convertible ARM: An adjustable-rate mortgage that allows the borrower to change the ARM to a fixed-rate mortgage within a specific time.

Cooperative (co-op): A type of multiple ownership in which the residents of a multiunit housing complex own shares in the cooperative corporation that owns the property, giving each resident the right to occupy a specific apartment or unit.

Credit history: A record of an individual's repayment of debt. Credit histories are reviewed by mortgage lenders as one of the underwriting criteria in determining credit risk.

Creditor: A person to whom money is owed.

Credit report: Is a report of an individual's credit history prepared by a credit bureau and used by a lender in determining a loan applicant's creditworthiness.

Crowdfunding: Crowdfunding is a financing method that involves funding a project with relatively modest contributions from a large group of individuals, rather than seeking substantial sums from a small number of investors. It is also a term used to describe and evolving method of raising money through the Internet and social media outlets.

D

Debt-to-income ratio (back-end ratio): The total mortgage payment plus other monthly expenses (e.g., credit card payments, car loan payments, etc.) divided by the gross monthly income, expressed as a percentage. Debt-to-income ratio for housing, which is also known as the front-end ratio, is a variation of the debt-to-income ratio (DTI) that calculates how much of a person's gross income is going towards housing costs. If a homeowner has a mortgage, the front-end DTI ratio is usually calculated as housing expenses (such as mortgage payments, mortgage insurance, etc.) divided by gross income, expressed as a percentage.

Deed: The written document conveying real property.

Deed-in-lieu: Short for "deed in lieu of foreclosure," this conveys title to the lender when the borrower is in default and wants to avoid foreclosure. The lender may or may not cease foreclosure activities if a borrower asks to provide a deed-in-lieu. Regardless of whether the lender accepts the deed-in-lieu, the avoidance and non-repayment of debt will most likely show on a credit history. What a deed-in-lieu may prevent is having the documents preparatory to a foreclosure being recorded and becoming a matter of public record.

Deed of trust: A deed of trust is used to convey the "dormant title" to the land to another person or company as a "trustee" in order to secure debts or other obligations. The trustee is given the power of sale of the land encumbered in the event of a default by the borrower.

Default: When the borrower does not meet his or her obligations as defined by the loan agreement. This usually involves non-payment of money due, but can also involve other factors, such as failure to maintain adequate insurance or failure to properly maintain the property.

Default rate: An increased interest rate charged to a borrower when payments on a loan are overdue. This higher rate is applied to outstanding balances in arrears in addition to the regular interest charges for the debt. It is illegal to charge this rate on certain mortgage loans.

Department of Veterans Affairs (VA): An independent agency of the federal government that guarantees long-term, low, or no down payment mortgages to eligible veterans.

Dormant title: Under a deed of trust, a trustee is given title without ownership of the property. The trustee has "dormant title" because he or she can sell the property if the borrower defaults on the loan, but the trustee cannot use the property and does not own it.

Down payment: Cash paid up front to the seller.

Due-on-sale clause: Provision in a security instrument calling for automatic maturity in the event of sale or transfer of title by borrower.

E

Earnest money deposit: Cash paid up front to the seller to show the potential buyer has a definite interest in the property. This is normally paid to an impartial third party (escrow company) to hold until the transaction is completed or the deposit is forfeited.

Easement: A right of way giving persons other than the owner access to, or over, a property.

Eminent domain: The right of a government to take private property for public use upon payment of its fair market value. Eminent domain is the basis for condemnation proceedings.

Encroachment: An improvement that intrudes illegally on another's property.

Encumbrance: Anything that affects or limits the fee simple title to a property, such as mortgages, leases, easements, or restrictions.

Equal Credit Opportunity Act: Federal law that prohibits discrimination in a credit transaction on the basis of sex, marital status, race, color, religion, national origin, age, receipt of public assistance benefits, and/or the borrower's good faith exercise of the rights under the Consumer Credit Protection Act.

Equity: The value of the property over and above the financial obligations against it. For example, if a property is worth $200,000 and loans against it total $150,000, there is $50,000 of equity.

Escrow: An impartial third party who holds the financial instrument (check, cashier's check, bank wire, etc.) on behalf of the other two parties in a transaction. The funds are held by the escrow service until it receives the appropriate written or oral instructions, or until obligations have been fulfilled.

Escrow account: Once you close your purchase transaction, you may have an escrow account or impound account with your lender.

This means the amount you pay each month includes an amount above what would be required if you were only paying your principal and interest. The extra money is held in your impound account (escrow account) for the payment of items like property taxes and homeowner's insurance when they come due. The lender pays them with your money instead of you paying them yourself.

Eviction: The lawful expulsion of an occupant from real property.

Exclusive listing: A written contract that gives a licensed real estate agent the exclusive right to sell a property for a specified time.

Executor: A person named in a will to administer an estate. The court will appoint an administrator if no executor is named. "Executrix" is the feminine form.

F

Federal Housing Administration (FHA): An agency of the U.S. Department of Housing and Urban Development (HUD). Its main activity is the insuring of residential mortgage loans made by private lenders. The FHA sets standards for construction and underwriting but does not lend money or plan or construct housing.

Fee simple: The greatest possible interest a person can have in real estate.

Fee simple estate: An unconditional, unlimited estate of inheritance that represents the greatest estate and most extensive interest in land that can be enjoyed. It is of perpetual duration. When the real estate is in a condominium project, the unit owner is the exclusive owner only of the airspace within his or her portion of the building (the unit) and is an owner in common with respect to the land and other common portions of the property.

FHA mortgage: Along with VA loans, an FHA loan will often be referred to as a government backed loan.

Fair Housing Act: Prohibits discrimination in the sale, rental, and financing of dwellings, and in other housing-related transactions, based on race, color, national origin, religion, sex, familial status (including children under the age of 18 living with parents of legal custodians, pregnant women, and people securing custody of children under the age of 18), and handicap (disability).

Fannie Mae Federal National Mortgage Association (FNMA): A government-sponsored enterprise (GSE) that was created in 1938 to expand the flow of mortgage money by developing a secondary mortgage market. Fannie Mae is a publicly traded company that operates under a congressional charter that directs Fannie Mae to channel its efforts into increasing the availability and affordability of home ownership for low, moderate, and middle-income Americans.

Finance charge: The cost of credit, which is either collected at or before the loan closing.

Firm commitment: A lender's agreement to make a loan to a specific borrower on a specific property.

First mortgage: The mortgage that is in first place among any loans recorded against a property. Usually refers to the date on which loans are recorded, but there are exceptions.

Fixed-rate mortgage (FRM): A mortgage in which the interest rate does not change throughout the term of the loan.

Fixture: Personal property that becomes real property when attached in a permanent manner to real estate.

Flood insurance: This is the insurance coverage that is required in designated areas to protect the borrower and lender against loss due to flooding.

Foreclosure: The process used by a lender to terminate the borrower's interest in a property due to a default in the loan, often ending in the lender selling the property and using the proceeds to satisfy the mortgage.

Freddie Mac (Federal Home Loan Mortgage Corp (FHLMC)): A stockholder-owned, government-sponsored enterprise (GSE) chartered by Congress in 1970 to keep money flowing to mortgage lenders in support of homeownership and rental housing for middle income Americans. The FHLMC purchases, guarantees and securitizes mortgages to form mortgage-backed securities. The mortgage-backed securities that it issues tend to be very liquid and carry a credit rating close to that of U.S. Treasuries.

G

Good faith estimate: An estimate of settlement costs that the applicant may incur at loan closing.

Government National Mortgage Association (Ginnie Mae): A government-owned corporation within the U.S. Department of Housing and Urban Development (HUD). Created by Congress on September 1, 1968, GNMA performs the same role as Fannie Mae and Freddie Mac in providing funds to lenders for making home loans. The difference is that Ginnie Mae provides funds for government loans (FHA and VA).

Grant deed: The most commonly used deed in California. It conveys all the title that the grantor has and any title that the grantor may acquire in the future.

Grantee: The person to whom an interest in real property is conveyed.

Grantor: The person conveying an interest in real property.

Gross monthly income: The borrower's total earnings per month before expenses and income taxes are deducted, but after business expenses are deducted.

H

Hazard insurance: This is the insurance coverage that insures against damage to a property from fire, wind, or other hazards. This is separate from flood insurance.

Home equity line of credit: A mortgage loan, generally in a subordinate position, which allows the borrower to draw funds in different increments from the loan as needed.

Home inspection: A thorough inspection by a professional that evaluates the structural and mechanical condition of a property. A satisfactory home inspection is often included as a contingency by the purchaser.

Homeowner's association: A nonprofit association that manages the common areas of a planned unit development (PUD) or condominium project. In a condominium project, it has no ownership interest in the common elements. In a PUD project, it holds title to the common elements.

Homeowner's insurance: An insurance policy that combines personal liability insurance and hazard insurance coverage for a dwelling and its contents.

Homeowner's warranty: A type of insurance often purchased by homebuyers that will cover repairs to certain items, such as heating or air conditioning, should they break down within the coverage period. The buyer often requests that the seller pay for this coverage as a condition of the sale, but either party can pay.

Housing expense ratio (front-end ratio): This is the percentage of gross monthly income that goes toward paying housing expenses (see also debt-to-income ratio).

HUD-1 settlement statement: A document that provides an itemized listing of the funds that were paid at closing. Items that appear on the statement include real estate commissions, loan fees, points, and initial escrow (impound) amounts. Each type of expense goes on a specific numbered line on the sheet. The totals at the bottom of the HUD-1 statement define the seller's net proceeds and the buyer's net payment at closing. It is called a HUD-1 because the form is printed by the Department of Housing and Urban Development (HUD). The HUD-1 statement is also known as the "closing statement" or "settlement sheet."

I

Interest only loan: Is a mortgage that requires only the accrued interest (and no principal) to be paid for a specified term of the loan.

J

Joint tenancy: A form of ownership or taking of title to a property, which means that each party owns the whole property and that ownership, is not separate. In the event of the death of one party, the survivor owns the property in its entirety.

Judgment: A decision made by a court of law. In judgments that require the repayment of a debt, the court may place a lien against the debtor's real property as collateral for the judgment's creditor.

Judicial foreclosure: A type of foreclosure proceeding used in some states that is handled as a civil lawsuit and conducted entirely under the auspices of a court. Other states use non-judicial foreclosure.

Jumbo loan: A loan that exceeds Fannie Mae and Freddie Mac's loan limits, currently at $417,000. This is also called a nonconforming loan. Freddie Mac and Fannie Mae loans are referred to as conforming loans.

k

L

Late charge: The penalty a borrower must pay when a payment is not made for a stated number of days. On a first trust deed or mortgage, this is usually fifteen days.

Lease: A written agreement between the property owner and a tenant that stipulates the payment and conditions under which the tenant may possess the real estate for a specified period of time.

Lease option: An alternative financing option that allows homebuyers to lease a home with an option to buy. Each month's rent payment may consist of not only the rent, but also an additional amount that can be applied toward the down payment on an already specified price.

Leasehold estate: A way of holding title to a property wherein the mortgagor does not actually own the property, but rather has a recorded long-term lease on it.

Legal description: A property description recognized by law that is sufficient to locate and identify the property without oral testimony.

Lender: A term that can refer to the institution making the loan or to the individual representing the firm. For example, loan officers are often referred to as "lenders."

Liabilities: A person's financial obligations. Liabilities include long-term and short-term debt, as well as any other amounts that are owed to others.

Liability insurance: Insurance coverage that offers protection against claims alleging that a property owner's negligence or inappropriate action resulted in bodily injury or property damage to another party. It is usually part of a homeowner's insurance policy.

Lien: A legal claim against a property that must be paid off when the property is sold. A mortgage or first trust deed is considered a lien.

Line of credit: An agreement by a commercial bank or other financial institution to extend credit up to a certain amount for a certain period of time to a specified borrower.

Liquid asset: A cash asset or an asset that is easily converted into cash.

Loan: A sum of borrowed money (principal) that is generally repaid with interest.

Loan officer: Also referred to by a variety of other terms, such as lender, loan representative, loan rep, account executive, and others. The loan officer serves several functions and has various responsibilities: soliciting loans, representing the lending institution, and representing the borrower to the lending institution.

Loan origination: How a lender refers to the process of obtaining new loans.

Loan servicing: After you obtain a loan, the company you make the payments to is "servicing" your loan. They process payments, send statements, manage the escrow/impound account, provide collection efforts on delinquent loans, ensure that insurance and property taxes are made on the property, handle pay-offs and assumptions, and provide a variety of other services.

Loan-to-value ratio: The relationship, expressed in a percentage, between the amount of the mortgage and the appraised value/ purchase price of the property. For example, on a loan of $65,000 against a property value of $100,000, the LTV is 65%.

M

Maturity: The date on which the principal balance of a loan, bond, or other financial instrument becomes due and payable.

Merged credit report: A credit report that reports the raw data pulled from two or more of the major credit repositories. Contrast with a residential mortgage credit report (RMCR) or a standard factual credit report.

Mezzanine loan: a second lien or a junior lien.

Modification: Occasionally, a lender will agree to modify the terms of your mortgage without requiring you to refinance. If any changes are made, it is called a modification.

Mortgage: A legal document that pledges a property to the lender as security for payment of a debt. Instead of mortgages, some states use trust deeds. Another way of stating this is the security instrument in which real property is pledged by the borrower to the lender as security for the repayment of a loan.

Mortgage broker: A mortgage company that originates loans, then places those loans with a variety of other lending institutions with which they usually have pre-established relationships.

Mortgage insurance (MI): Insurance that covers the lender against some of the losses incurred as a result of a default on a home loan. It is often mistakenly referred to as PMI, which is actually the name of one of the larger mortgage insurers. Mortgage insurance is usually required in one form or another on all loans that have a loan-to-value (LTV) ratio higher than 80%. Mortgages above 80% LTVs that call themselves "No MI" loans are usually made at a higher interest rate. Instead of the borrower paying the mortgage insurance premiums directly, they pay a higher interest rate to the lender, which then pays the mortgage insurance itself. Also, FHA loans and certain first-time homebuyer programs require mortgage insurance regardless of the loan-to-value (LTV).

Mortgage insurance premium (MIP): This is the amount paid by a mortgagor for mortgage insurance, either to a government agency such as the Federal Housing Administration (FHA) or to a private mortgage insurance (MI) company.

Mortgagee: The lender in a mortgage agreement.

Mortgagor: The borrower in a mortgage agreement.

Multi-dwelling units: Properties that provide separate housing units for more than one family, although they secure only a single mortgage.

N

Negative amortization: Some adjustable-rate mortgages allow the interest rate to fluctuate independently of a required minimum payment. If a borrower makes the minimum payment, it may not cover all of the interest that would normally be due at the current interest rate. In essence, the borrower is deferring the interest payment, which is why this is called "deferred interest." The deferred interest is added to the balance of the loan and the loan balance grows larger instead of smaller, which is called negative amortization.

No cash-out refinance: A refinance transaction that is not intended to put cash in the hand of the borrower. Instead, the new balance is calculated to cover the balance due on the current loan and any costs associated with obtaining the new mortgage. This is often referred to as a "rate and term refinance."

No-cost loan: Many lenders offer loans that you can obtain at "no cost." You should inquire whether this means there are no "lender" costs associated with the loan, or if it also covers the other costs you would normally have in a purchase or refinance transaction, such as title insurance, escrow fees, settlement fees, appraisal, recording fees, notary fees, and others. These are fees and costs that may be associated with buying a home or obtaining a loan, but not charged directly by the lender. Keep in mind that, like a "no-point" loan, the interest rate will be higher than if you obtain a loan that has costs associated with it.

Non-conforming loans: A non-conforming loan is a loan that fails to meet bank criteria for funding. Reasons include that the loan amount is higher than the conforming loan limit (for mortgage loans), lack of sufficient credit, the unorthodox nature of the use of funds, or the collateral backing it. In many cases, non-conforming loans can be funded by hard money lenders or private institutions/money. A large portion of real-estate loans qualifies as non-conforming because either the borrower's financial status or the property type does not meet bank guidelines. Non-conforming loans can be either A-paper or subprime loans.

Note: See Promissory Note.

Note Rate: The interest rate shown on the promissory note. It includes only the interest and does not include any other fees of the loan as the APR (Annual Percentage Rate) would.

Notice of default: A formal written notice to a borrower that a default has occurred and that legal action may be taken.

O

Original principal balance: The total amount of principal owed on a mortgage before any payments are made.

Origination fee: On a government loan, the loan origination fee is 1% of the loan amount, but additional points may be charged which are called "discount points." One point equals 1% of the loan amount. On a conventional loan, the loan origination fee refers to the total number of points a borrower pays.

Origination Fee: Compensation paid to a lender to originate and close a loan. Sometimes expressed in the form of points, in which case one point is equal to 1%.

Owner financing: A property purchase transaction in which the property seller provides all or part of the financing.

P

Partial payment: A payment that is not sufficient to cover the scheduled monthly payment on a mortgage loan. Normally, a lender will not accept a partial payment, but in times of hardship, you can make this request of the loan servicing collection department.

Payment change date: The date when a new monthly payment amount takes effect on an adjustable-rate mortgage (ARM) or a graduated-payment mortgage (GPM). Generally, the payment change date occurs in the month immediately after the interest rate adjustment date.

Personal property: Any property that is not real property.

PITI (Principal, Interest, Taxes, and Insurance): The four components of a monthly mortgage payment on impounded loans. Principal refers to the part of the monthly payment that reduces the remaining balance of the mortgage. Interest is the fee charged for borrowing money. Taxes and insurance refer to the amounts that are paid into an escrow account each month for property taxes and mortgage and hazard insurance.

Planned unit development (PUD): A type of ownership where individuals actually own the building or unit they live in, but common areas are owned jointly with the other members of the development or association. Contrast with condominium, where an individual actually owns the airspace of his unit, but the buildings and common areas are owned jointly with the others in the development or association.

Point: A point is 1% of the amount of the mortgage.

Power of attorney: A legal document that authorizes another person to act on one's behalf. A power of attorney can grant complete authority or can be limited to certain acts and/or certain periods of time.

Pre-approval: A loosely used term which is generally taken to mean that a borrower has completed a loan application and provided debt, income, and savings documentation, which an underwriter has reviewed and approved. A pre-approval is usually done at a certain loan amount and making assumptions about what the interest rate will actually be at the time the loan is actually made, as well as estimates for the amount that will be paid for property taxes, insurance, and others. A pre-approval applies only to the borrower. Once a property is chosen, it must also meet the underwriting guidelines of the lender.

Prepayment: Any amount paid to reduce the principal balance of a loan before the due date. This is the payment in full on a mortgage that may result from the sale of the property, the owner's decision to pay off the loan in full, or as the result of foreclosure. In each case, prepayment means that payment occurs before the loan has been fully amortized.

Prepayment Penalty: A fee that is sometimes charged to a borrower for paying off a debt early.

Pre-qualification: This usually refers to the loan officer's written opinion of the ability of a borrower to qualify for a home loan, after the loan officer has made inquiries about debt, income, and savings. The information provided to the loan officer may have been presented verbally or in the form of documentation, and the loan officer may or may not have reviewed a credit report on the borrower.

Prime rate: The interest rate that banks charge to their preferred customers. Changes in the prime rate are widely publicized in the news media and are used as the indexes in some adjustable-rate mortgages, especially home equity lines of credit. Changes in the prime rate do not directly affect other types of mortgages, but the same factors that influence the prime rate also affect the interest rates of mortgage loans.

Principal: The amount borrowed or remaining unpaid balance. This is the part of the monthly payment that reduces the remaining balance of the mortgage.

Principal balance: The outstanding balance of principal on a mortgage. The principal balance does not include interest or any other charges. See remaining balance.

Private Mortgage Insurance (PMI): Protects lenders against borrower defaults. Generally required on mortgages where the loan to value ratio is more than 80%.

Promissory Note: A written, dated, and signed two-party instrument containing an unconditional promise by the maker to pay a definite sum of money to a payee on demand or at a specified future date, which could include multiple payments over time.

Purchase agreement: A written contract signed by the buyer and seller stating the terms and conditions under which a property will be sold.

Q

Qualification: The process of determining whether a prospective borrower has the ability— meaning sufficient assets and income— to repay a loan. Qualification is sometimes referred to as pre-qualification because it is subject to verification of the information provided by the applicant. Qualification is short of approval because it does not take account of the credit history of the borrower. Qualified borrowers may ultimately be turned down because, while they have demonstrated the capacity to repay, a poor credit history suggests that they may be unwilling to pay.

Quit Claim Deed (QCD): A deed that transfers, without warranty, whatever interest or title a grantor may have at the time the conveyance is made.

R

Real estate agent: A person licensed to negotiate and transact the sale of real estate.

Real Estate Owned (REO): Property acquired by a lender, through foreclosure, which is held as inventory.

Real Estate Settlement Procedures Act (RESPA): RESPA requires lenders and brokers to provide borrowers with information on settlement costs and mortgage servicing transfers at the time of application.

Real property: Land and appurtenances, including anything of a permanent nature such as structures, trees, minerals, and the interest, benefits, and inherent rights thereof.

Realtor: A real estate agent, broker, or an associate who holds active membership in a local real estate board that is affiliated with the National Association of Realtors.

Recorder: The public official who keeps records of transactions that affect real property in the area. This is sometimes known as a "Registrar of Deeds" or "County Clerk."

Recording: The noting in the registrar's office of the details of a properly executed legal document, such as a deed, a mortgage note, a satisfaction of mortgage, or an extension of mortgage, thereby making it a part of the public record.

Refinance transaction: The process of paying off one loan with the proceeds from a new loan using the same property as security.

Remaining balance: The amount of principal that has not yet been repaid. See principal balance.

Rescission: The cancellation of a transaction, stipulated by state and federal law that allows refinancing borrowers to cancel the loan. The general rescission period is three days (not including Sunday or federal holidays) from the signing date. This only applies to owner-occupied refinances.

Right of first refusal: A provision in an agreement that requires the owner of a property to give another party the first opportunity to purchase or lease the property before he or she offers it for sale or lease to others.

Right of ingress or egress: The right to enter or leave designated premises.

Right of survivorship: In joint tenancy, the right of survivors to acquire the interest of a deceased joint tenant.

S

Sale-leaseback: A technique in which a seller deeds property to a buyer for a consideration, and the buyer simultaneously leases the property back to the seller.

Second mortgage: A mortgage that has a lien position subordinate to the first mortgage.

Secondary Mortgage Market: The segment of the mortgage market where mortgages are resold, not where mortgages are originated. Mortgages in this market are often grouped together based on risk, size, and structure, and are then sold.

Secured loan: A loan that is backed by collateral.

Security: The property that will be pledged as collateral for a loan.

Self-directed IRA: An individual retirement account in which a custodian handles alternative investments at the direction of the account owner. This arrangement enables private money investors to make hard money loans from their retirement accounts.

Seller carry-back: An agreement in which the owner of a property provides financing, often in combination with an assumable mortgage.

Servicer: An organization that collects principal and interest payments from borrowers and manages borrowers' escrow accounts. The servicer often services mortgages that have been purchased by an investor in the secondary mortgage market.

Servicing: The collection of mortgage payments from borrowers and related to the responsibilities of a loan servicer.

Settlement statement: See HUD-1 Settlement Statement

Short Sale: Arrangement between a mortgagor (borrower) and mortgagee (lender) through which the mortgagor retires the mortgage obligation with a payment of something less than the total outstanding principal balance. Any principal forgiven in the transaction is considered by the IRS to be taxable income to the borrower (see www.irs.gov for current tax information).

Simple Interest: Interest computed solely on the principal balance.

Stay: The automatic prohibition of collection actions against a debtor in a bankruptcy filing.

Subdivision: A housing development that is created by dividing a tract of land into individual lots for sale or lease.

Subordinate financing: Any mortgage or other lien that has a priority that is lower than that of the first mortgage.

Survey: A drawing or map showing the precise legal boundaries of a property, the location of improvements, easements, rights of way, encroachments, and other physical features.

Sweat equity: Contribution to the construction or rehabilitation of a property in the form of labor or services rather than cash.

T

Takeout Loan: a long-term loan replacing a short term or interim loan (e.g., a construction loan).

Tenancy in common: As opposed to joint tenancy, when there are two or more individuals on title to a piece of property, this type of ownership does not pass ownership to the others in the event of death.

Time Value of Money: A core finance principle stating that money is worth more the sooner it is received.

Title: The right to the ownership and possession of any item that may be legally recognized as belonging to someone or something. In its most basic sense, title is the recognition of ownership.

Title Company: A company that specializes in examining and insuring titles to real estate.

Title Search: An examination of public records to determine and confirm a property's legal ownership and find out what claims are on the property. A title search is usually performed by a title company or an attorney who researches the vested owner, the liens or other judgments on the property, the loans on the property, and the property taxes due.

Title Insurance (Lender's policy): An insurance policy that insures a lender against errors in the title that were not discovered in the title search.

Title Insurance (Owner's policy): An insurance policy certifying an owner has the title to a house and the right to transfer it to another.

Transfer of ownership: Any means by which the ownership of a property changes hands. Lenders consider all of the following situations to be a transfer of ownership: the purchase of a property "subject to" the mortgage, the assumption of the mortgage debt by the property purchaser, and any exchange of possession of the property under a land sales contract or any other land trust device.

Transfer tax: State or local tax payable when title passes from one owner to another.

Truth-in-Lending Act: Federal law requiring disclosure of the Annual Percentage Rate to home buyers within a short period of applying for a loan. Its purpose is to help borrowers understand the actual cost of borrowing money, which allows them to compare costs among lenders.

Trustee: A fiduciary who holds or controls property for the benefit of another.

U

Underwriting: Is the process by which the guidelines established are applied to a loan application to ensure that safe and secure loans are issued. Some of the things that are considered are the property value, the borrower's ability to make the payments, the borrower's credit, and the loan-to-value ratio.

Unlimited Personal Guarantee: A guarantee by a borrower to a lender for the entire outstanding loan amount plus legal fees, accrued interest, and costs associated with collecting the loan. This type of guarantee entitles the lender to look to the borrower's personal assets to recover any unrealized balance due in which foreclosure and re-sale of the asset does not satisfy the debt.

Unrelated Business Income Tax (UBIT): The tax on unrelated business taxable income (UBTI). This typically refers to income earned on retirement income that does not qualify as tax deferred.

Usury: Charging a greater payment or interest rate for the lending of money than is permitted by law. Mortgage brokers are often exempt from usury laws, which is why private money transactions can be priced higher than usury laws permit if otherwise transacted between private individuals.

V

VA mortgage: A mortgage that is guaranteed by the Department of Veterans Affairs (VA).

Variable Rate: An interest rate that changes periodically in relation to an index. Payments may increase or decrease accordingly.

Veterans Administration (VA): An agency of the federal government that guarantees residential mortgages made to eligible veterans of the military services. The guarantee protects the lender against loss and thus encourages lenders to make mortgages to veterans.

Voluntary Lien: A lien internationally created or entered into by a debtor.

W

Waiver of escrows: Authorization by the lender for the borrower to pay taxes and insurance directly. This is in contrast to the standard procedure where the lender adds a charge to the monthly mortgage payment that is deposited in an escrow account, from which the lender pays the borrower's taxes and insurance when they are due. On some loans, lenders will not waive escrows, and on loans where waiver is permitted, lenders are likely either to charge for it in the form of a small increase in points, or restrict it to borrowers making a large down payment.

Wrap-Around-Mortgage: A mortgage incorporating the balance due under a prior mortgage. In other words, it is a mortgage on a property that already has a mortgage, where the new lender assumes the payment obligation on the old mortgage. Wrap-around mortgages arise when the current market rate is above the rate on the existing mortgage, and home sellers are frequently the lender. If the mortgage has a due-on-sale clause, this will prevent that a wrap-around mortgage be done in connection with sale of a property.

Y

Yield-Spread premium abuse: The practice by mortgage brokers of pocketing a rebate from the lender for delivering a high-rate loan, without the knowledge of the borrower.

Z

References

Abbott, R. (2012). Private mortgage investing: Your Path to Creating Passive Income and Building Wealth. USA: Author House.

Adams, P. E. (n. d.). Business partnerships need pre-nuptial agreements. Adam Hall Publishing Retrieved April 16, 2014 from http://www.adams-hall.com/bupaneprag.html

Ahluwalia, A. (2007). Make your money make money for you: Step-by-step guide to Trust Deed Investing and Financial Independence. Bloomington, Indiana: Author House.

Alvi, S. (2010, August 7). Efficient markets do not exist: *A Primer on Perpetual Market Disequilibrium Hypothesis*. Retrieved August 10, 2014 from, http://seekingalpha.com/instablog/668504-sahil-alvi/86211-efficient-markets-do-not-exist-a-primer-on-perpetual-market-disequilibrium-hypothesis

Amerinotexchange (n. d.). Specializing in the purchase of mortgage notes and business Notes. Retrieved July 22, 2014 from http://www.amerinotexchange.com/

Annuity Company Ratings. (n. d.). Compare annuity rates. Retrieved August 23, 2014 from http://www.freeannuityrates.com/annuities/annuity-company-ratings.php

Baker, J. (n. d.). Divorce Statistics: Forest Institute of Professional Psychology. Retrieved August 3, 2014 from http://www.divorcestatistics.org/

Barnes,T. B. & Walker, A.H. (n.d.). Seller-Financing Restrictions Under The Dodd-Frank Act. Retrieved November 22, 2019 from https://barneswalker.com/seller-financing-restrictions-under-the-dodd-frank-act/

Beggs, L. (2008). Trading losses. Retrieved October 27, 2013, http://www.isnare.com/?aid=305308&ca=Finances

Bishop, K. (1989, May 31). San Francisco grants recognition to couples that aren't married. New York Times. Retrieved March 29, 2014 from http://www.yourtradingcoach.com/Videos-Money-Management/Trading-Loss.

Burns, A. F., & Mitchell, W. C. (1946). Measuring business cycles. New York: National Bureau of Economic Research.

Burke, Jr., D. B. (1986, § 1.1, p. 2.). Law of title insurance. Little Brown & Company. Retrieved July 26, 2014 from http://www.ask.com/wiki/Title_insurance

Callahan, J. (2014, June 29). Dodd-Frank Act: Six Months In and the Sky Is Not Falling! Retrieved August 1, 2014 from, http://www.advantaira.com/blog/dodd-frank-act-part-two-six-months-after-the-dfa-and-the-sky-is-still-not-falling/

Carney, J. L. (2011). Four step guide to private lending profits. Earn 10% to 20% Return on Investment without Dealing with Tenants, Toilets, or Trash. USA: Insight Press

Chevreau, J. (2010). You need a 100% gain to erase a 50% loss. Retrieved October 27, 2013, from http://indonesiastockmarket.com/index/you-need-a-100-gain.

CFPB Consumer Laws and Regulations (n. d.). The SAFE Act. Retrieved February 13, 2014 from, http://consumerfinance.gov/f/201203_cfpb_update_SAFE_Act_Exam_Procedures.pdf

Clark, B. (2011, Sept 15). The history and evolution of crowdfunding. Retrieved May 5, 2015 from, http://mashable.com/2011/09/15/crowdfunding-history/

Clarke, P. (n. d.). Falsifying documents. Retrieved December 28, 2014 from http://www.legalmatch.com/law-library/article/falsifying-documents.htm

Colao, J. J. (2012, March 21). Breaking down the JOBS Act: Inside the Bill that would American Business. Retrieved May 5, 2015 from,http://www.forbes.com/sites/jjcoleo/2012/03/21/jobs-act/

Commerce Clause (n. d.). Retrieved August 26, 2014 from, http://www.law.cornell.edu/wex/commerce_clause

Congress.Gov (2018). Economic Growth, Regulatory Relief, and Consumer Protection Act.Retrieved November 11, 2019 from https://www.congress.gov/bill/115th-congress/senate-bill/2155

Cornet, B. (2012, 2013). QM and QRM rules for mortgages: Let the Confusion Begin. Retrieved March 28, 2014 from http://www.homebuyinginstitute.com/news/qm-qrm-confusion-232/

Coronet, B. (2014, January 6). New lending rules should not affect down payments in 2014.Retrieved January 25, 2014 from, http://www.homebuyinginstitute.com/news/down-payment-requirements-520/

CRS.Gov (June 6, 2018). Economic Growth, Regulatory Relief, and Consumer Protection Act (P.L. 115-174). Retrieved November 11, 2019 from https://fas.org/sgp/crs/misc/R45073.pdf

Derivatives. (n. d.). Office of the comptroller of the currency: Ensuring a Safe and Sound Federal Banking System for all Americans. Retrieved July 5, 2014 from http://www.occ.gov/topics/capital-markets/financial-markets/trading/derivatives/index-derivatives.html

Dawson, S. L. (2010). Series LLC and bankruptcy: When the Series Finds Itself in Trouble. Retrieved August 2, 2014 from http://www.djcl.org/PDF/35-2/dawson.pdf Di Florio, C. V. (2012). Conflict of interest and risk governance. Retrieved April 18, 2014 from http://www.sec.gov/News/Speech/Detail/Speech/1365171491600#.U1GLMsuPLay

Dojima Rice Exchange. (n. d.). Retrieved August 20, 2014 from, http://en.wikipedia.org/wiki/D%C5%8Djima_Rice_Exchange

Domaszewiez, C. J. (2002). Avoid market loss with trust deed investing. The How-to Book on Investing in Trust Deeds. New York, NY: Writers Club Press.

Domestic Partnership. (n. d.). Retrieved June 12, 2014 from, http://en.wikipedia.org/wiki/Domestic_partnership

Drake, D. (n. d.). Crowdfunding: It's no Longer a Buzzword. Retrieved May 5, 2015 from, http://www.crowdfunding.org/editorial//crowdfunding-its-no-longer-a-buzzword/32268

Dukeminier, J., Johanson, S. M., Lindgren, J. & Sitkoff, R. H. (2005). Will, trusts, and estates (7th ed.). New York, N.Y: Aspen Publishers

Dungey, D. (2007, March 6). Unwinding the fraud for bubbles. Retrieved December 26, 2014 from, http://www.calculatedriskblog.com/2007/03/unwinding-fraud-for-bubbles.html

EPRA/NAREIT Global Real Estate Index Series. (2012, December 18). FTSE. Retrieved June 26, 2014 http://www.ftse.com/Indices/FTSE_EPRA_NAREIT_Global_Real_Estate_Inde Series/index.jsp

ETFs. (n. d.). Securities and exchange commission. Retrieved July 12, 2014 from, http://www.sec.gov/answers/etf.htm

Evergeht, G. (2007, January 17). Property tax appeals and protests. Retrieved October 13, 2014 from, http://ezinearticles.com/?Property-Tax-Appeals-and-Protests&id=421556

Foreclosure HQ. (n. d.). Shedding light on the dark topic. *What is a Strict Foreclosure.* Retrieved August 25, 2014 from http://www.foreclosure-hq.com/general/strict-foreclosure.html

FreeAnnuityRates.com. (n. d.). Compare annuity rates. Retrieved August 6, 2014 from, http://www.freeannuityrates.com/annuities/article.php?title=Retirement-Annuity-Guide

Fink, J. (2011). The great investment truth behind simple arithmetic. Retrieved February 18, 2014, from http://www.investingdaily.com/14485/the-great-investment-truth-behind-simple-arithmetic/

Friedman, M., & Jacobson-Schwartz, A. (1963). A Monetary History of the United States, 1867 960. A Study by the National Bureau of Economic Research. New York, N.Y: Princeton: Princeton University Press for NBER, 1963.

Fydenkevez, G. (n. d.). Private commercial mortgage lenders are lending, growing and thriving during this credit crisis. Retrieved March 24, 2014 from http://ezinearticles.com/?Private-

Commercial-Mortgage-Lenders-Are-Lending,-Growing-and-Thriving-During-This-Credit Crisis & id=1711327

Gallagher, C. (2011, June 9). Truth in saving act. Retrieved August 21, 2014 from http://www.jdsupra.com/legalnews/truth-in-savings-act-23711/

Giveforward (n. d.). Crowd funding: A Brief History. Retrieved May 5, 2015 from, http://www.giveforward.com/p/crowdfunding/Crowd-funding-websites.

Glaser, B. G., & Strauss, A. L. (1967). The discovery of grounded theory. Chicago, IL: Aldaline Publishing Company.

Gleeson, P. (2013). The average stock market loss. Retrieved October 19, 2013, from http://www.economicshelp.org

Guest, G., Bunce, A., & Johnson, L. (2006) How many interviews are enough? An Experiment with Data Saturation and Variability. Retrieved October 4, 2014 from, http://fmx.sagepub.com/content/18/1/59.abstract

Gustini, R. J., Spencer, L. H., & Butcher, T. M. (2013, February 26). Qualified mortgages versus qualified residential mortgages. Retrieved March 27, 2014 from http://www.nixonpeabody.com/files/155344_RFI_Alert_26FEB2013.pdf

Hubbard, D. W. (2009). The failure of risk management: Why It's Broken and How to fix it. Wiley & Sons.

Hudson's bay company. (n. d.). Retrieved July 1, 2014 from http://en.wikipedia.org/wiki/Hudson%27s_Bay_Company

Hudson's Bay Company: 1670. (n. d.). The loyal Edmonton regiment military museum. Retrieved July 1, 2014 from http://www.lermuseum.org/en/chronology/new-france-1600-1730/1650-1730/hudsons-bay-company-1670/? vm=r

Infoplease. (n. d.). A brief history of checking. Retrieved June 24, 2014 from http://www.infoplease.com/ipa/A0001522.html

ISO/DIS 31000 (2009). Risk management- principals and guidelines on implementation.

International Organization for Standardization. Retrieved August 15, 2014 from, http://www.iso.org/iso/iso_catalogue/catalogue_tc/catalogue_detail.htm?csnumber=43170

Investment Company Act of 1940, (2008, February 27). Release No. 28171. Retrieved September 3, 2014 from, http://www.sec.gov/rules/ic/2008/ic-28171.pdf

Investopedia (n. d.). Opportunity cost. Retrieved October 27, 2013, from http://www.investopedia.com/terms/o/opportunity cost.asp

Investopedia (n. d.). Section 1244 stock. Retrieved January 19, 2015 from, http://www.investopedia.com/terms/s/Section-1244-stock.asp.

Investor Alert. (2011, September). Self-directed IRAs and the risk of fraud. Retrieved August 30, 2014 from, http://www.sec.gov/investor/alerts/sdira.pdf

Investor Bulletin (n. d.) Interest Rate Risk: When Interest Rates Go Up, Prices of Fixed-Rate Bonds Fall. Retrieved October 13, 2014 from, http://www.sec.gov/investor/alert/ib_Interestraterisk.pdf

IRS.gov (n.d.). Limited Liability Company (LLC). Retrieved November 7, 2019 from, https://www.irs.gov/businesses/small-businesses-self-employed/limited-liability-company-llc

Johnson, A. (2014, July 22). What is a deed in lieu of foreclosure? Retrieved August 25, 2014 from http://www.ehow.com/info_8110338_deed-lieu-foreclosure.html

Johnston, M. (2014, May 22). Brief history of ETFs. Retrieved July 4, 2014 from http://etfdb.com/etf-education/brief-history-of-etfs/

Klarman, S. A. (1957, 1991). Margin of safety: risk-averse investing strategies for the thoughtful investor. New York, NY: Harper Business.

Kumar, A., McDonough, M. (2013, June 29). The basics of risk management. Retrieved February 21, 2013 from, http://www.brighthubpm.com/risk-management/71742-the-basics-of-risk-management/

Kaufman, S. (2019). Zeus Crowdfunding™. Retrieved from https://zeuslending.com/zeuscrowdfunding/about/#our-company

LaMance, K. (n. d.). Terminating a tenancy by the entirety. Retrieved August 3, 2014 from http://www.legalmatch.com/law-library/article/terminating-a-tenancy-by-the-entirety.html

LaMance, K. (n. d.). White collar crimes lawyers. Retrieved December 28, 2014 from http://www.legalmatch.com/law-library/article/white-collar-crimes.html

Larson, A. (2010, December). Piercing the Corporate Veil. Retrieved October 13, 2014 from, http://www.expertlaw.com/library/business/corporate_veil.html

Laurence, B. (n. d.). The LLC operating agreement. Create an Operating Agreement to Limit your Liability. Retrieved August 1, 2014 from http://www.nolo.com/legal-encyclopedia/llc-operating-agreement-30232.html

Legal Alerts. (2012, July6). Junior lien assignee allowed deficiency judgment after senior lien non-judicial foreclosure. Retrieved August 25, 2014 from http://www.bbklaw.com/?t=40&an=13305&format=xml

Lemke, T. P., Lins, G.T. & Smith, A.T. (2002) Regulation of Investment Companies. Securities Law Series (7th ed.). Matthew Bender & Company.

Lo, B. & Field, M. J. (2009). Conflict of interest in medical research. Retrieved April 18, 2014 from http://en.wikipedia.org/wiki/Conflict_of_interest#cite_note-1

Lofsgordon, A. (n.d.). The Mortgage Forgiveness Debt Relief Act gives some taxpayers a break. Retrieved January 23, 2020 from https://www.nolo.com/legal-encyclopedia/canceled-mortgage-debt-tax-time-36146.html

Maeda, H., Clark, T. B., & Tabacchi, M. S. (2011). Private mortgage investing: How to Earn 12% or more on your Savings, Investments, IRA accounts, and Personal Equity (2nd ed.). Ocala, FL: Atlantic Publishing Group.

M & G Investments. (n. d.). Retrieved September 2, 2014 from, http://en.wikipedia.org/wiki/M%26G_Investments; http://www.mandg.co.uk/investor/

Mahony, R. (2014). Why joint tenancy may create income tax problems. Retrieved January 16, 2014 from, http://mahonytrust.com/tenancy.htm

Manier, J. (2013, April 17). Private mortgage loans offer attractive yields. Retrieved April 17th, 2014 from http://www.nuwireinvestor.com/articles/private-mortgage-loans-offer-attractive-investment-yields-60706.aspx

Marshall, C. & Rossman, G. B. (2011). Designing qualitative research (5th ed.). Thousand Oaks, CA: Sage.

Martel, J. (2013, March 5). Future of Fannie and Freddie. Retrieved September 4, 2014, from http://www.bankrate.com/financing/mortgages/future-of-fannie-and-freddie/

McKean, E. (2005). The new oxford American dictionary (2nd ed.). Oxford: Oxford University Press.

Merriam, S. B. (1998). Qualitative research and case study applications in education. San Francisco, CA: Jossey-Bass.

Metropolitan Statistical Area. (n. d). Retrieved July 2, 2014 from, http://en.wikipedia.org/wiki/Metropolitan_statistical_area

Mortgage Scams: Appraisal Fraud. (n. d.). Retrieved September 2, 2014 from http://www.fraudguides.com/mortgage-appraisal-fraud.asp

Moskowitz, J. M., & Napoliello, M. E. (2004). Spark: The orchestra funding revolution. lending your way to real estate millions. Newport Beach, CA: Literary Press.

Mott, A. (n. d.). IRS rules for the cancellation of debt. Retrieved November 10, 2014 from, http://wiki.fool.com/IRS_Rules_For_Cancellation_of_Debt.

NBER (2010). US business cycle expansions and contractions. Retrieved January 16th, 2014 from, http://www.nber.org/cycles.html#announcements. Nursing Research, 40(1), 120-123.

Nelson, S. L. (n. d.). S corporations explained. Retrieved August 2, 2014 from http://www.scorporationsexplained.com/what-is-a-Qualified-Subchapter-S-Subsidiary.htm

Noked, N. (2013, December 6). JOBS Act Title III crowdfunding moves closer to reality. Retrieved May 11, 2015 from, http://corpgov.law.harvard.edu/2013/12/06/jobs-act-title iii-Crowdfunding-moves-closer-to-reality/

Norton, R. (n.d.). Unintended Consequences. Retrieved November 11, 2019 from https://www.econlib.org/library/Enc/UnintendedConsequences.html

Office of Inspector General, (2006, June). Challenges and FDIC efforts related to predatory lending. Retrieved November 25, 2014 from, http://fdicoig.gov/reports06/06011.pdf

O'Connell, B. (n. d.). Real estate and crowdfunding: A New Path for Investors. Retrieved May 8, 2015 from, http://www.

investopedia.com/articles/investing/072514/real-estate-and-crowdfunding-new-path-investors.asp.

Oxford Dictionaries (n. d.). Investors and crowdfunding. Retrieved May 5, 2015 from, http://www.oxforddictionaries.com/us/definition/american_english/crowdfunding.

Patton, M. (1990). Qualitative evaluation and research methods (pp. 169-186). Beverly Hills. CA: Sage.

Pecora Commission (n. d.). Retrieved July 5, 2014 from http://en.wikipedia.org/wiki/ Pecora_Commission.

Pettinger, T. (2012). Causes of boom and bust cycles. Retrieved October 19, 2013, from http://www.economicshelp.org.

Piercing the Corporate Veil (2010 September, 14). Retrieved April 2, 2014 from http://pcm.me/piercing-the-corporate-veil

Pinto, J. E. (2011, February 5). Government housing policies in the lead-up to the financial crisis: A Forensic Study. Retrieved July 17, 2014 from http://www.aei.org/papers/economics/financial-services/housing-finance/government-housing-policies-in-the-lead-up-to-the-financial-crisis-a-forensic-study/

Pratt, S. P., & Niculita, A. V. (2008). Valuing a business: The Analysis and Appraisal of Closely Held Businesses, (5th ed.) p.39. New York: McGraw Hill.

Private Money Investing. (n. d.). Retrieved April 20, 2014 from, http://en.wikipedia.org/wiki/Private_money_investing

PRWeb. (n. d.). Subprime loans are back: Hard Money Real Estate Loans Make Up 3.7% of All

New Loan Origination Types In 2013, According To Alternative Lending Magazine Analysis. Retrieved August 12, 2014 from, http://www.prweb.com/releases/newsprimeLenders_2013/hardmoneysubprimeloans/prweb10574182.htm

Quoteinvestigator (2016, March 5). If You Think Education Is Expensive, Try Ignorance. Retrieved from https://quoteinvestigator.com/2016/05/03/expense/

Real Estate Investment Trust, (n. d.). Retrieved August 1, 2014 from, http://en.wikipedia.org/wiki/Real_estate_investment_trust

Regulation DD Truth in Savings. (n. d.). Retrieved September 1, 2014 from http://www.federalreserve.gov/boarddocs/supmanual/cch/tis.pdf

REIT Basics (n. d.). Investing. Retrieved November 10, 2014 from, https://www.reit.com/investing/reit-basics.

Ridgway, L. M. (n. d.). The potential risks of joint tenancy. Retrieved January 16, 2014 from, http://www.martharidgwaylaw.com/JointTenancy.Dangers.pdf

Risk management. (n. d..). Retrieved February 21, 2014 from http://en.wikipedia.org/wiki/Risk_management

Ritholtz, B. (2012, January 4).Small business success/failure rates. Retrieved August 4, 2014 from http://www.ritholtz.com/blog/2012/01/small-business-successfailure-rates/

Romer, D. C. (n. d.). The concise encyclopedia of economics business cycles. *Library of Economics and Liberty*. Retrieved January 16th, 2014 from, http://www.econlib.org/library/Enc/BusinessCycles.html

Romer, C. D. (1999). Changes in Business Cycles: Evidence and Explanations. *Journal of Economic Perspectives* 13 (Spring 1999): 23–44.

Romer, C. D. (1954). Remeasuring business cycles. *Journal of Economic History* 54 (September 1994): 573–609.

Ruggeri, A. (2009, September 29). Pecora hearings a model for financial crisis investigation. Congress could learn from Pecora's 1930s investigation of the stock market crash. Retrieved July 5, 2014 fromhttp://www.usnews.com/news/

history/articles/2009/09/29/Pecora-hearings-a-model-for-financial-crisis-investigation

Rutledge, T. E. (2009). Again, for the Want of a Theory: The Challenge of the "Series" to Business Organization Law, 46 Am. Bus. Law J. 311 at 313-15. Retrieved August 2, 2014 from http://en.wikipedia.org/wiki/Series_LLC

Saunders, B., Sim, J., Kingstone, T., Baker, S., Waterfield, J., Bartlam, B., Burroughs, H., and Jinks, C. (2018). Saturation in qualitative research: exploring its conceptualization and operationalization. *Quality & quantity, 52*(4), 1893–1907. Retrieved from https://www.ncbi.nlm.nih.gov/pmc/articles/PMC5993836/ doi:10.1007/s11135-017-0574-8

Scrofano, J. (n. d.). Right of redemption laws in the state of Florida. Retrieved January 3, 2015 from, http://www.ehow.com/list_6113269_right-redemption-laws-florida.html

Sec Concept Release (2001, November 8). Actively managed ETFs. Release # IC-25258 Retrieved July2, 2014 from, http://www.sec.gov/rules/concept/ic-25258.htm

Sec.org. (2013, Oct. 23). Sec issues proposed on crowdfunding. Retrieved May 6, 2015 from, http://www.sec.org/News/PressRelease/Deatil/PressRealease 1370540017677.

Security Exchange Commission (n. d.). Questions you should ask about your investments. Retrieved February 18, 2014 from, http://www.sec.gov/investor/pubs/askquestions.htm

Segal, T. (2019, April 6). Understanding the Five Cs of Credit. Retrieved November 25, 2019 from, https://www.investopedia.com/ask/answers/040115/what-most-important-c-five-cs-credit.asp

Sin, K. F. (1998). The legal nature of the unit trust. Clarendon Press

Single Member LLCs. (n. d.). Retrieved August 10, 2014 from, http://www.irs.gov/Businesses/Small-Businesses-&-Self-Employed/Single-Member-Limited-Liability-Companies

Single-Purpose Entity (n. d.). Retrieved September 2, 2014 from, http://financial-dictionary.thefreedictionary.com/single-purpose+entity

Slagle, J. (2008, February 26). Trading strategy: How to cut your Losses and let your Profits Run, The Core Any Trading Strategy. Retrieved August 15, 2014 from http://ezinearticles.com/?Trading-Strategy---How-To-Cut-Your-Losses-And-Let-Your-Profits-Run,-The-Core-Of-Any-Trading-Strategy & id=1010836

Stafford, M. (2010, June 17). Limited liability company is an "unincorporated association for purpose of CAFA. Retrieved February 19, 2015 from, http://www.cafalawblog.com/case-summaries/limited-liability-company-is-an unincorporated-association-for-the-purpose-of-cafa

Star, L (2013). Which states are deed trust states? Retrieved October 26, 2013, from http://www.ehow.com/print/about_5488538_states-deed-trust-states.html.

Staub, K. D. (n. d). What is a series LLC? Retrieved August 2, 2014 from, http://www.limitedliabilitycompanycenter.com/series_llc.html

Stratis, G., & Snow, N. (n. d.). Business continuity planning: A Case History. Retrieved February 21, 2014 from, http://www.drj.com/drworld/content/w3_018.htm

Stuntz, J. A. (2005). Hers, His, and theirs: *Community Property Law in Spain and Early Texas,* Lubbock, Texas: Texas Tech University Press.

Thelawdictionary. (n. d.). What is security instrument? Retrieved August 3, 2014 from, http://thelawdictionary.org/security-instrument/

Title I-Investment Companies. (n. d.). Retrieved August 23, 2014 from, http://Legislin.org/us/pl-76-768

Truth-in-Savings Act. (n. d.). Regulation DD. Retrieved June 30, 2014 from http://www.federalreserve.gov/boarddocs/supmanual/cch/200601/tis.pdf

Twyman, T. (n. d.). What is a strict foreclosure? Retrieved August 24, 2014 from http://www.ehow.com/info_7736076_strict-foreclosure.html

USA.gov. (n. d.). SAFE mortgage licensing act. Retrieved August 25, 2014 from http://www.hud.gov/offices/hsg/ramh/safe/smlicact.cfm

US Securities and Exchange Commission. (n. d.). Mutual funds. Retrieved September 4, 2014 from, http://www.sec.gov/answers/mutfund.htm

Usury (n. d.). Retrieved July 10, 2014 from http://en.wikipedia.org/wiki/Usury

Unit Investment Trusts (UITs). (n. d). Retrieved September 5, 2014 from http://www.sec.gov/answers/uit.htm

Unit Trust. (n. d.). Retrieved September 5, 2014 from, http://en.wikipedia.org/wiki/Unit_trust

Virtual-Strategy Magazine (2015, May 4). Real estate crowdfunding platform opens doors nationwide. Retrieved May 8, 2015 from, http://www.virtual-startegy.com/2015/05/04/real-estate-crowdfunding-platform-opens-doors-nationwide/#ax32ZstUf6j

Wang, S. (2013, March 19). HBC history presentation. Retrieved October 13. 2014 from, http://prezi.com/0rzuekjkdrh5/hbc-history-presentation/

Wealth Strategy Report (n. d.). The 3.8% Medicare surtax on investment income. Retrieved July 18, 2014 from http://www.ustrust.com/Publish/Content/application/pdf/GWMOL/3.8_Medicare_Surtax.pdf

Wilkerson, L. (2011, May 25). Death of the boy plunger. (1940). Retrieved August 1, 2014 from http://www.open.salon. com/blog/laura_wilkerson/2011/05/25/death_of_the_boy_ plunger_1940

Winter, G. (2012). Frequently asked questions about private mortgage investments. Retrieved May 22, 2014 http:// privatemortgageinvestment.com/privatemortgageinvestment.

Wisegeek. (n. d.). What is an escrow settlement? Retrieved July 23, 2014 from, http://www.wisegeek.net/what-is-an-escrow-settlement.htm

Index

Further Reading Recommendations

Throughout the book, the author has stated numerous times that the learning curve for safe real estate and private mortgage investing is quite steep. While initially, it is advisable to seek the mentorship of an ethical and experienced broker/lender or a knowledgeable, hard mortgage investor to learn the underwriting guidelines and the due diligence process to evaluate the loan opportunities, the ultimate responsibility for the safety of the investments lies with the investor.

Most of the learning that takes place in the private mortgage lending industry occurs by happenstance. There are no formal or structured educational programs to learn this type of information. However, there are a few helpful books available on the subject listed below as recommended reading.

The research project undertaken to write this book will provide an additional unbiased source of information that will serve to develop the necessary educational foundation to begin the process of learning the intricacies of this unique and valuable investment vehicle.

List of books for further reading:

Abbott, R. (2012). Private mortgage investing: Your Path to Creating Passive Income and Building Wealth. USA: Author House.

Ahluwalia, A. (2007). Make your money make money for you: Step-by-step guide to Trust Deed Investing and Financial Independence. Bloomington, Indiana: Author House.

Burns, A. F. & Wesley, C. M. (1946). Measuring business cycles. New York: National Bureau of Economic Research.

Domaszewiez, C. J. (2002). Avoid market loss with trust deed investing. The How-to Book on Investing in Trust Deeds. New York, NY: Writers Club Press.

Hubbard, D. W. (2009). The failure of risk management: Why It's Broken and How to fix it. Wiley & Sons.

Hrimnak, J. (2008). Breaking the wealth code. How You can Earn your First Million and Create a Lifetime of Wealth. Scottsdale, Arizona: Forbes Success Strategies.

Lee, C. J. (2011). Four step guide to private lending profits. Earn 10% to 20% Return on Investment without Dealing with Tenants, Toilets, or Trash. USA: Insight Press

Maeda, H., Clark, T. B. & Tabacchi, M. S. (2011). Private mortgage investing: How to Earn 12% or more on your Savings, Investments, IRA accounts, and Personal Equity (2nd ed.). Ocala, FL: Atlantic Publishing Group.

Moskowitz, J. M. & Napoliello, M. E. (2004). Spark: The Orchestra Funding Revolution.

Lending your way to Real Estate Millions. Newport Beach, CA: Literary Press.

Pratt, S. P. & Niculita, A. V. (2008). Valuing a business: The Analysis and Appraisal of Closely Held Businesses, (5th ed.) New York: McGraw Hill.